Buying Louisiana

"Hoisting of American Colors over Louisiana"
Main Plaza, New Orleans, Painting by Thure de Thulstrup

Buying Louisiana

*An Eyewitness's Account
of the
Louisiana Purchase*

Josée Clerens

Foley Square

Buying Louisiana: An Eyewitness's Account of the Louisiana Purchase
New Hardbound Edition

Although the author and publisher have made every effort to ensure the accuracy and completeness of information contained in this book, we assume no responsibility for errors, inaccuracies, omissions or inconsistencies herein. Any slights of people, places, or organizations are purely unintentional.

Publication date: July 4, 2014
Original Paperback edition published 2000, iUniverse

Hardbound Edition ISBN: 978-0-9760846-7-9
Softcover Edition ISBN: 978-0-9760846-8-6

Library of Congress Control Number: 2014934276

Manufactured in the United States of America.

10 9 8 7 6 5 4 3 2 1

www.BuyingLouisiana.com.

Cover and Book Design by John Clifton
john@johnclifton.net

Key to Personages on the Cover
1. Napoleon Bonaparte
2. President Thomas Jefferson
3. Charles Maurice de Talleyrand
4. King Carlos IV of Spain
5. Queen Maria Luisa of Spain

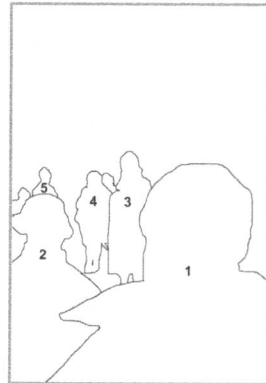

Foley Square Books • 175 West 87th Street, Room 27E • New York, NY 10024
212-724-1578 • EMAIL: *info@FoleySquareBooks.com*

CONTENTS

Contents

DIPLOMACY, *n*. The patriotic art of lying for one's country.

– Ambrose Bierce, *The Devil's Dictionary*

Acknowledgements

For their gracious help and support, I would like to express my gratitude to the late Quentin Crisp, Yvonne Lynn, and Mark Rosin. Firstly, lastly, in between and above all, I thank my sweetheart of a husband, John Clifton.

ABOUT THE AUTHOR

Born in Belgium and a naturalized citizen of the United States, Josée Clerens has cultivated a passion for America's past that has propelled her on an insatiable journey of historical discovery. Combining her knowledge of things American and her novelistic style, she is able to relate real events in a way that puts readers in the middle of the story.

Ms. Clerens co-authored *Sparky Fights Back: A Little Dog's Big Battle Against Cancer*, which was an award finalist for best book of the year by the Dog Writers of America. She has written many short stories, published in various periodicals. She was for several years a regular contributor to newspapers in her native Flanders, writing accounts of everyday life in the United States as Our Woman in America.

Ms. Clerens lives in New York City.

A Preface by Philip Crittenden, Chronicler of These Events

The Jefferson administration's lauding of James Monroe while ignoring the inestimable contributions of Chancellor Livingston is highly unfair to the Chancellor, who is not here to speak for himself. It can be argued that Monroe, too, is still abroad, but what need is there to quarrel with praise? The Livingston clan, meanwhile, has tossed aside its internal bickerings to howl in concert at the Government bias, revealing its own.

All of this chauvinistic clamor prompts an impartial witness such as myself to give an account of what really happened in Paris, and leave to the American people the awarding of credit and the distribution of honors.

Also, I have returned from France no richer than I left and very shortly shall have to generate an income compatible with the expectations of Mrs. Hagedoorn, who possesses the quarter-and-bits-obsessed mind of widowed ladies everywhere who are forced to take in lodgers.

The fact that Necessity (in the guise of the meritorious Mrs. H.) is lurking over my shoulder oughtn't to obscure my view. To those who whisper that I was in the pay of the Chancellor while in Paris, claiming that my testimony must inevitably be colored by the circumstance, I can only reply: Would they I had toiled without remuneration? — for the sheer pleasure of copying tedious documents and transcribing ungainly script? Would my testimony prove less tainted in the event I, a virtual pauper, had offered my talents (such as they are) gratis to one of the wealthiest landowners in New York? Come, come, my friends, let's keep our heads.

What you are about to read isn't the last word (though it may be the first) on the Louisiana Purchase. The factors and circumstances — to say nothing of the number of people — contriving toward that turn of events are spread over two continents and several countries. It would be unlikely for any one person to be acquainted with all of the personages involved, or to be familiar with every landscape and drawing room mentioned.

Consequently, this cannot be a story constructed wholly from first-hand knowledge. I have found it necessary in many cases to rely on information of-fered me by witnesses (friends, colleagues, family members, etc.). And, since scattered accounts don't tend to arrange themselves naturally — à la Madame Récamier — into a form of blissfully-flowing lines, what follows is a patchwork quilt of scenes leading up to and culminating into that momentous event.

A good case in point: While I can count among my indelible impressions a single encounter with the yellow mud of Washington City, a single viewing of President Jefferson has proven our President no match for the mud. A fact that might have constituted a serious hurdle, for, in order to present a comprehen-sive whole, I must go back about a year, to the President's House and the ex-traordinary man who occupies it.

However, I have known the President's private secretary, Captain Meri-wether Lewis, since time immemorial, or ever since our army days in Pitts-burgh, and, as chance would have it, ran into him in Philadelphia earlier this summer. This, truly, was a case of luck, as both of us were stranded in the Pennsylvania capital — Lewis through the courtesy of a lame horse, I through the good offices of a sea captain who, alarmed at rumors of the yellow fever rag-ing in New York City (well founded, it later appeared), refused to lay anchor there.

When you consider, then, that Lewis was, quite literally, at Jefferson's elbow during the crisis which precipitated this entire affair, it strikes me, as it must strike anyone who has ever spent an afternoon at the card tables, that Luck is rarely arbitrary.

— P. C.

NOVEMBER

The President was already at his desk. Meriwether Lewis could barely distinguish the familiar maps on the study's walls in the faint November dawn, but Jefferson's pen scratched over the surface of the paper with the confidence of one who could see where others couldn't. The mockingbird perched atop the presidential shoulder displayed a similar confidence.

For a man, president or not, to have kept the eyesight of a twenty-year old at sixty was remarkable enough, Lewis thought, though he was careful not to say so. Jefferson had a way of reacting to your wonder that got in the way of it. Convinced that stepping into a bowl of cold water at daybreak was the key to healthy blood; that daily tearing on a horse through the swamps of Washington kept your teeth put; that jumping out of bed every morning before the sun could catch you in it saved your eyes, he seemed bent on convincing others.

A timid ray of light came spinning through the window and, in a burst of avian delight, the bird let loose with a penetrating warble. The scratching of the pen ceased. "Not in my ear, please," Jefferson whispered. His grey-blue eyes smiled at the warbler, then at Lewis. "You seem in good spirits this morning, Meriwether."

Lewis shrugged. It took his spirits a while to warm up to the day, as the President well knew. There was little Jefferson did *not* well know about Lewis, and, by the same token, not much that Lewis didn't well know about Jefferson. Except for a brief spell in the woods of Georgia, Lewis had lived all of his early life at Locust Hill, a mere stone's throw from Monticello, from whose rolling heights its owner used to summon young, fatherless Meriwether with a mirror reflecting the sun. Like Monticello, the President's House held no secrets for Lewis who, in his position of private secretary, was a combination of confidant, errand boy, and son to the present occupant.

"Have you had breakfast?" the President asked.

"Only a cup of coffee."

"We shall have it together." Jefferson lifted his tall, rambling frame out of the chair, sending the bird spiraling toward the bookcase. "Have you reminded Mrs. Madison about hosting the dinner this afternoon?"

Lewis smiled. "Mrs. Madison doesn't need to be reminded about hosting a dinner at the President's House."

Jefferson hesitated at the door, as if wondering whether he ought to find this amusing. "I was merely suggesting that, if her husband is still ill, Mrs. Madison might be reluctant to leave his side."

Lewis kept on smiling. He was used to the President saying one thing and meaning another. It came with the Jeffersonian mental territory. "Mr. Madison is always ill. Mrs. Madison will be here this afternoon if she has to be carried in on a stretcher."

Jefferson's hesitation vanished into a grin. "Now, Meriwether . . . " Both men laughed as they made their way through the corridor and into the dining room.

Outside in the yard, near the outhouses, an old slave was covering a sweating horse with a blanket. The horse started urinating, sending up clouds of steam and causing the old man to curse and jump aside. When the downpour stopped, he led the snorting animal out of the yard, in the direction of 14th and G Streets where the stables were located. The exhausted, dirt-streaked courier stood gaping after his departing horse in the bleak morning, his expression and posture typical of the messenger who has spent several days on the roads — relieved to be free of his mount, with his thighs curved as though he were still on it.

A black porter, yawning in his crumpled uniform, deposited the fresh dispatches on the dining room table, lingering near the President and Lewis by the window to take in the scene, a look of benign contempt on his face. When the courier tottered off toward the kitchen, the porter started for the door, nearly upsetting the turbaned, mud-colored woman waddling inside with a covered breakfast tray.

Lewis was halfway through his kidney stew when he noticed the President hadn't touched his toast. His eyes went to an envelope marked "urgent", then gazed questioningly at his employer. "What is it?"

"I must confer with Mr. Madison at once," Jefferson replied, more to himself than to his secretary.

"At this hour of the day, sir?"

"At this, or at any other hour of the day, Captain Lewis, Mr. Madison is the Secretary of State. He will be expecting me."

"Bad news?"

"The Spanish Intendant has closed the port of New Orleans to all American ships. The Westerners are threatening to take New Orleans by force." Jefferson made for the door, then, realizing he was still in his faded red flannel robe, went upstairs to change.

The mile stretch of road called Pennsylvania Avenue was a sea of yellow mud. The heavy rains of the past days had swollen the Tiber Creek beyond its borders, overflowing the Avenue and leaving catfish stranded on its receding. The subdued cacophony of animal and bird noises rising from the bowels of the swampy wilderness was punctuated by the furious quacking of wild ducks and croaking frogs. A rabbit coursed into the alder bushes at Jefferson's approach.

Jefferson saw himself forced to abandon his usual stride. At every step he sank away in the clayey wet soil that clung to his boots like suction pistons. Even so, he preferred being mired in the mud to having his soles lacerated by the white chips of the narrow sidewalk and his breeches splattered with the white muck oozing from them. Mud could be brushed off when dry. It was a preference remembered by his subconscious, for his conscious mind was intent on what was the first serious crisis of his administration. He was determined to do better than either of his predecessors.

Adams, quarrelsome and arrogant, had distinguished himself primarily by alienating everyone in his Cabinet, spending the closing months of his Presidency surrounded by incompetents. A feisty bulldog who, for all his intelligence, ran and barked at all who approached.

Washington was merely vain. The vanity of an old peacock, preening, posturing, knowing himself to be much admired. Washington's main virtue while in office was his distrust of taking action based on impulse. It was a virtue born of necessity. The Father of the Country was slow of comprehension. His was not a mind able to take in a situation at a glance. Both men were honest. Jefferson needed no convincing on that score. No doubt more honest than himself. But honesty in political life was a dubious quality, not altogether a desirable one. The object of the President was the preservation of the Union, the wellbeing of the American people, and in bearing this in mind he knew himself to be as good, or better, than Adams or Washington.

This wasn't self-flattery. He was too proficient in the art of flattering others to want to delude himself. If one could be careless of the truth with others, one oughtn't to take such liberties with oneself. No longer the greenhorn who had botched the governorship of Virginia, he chose to believe that four years in France as United States Minister, and three in Washington's administration as Secretary of State, had furnished him with the necessary political maturity, which, coupled with a little foresight, would guide his Presidency into keeping the several States united and prosperous. And without the use of the Mississippi River and New Orleans, its mouth, the western states were unable to prosper.

He stopped battling the mud for a moment to catch his breath. Aside from a coal-and-wood carter coming from the direction of Georgetown, not a human soul was to be seen in the hazy morning. No sounds emerged from the few frame or brick dwellings sitting helter-skelter along the Avenue. A candle flame wavered disconsolately behind one of the upper story windows of Blodgett's Hotel. The immigrants, packed a dozen to a room on Blodgett's unfinished top floor, were getting ready to continue their daily toils at converting Washington into a city. Often, on returning from his afternoon ride on Wildair, Jefferson would stop to chat with their foreman. Right now he was grateful for the empty road, though he would rather have met with one of those poor wretches than come across any Federalist.

Congressmen, Federalist and Republican-Democrat alike, were

steadily trickling into town from every part of the country. The fact that Congress had yet to meet was a lucky coincidence, allowing the Cabinet a head start to discuss policy, for he could rest assured that the opposition would pounce on this issue and run with it, howling for war.

Not that the West wasn't justified in wanting to take New Orleans by force if Spain didn't relent. A country had a right to the use of its rivers and their mouths. To dispute such a right was to ignore one of the laws of nature. Of course it wasn't Spain, the power at work in New Orleans. Spain had ceded the Louisiana Territory to France. Bonaparte had wheedled it out of the hands of the credulous Carlos IV, in exchange for a few Tuscan provinces to be made into the Kingdom of Etruria for his daughter, a kingdom existing only in the imagination of the wily First Consul of France.

The implications inherent in this secret transaction were ominous. With a man thirsting for power and glory at her head, France was an undesirable neighbor to the United States. Britain, too, was alarmed at a French takeover so near her own colonies in the New World. Events in Saint Domingue were being closely watched, for if Bonaparte's generals succeeded in keeping down the insurrection and stabilizing French rule there, the French army would descend on Louisiana, after which it would be only a matter of time before it marched on the neighboring territories. The closure of New Orleans as a port of trade to the Americans was only the beginning — a mere opening sample of things to come.

The Madisons' cupolaed house loomed somberly amongst the trees on F Street, attaining a grandeur in the shadowy morning light it didn't possess in the day. The icy feel of the iron bell handle penetrated Jefferson's knit glove. He almost jumped as its hysterical shrieking reverberated through his ears. The people inside were used to the diabolical noise apparently, for no one came running to prevent its recurrence. Finally, the sound of slippers dragging over the tiles signaled the approach of old Livinus.

When the elderly slave opened the door, the slight silhouette of the

Secretary of State appeared in the hall, booted and bundled as though for an excursion into the arctic.

"Mr. Jefferson, sir." Madison's lisp bore testimony to his excitement. "I was just about to come to see you." Relief at being spared the ordeal spread over his pale, delicately lined face as he unbundled, piling mufflers, hat, and overcoat onto the extended arms of Livinus, who watched these premature comings and goings with a critical eye.

"Let's go to my study. It's warm there." Taking three steps to Jefferson's every muddy two, Madison rushed ahead of the nearly one-foot-taller President, waiting for both to be safely within the heated confines of the study to say: "Governor Claiborne has informed you, then."

"We must immediately lodge a strong protest with the Spanish Minister," Jefferson replied.

The President and his Secretary of State spoke softly, bringing down their naturally small speaking voices to a near whisper, in deference to those still asleep in the house. "I prepared a draft." Madison reached inside the pocket of his worsted coat for the letter and handed it to Jefferson. "I had thought you could go over it and I would drop it off at Yrujo's on my way back."

"Yrujo's in Philadelphia. We'll have to send it there. Can you make a little light, Jemmy?"

Madison lit the oil lamp on his desk and pushed it to the President's side, after which he went stirring in the coals of the fireplace, throwing on an additional log to provoke the flames into new ardor. Yrujo wasn't alone in coming to Washington City only when his presence was required, he thought. Federalists and Republican-Democrats were of one mind when it came to listing the inconveniences of living in the Capital, a city in name only. Adams had been the first President to take up residence in the unfinished President's House, standing its leaky roofs and drafty rooms all of two months before fleeing for the comforts of New England. Jefferson, perennially engaged in tearing down and building up Monticello, saw nothing particularly unusual in sitting amongst flying bricks and mortar.

In summer even he, of course, deserted Washington City, along with everyone else. Except maybe for the industrious Gallatin, the Swiss-born Secretary of the Treasury, whose sense of duty surpassed his fear of the putrescent, yellow fever-inducing gases rising from the swamps in the miasmic heat. Or else he thought himself immune. Survivors of past yellow plagues often harbored this belief. Not so Dolley.

Having lost her first husband, youngest son, and in-laws to the epidemic that had claimed four thousand lives in Philadelphia nine years earlier, Dolley didn't wait for the arrival of the first heat wave to repair to Montpelier and its pure Piedmont air. Jefferson had gone so far as to directly subject his daughters and house slaves to the dread disease—a newfangled practice called inoculation, viewed with terror by many people, and with good reason, Madison thought. But Jefferson always stopped to investigate newfangled ideas. It was in his nature. He couldn't help himself.

"Excellent, Mr. Madison. It can be dispatched as soon as we've made a copy."

"I've made a copy."

Jefferson smiled. "Ah, Jemmy, what would I do without you?"

The Secretary of State looked pleased. "Shall I draw up the protest to the Governor of Louisiana along the same lines? I take it you do want to protest to him?"

"Absolutely. You know . . . " The President paused to loosen his corduroy waistcoat (the room was stifling hot). "Isn't it curious that the Spanish government should close the port at a time when everybody in the world knows they have ceded Louisiana to France? On whose orders are the officials in New Orleans acting, I wonder?"

A devotee of chess, Madison wasn't in the habit committing himself in a hurry. "Curious indeed. But until the Spanish admit to the cession, we haven't got any choice but to address ourselves to them. Officially, Spain is responsible for the move, regardless of whom might be directing her from the wings. And, whether we like it or not, Mr. Jefferson, she is perfectly within her rights legally, the Treaty granting us right of entrance having expired four years ago."

"Then why not close the port four years ago? Why allow business as usual until now? Because Bonaparte is manipulating the strings, Jemmy, I'm convinced of it."

"That certainly would explain Livingston's failure to get us the port from the French for cash. In his last letter he seems more discouraged than ever. Remind me to show it to you before you leave."

"I can imagine . . . " Jefferson's blue eyes rolled upward, resting on the brass weight of the clock. (If the weight weren't pulled down soon, the clock would stop.) " . . . considering Livingston's disposition."

The President's remark wasn't meant to amuse, Madison knew, nor did it refer to Livingston's temperament *per se*. Rather it meant that the American Minister in Paris, who had deserted the Federalist ranks only recently out of political motive, couldn't be trusted to exert himself for the administration to the extent a convinced Democrat would. Livingston's appointment was a reward to the mighty Livingston clan of New York for having helped sway that state into the Jefferson camp in 1801. For all this, the appointee was well qualified for his post, Madison decided. "Of course, the situation may have changed considerably in the interval." Livingston's letter was dated two months in the past.

"I don't mind telling you, Mr. Madison, that I devoutly wish for the day when ships will be able to cruise faster. I'll console myself for the time being with the knowledge that Yrujo, at least, can be reached within two days. Inform Livingston, and Pinckney in Madrid, and take special care when you answer Governor Claiborne."

The young Governor of the Mississippi Territory was as hot-headed as the Westerners he governed, proposing to gather his militia and storm New Orleans tomorrow. Such impetuousness had to be curbed. "I, too, will write him. Try to calm him down. War is a last resort. It isn't as though the Mississippi River itself were sealed off. The people affected by the closure can't be expected to make these fine legal distinctions, but Governor Claiborne ought to. Even assuming that Bonaparte plans to occupy Louisiana, he can hardly do so without a considerable fleet, the assembling of which would attract much notice of which we would have been informed. This not being the case, our object must be to reclaim our rights by pacific means. What do you think, Jemmy?"

"I agree." The very word war carried a connotation of physical violence repellent to Madison. "If it were up to me, I wouldn't even mention the incident in your address to Congress. Why bring the matter to the attention of the whole nation?"

"Well I haven't, of course, in the speech I drafted . . . Jefferson reached for the coat hanging on the back of his chair, retrieving a set of folded papers he deposited in Madison's hands. "When you have time, maybe you will have a look at these and give me your sugges —" He stopped abruptly as the inner door to the study opened, showing a visibly distraught Mrs. Madison.

"Oh, Mr. Jefferson . . . " Obviously expecting to find her husband alone, Dolley Madison's dark blue eyes darted across the room as if looking for an exit, apparently oblivious to the fact that she was standing in one.

Jefferson, who had risen automatically at her sight, nodded assent to Madison's request to be excused for a few moments. "The reports of the fever raging in the French Islands disturb her sleep," he whispered before going over to his wife and leading her outside the study.

A kind lie, Jefferson thought. Mrs. Madison's nightmares had nothing to do with yellow fever. Jemmy had told him all about it. Poor Dolley. Her obsession with clothes was such that she had recurring dreams of being robbed of them. A peculiar fear, it struck Jefferson. Personally, he found himself at the other end of the spectrum, inviting criticism for his indifference to outward appearance. There was a time when silks and ruffles had meant a great deal to him. Still, the only conceivable nightmares their possession could have caused was how to pay the tailor. But then, he hadn't been raised a Quaker like Dolley Madison, forced to go about dressed in sack cloth, forbidden the wear of those frills and ornaments favored by women the world over.

The Society of Friends, as the Quakers referred to themselves, didn't believe in dress as a means to decorate the body. The Society also deplored slavery, inducing the now late John Payne, Dolley's father, to set free his slaves and leave Virginia for Philadelphia and the community of Quakers there. A move which had brought the Paynes to the brink of poverty.

As the eldest child, Dolley probably had been more deeply affected by these events than had her siblings. In any event, when the Friends expelled her from their Society upon her becoming Mrs. Madison, Dolley dropped her Quaker's garb like a mallard his feathers, setting to a mode of dress which featured to excess all the garniture and embellishments denied her heretofore (There were those who claimed that she had exchanged her religion for a wardrobe).

And, as she had come to attach great value to this accumulation of apparel, she inevitably assumed that others, too, ascribed great worth to it, which, according to Madison, accounted for the bad dreams. That wasn't to say that much in her collection hadn't cost a pretty penny, only that most ladies were bound to hesitate before stepping into the garments coveted by Mrs. Madison, even if invited to.

Her headdress alone had a way of startling people, consisting of elaborately wound, bejeweled and plumed turbans, or similarly complicated constructions, in colors that announced themselves halfway across a room. Being taller than Jemmy, who was conservative in dress, Dolley's towering headgear did nothing to soften the impression of contrasting height and taste, making the Madisons a couple strangers tended to stare at.

The clock made an abrupt, scraping sound, in preparation of striking the hour. Only seven. It seemed to Jefferson that half a day had passed since his rising that morning. He waited till the last stroke had died to walk resolutely toward the clock, grasping the brass weights on either end of the chain in both hands. The pendulum wavered momentarily, the chain rattling as he reversed the position of the weights. He went on to repeat the exercise with the second set of weights. There! The sight would bother him no more.

A slight knock and Madison opened the door, a smile crossing his face on seeing the President standing near the clock. Jefferson didn't mind sitting down to supper in a room with the ceiling missing, but he wouldn't tolerate a portrait frame deviating from its right angle or, as in this case, a timepiece about to deviate from its function. "Mrs. Madison would like to know if you have eaten breakfast, Mr. Jefferson?"

"A good question, Mr. Madison, since I am unable to answer it off-hand." His being in the dining room with Captain Lewis seemed hours ago. "Probably not. How is Mrs. Madison feeling?"

A bright-faced Dolley appearing behind her husband supplied the answer herself. "Mrs. Madison is in fine spirits, thank you, Mr. Jefferson. I expect you will join us at the breakfast table. I couldn't permit a gentleman to depart from here retaining the memory of my disheveled hair."

"As a gentleman my memory would refuse to retain an image such as you describe, Mrs. Madison," the President replied gallantly. It happened to be true as well, for if Mrs. Madison's coiffure had been disheveled, he hadn't noticed. What he *had* noted, though, was that, even in the midst of her distress, she had thought to put on a lavishly embroidered yellow morning coat, presently discarded in favor of a vermilion one adorned with small glittering stones arranged in a flower design, the presumably tousled dark locks hidden beneath a cap of the same vermilion and bearing the same glittering flower motif.

Dear Dolley . . . If it was true, as Meriwether Lewis maintained, that she hadn't a thought in her head, it was equally true that she hadn't a malicious bone in her body. Lewis, who had never set foot in a French salon, was arrested by the facile witticisms of a Theodosia Burr, electing her in his amorous folly to be the standard from which to evaluate all other females. In a competition as unfair as that Dolley was bound to fall by the wayside, Jefferson mused. As for him, he would rather be blinded by a woman's gown than by her wit. He had encountered enough clever women in Paris, eternally meddling in men's affairs, to last him a lifetime.

Dolley took a few steps forward to bring her vermilion person within the circle of light cast by the oil lamp on the desk. "Jimmy tells me you have an urgent letter for Philadelphia, Mr. Jefferson. I had planned on leaving for Philadelphia tomorrow, but I would be happy to start out on the trip today if it would be of help."

Jefferson's face lit up. "That would be splendid, Mrs. Madison!" The post was slow and not always reliable. "Splendid indeed. If it wouldn't be too inconvenient."

Madison's doting eyes smiled up at his buxom wife, then at the President. "Thinking the Spanish Minister in town, it didn't occur to me to mention Mrs. Madison's intended shopping trip earlier."

"Which reminds me . . . " Both Jefferson daughters were planning to come to Washington City later in the month and stay to spend the holidays. "Martha has written me to ask if you would buy her a wig in Philadelphia, Mrs. Madison." He had kept forgetting to ask.

"Did she think to send a lock of hair so the color can be matched?"

"As a matter of fact, yes, she did." It was inside the letter. "I'll have it sent over right away. Are you sure you wouldn't mind the additional errand?"

"My dear Mr. Jefferson . . . " Dolley's smile glowed in unison with her ensemble. "It will be my pleasure."

Of course the President was mistaken in assuming Bonaparte to be behind the move, as I had occasion to discover later, in Paris, working for the Chancellor. Bearing in mind the character of the French First Consul, this certainly was the reasonable conclusion to have reached and, consequently, it was a conclusion reached by many a reasonable man.

To what end should Spain, in the eleventh hour of her reign in Louisiana, suddenly close the port of New Orleans to foreign trade? A measure she knew was bound to provoke hostilities with the Americans?

The fury unleashed from stranded boats and thwarted and mired vessels was a beast untamed and frightening to behold. Mississippi boatmen are not the prettiest sight even at their sober best, and I shouldn't care to lead the reader before a veritable drunken mob of them, were it not that this mob, by its very untamed force, forged the major link in the chain of events to come.

Jefferson had cause to be worried. By the time news of the closure reached him, the west was in turmoil. And the authority presumed to keep order in the territory, the candidate he had appointed governor, was a mere boy.

NATCHEZ

November 1802

Natchez was in upheaval. You didn't need to leave the genteel reaches of Upper Natchez to see it, Governor Claiborne thought. A merchant in Monsieur Ude's Café the previous night claimed to have counted 500 flatboats. Standing amongst the chinaberry trees on the bluffs, the Governor easily believed it. The landing site below looked like an army had invaded it. Countless flatboats, skiffs, pirogues and other canoes, bateaux, keelboats, schooners, barges, rafts, and anything else able to withstand the Mississippi currents in coming downstream, were being unloaded and pulled ashore, dumped between barrels of whiskey, stocks of lumber, piles of smoked meat, otter, beaver and wildcat pelts, linseed, tallow, linen, swine, tobacco, and what have you.

In normal times the bulk of this traffic would proceed to New Orleans. With the port closed, there was nowhere else to go. How all these goods, the perishable ones in particular, were supposed to reach their ultimate destination, was a question Claiborne preferred not to consider, though judging from the flailing of arms and shaking of fists in the maze of deposited cargo and boats, it seemed very much on the minds of those below.

As he climbed down the bluffs in the morning sunlight, a clearing came into view where the various river craft were being demolished for lumber. There was nothing much unusual in that—every sidewalk in New Orleans had been laid with gunwales taken from the great flatboats—other than their considerable numbers, putting the rivermen at the mercy of the local sawmill operators. Another development provoking fits of temper.

How much longer could the West endure this humiliation at the hands of the Spanish before turning murderous? These men from Ohio, Kentucky, Indiana, Tennessee, and Pennsylvania were no bible-chewing Massachusetts Yankees or languid Virginian planters reciting Homer. The Westerner did not walk the earth the same way. This was a new breed of man, born and raised free, master of his own destiny, who had no patience with anything or anyone interfering with that freedom. Bill Claiborne sincerely hoped President Jefferson understood that.

The Spanish officials often complained of their Court in Madrid having no conception of life in the colonies. You didn't have to run that far from home to find governments understanding the local mentality. After the Mississippi Territory became American, President Adams had seen fit to send one of his Yankees to govern it. Possessed of the zeal to reform, Governor Winthrop Sargent had succeeded only in antagonizing planter and pauper alike. The planter of Upper Natchez had no taste for religion; the whores and pimps of Lower Natchez had no use for it; and the man in between, the settler, was too busy trying to survive to be interested. Few minded Sargent's quoting of the Scriptures, but all balked at his closing the grogshops on Sundays. What went on in Natchez-under-the-Hill was good for the entire town, and only an outsider like Sargent, bogged down in New England moral codes, would fail to grasp that.

All he would have to do right now was whistle, Claiborne thought, and the Hoosiers, Buckeyes, and Kaintucks would take to their boats, hooting and hollering at the prospect of wringing Spanish necks. The militia, however eager to float downriver, couldn't work up a fighting sweat like these Kaintucks. A good thing his faith in Mr. Jefferson was solid, else he might start whistling out of hand. As it was, he would just have to simmer down and wait for John Swaney's leather saddlebags to bring him the official go-ahead from the Palace in Washington.

Silver Street, the flat mile of gambling hovels, grogshops, and whorehouses in Lower Natchez where footsore boatmen returning from New Orleans counted on a last fling before continuing further on their trek back east, was being overrun with sharpers, peddlers, mulattos, bruisers, speculators, Flatheads, medicine men, yellow whores from New Orleans, card artists, and other adventurers come to investigate the possibilities of the situation, joining the assortment of tainted characters already present, all of them collaborating with the flow of volatile boatmen to clog its passage.

Mayor Brooks had his hands full. His men were everywhere, trying to build some order out of the chaos. The public stocks and jail could hold only those accused of crimes punishable by hanging. The rest had to be chased out of town after 39 lashes on the bare back. The miserable dwelling on the commons passing for a hospital had seen more cracked skulls than it could administer to.

A group of ragged, broke Kaintucks (all rivermen were called Kaintucks regardless of State of origin, as all were branded flatboatmen regardless of the craft on which they toiled), were bartering their shoes for hard biscuits and Indian cornmeal which was to serve them as sustenance on the long trip home. A slave trader carrying the fruits of his transaction in a bearskin back bag, an epicene preacher, and a peddler — his packhorse loaded with indigo linen shirts, red girdles, fancy calico, looking glasses, gunpowder,, and bullets — were waiting for the barter to conclude to join the men on the meandering trek though the wilderness. The Devil's Backbone wasn't a trail you ventured on alone.

There, behind the cover of cane, sumac, and trumpet flower; the pawpaws, catalpas, broom pines, magnolias, black-ash, and cypress, loomed the chimera of Micajah and Wiley Harpe (better known as the terrible Harpes), the Mason gang, Joseph Thompson Hare, and a stock of equally terrifying bandits determined to rob and quarter the passing traveler.

His black hair slicked down with bear oil, the Herculean half-breed regulating traffic before Madame Aivoges' sagging lodge — an establishment of some refinement, as the whores were reputed to wash themselves — tossed a tattooed brave into the crowd. The tattooed warrior — a Chickasaw it looked like — promptly set to snoring on the spot, invulnerable to the contempt of Madame Aivoges' muscle-flexing giant, oblivious to the kicks and curses of those trying to pass.

A black pig came squealing past, pursued by two barking dogs and the man who had allowed it to escape. The pig raced inside The Liquor Vault and House of Entertainment, mistaking its opening passage for the route to freedom.

His peripheral vision warned Claiborne of the oppressing proximity of two individuals. His coming down to take stock of the mood in person was foolish, he now realized. There was nothing happening in Lower Natchez which couldn't be observed comfortably from the polite porticoed mansions of Upper Natchez. It was a lot easier to identify with the plight of the people when you weren't stuck in the middle of them.

"This here kid's the Gov'nuh?" The Kaintuck speaking had eyes the color of the tobacco juice he generously distributed over the sinking flagstones, and teeth to match. The second seemed of milder aspect and well in his cups.

If he happened to forget that he looked younger than his 26 years, Bill Claiborne thought, there always was somebody obliging enough to remind him. When he had arrived in Washington to represent his adopted State of Tennessee (He was a Virginian by birth and education), he was 21 — underage actually — though no one told him to go home, just so, you'd have thought, the entire Congress could rile him about it. The tobacco-chewing pair positioned themselves in front of him, awaiting confirmation of their indirect question.

"I'm the Governor, yes."

"My, my, ain't we pretty . . . "

His buckskins and canvas shirt differed from theirs only in that they were still of one piece. He mustn't play into their hands and get himself upset. Claiborne smiled: "Seeing as I've got on the same bucks as you, it has to be I'm just naturally pretty."

This greatly entertained the one in one in his cups. The yellow-eyed one was harder to please. "When ya aimin' gone down to New Orleans, Gov'nuh boy?"

"First thing tomorrow." The decision was made right then and there. He had protested the closure of the port to the Governor of Louisiana right off. Governor de Salcedo had made a point of likewise replying right away that he knew nothing of the measure taken by Intendant Morales, who had gone over both his own and the Governor's head in taking it. No such instructions had come to him from Madrid, wrote de Salcedo, and he would immediately inform His Catholic Majesty of

Morales' insubordination. A well-bred visit to the Gouvernatorial Hotel in New Orleans wasn't exactly what his Kaintuck chums had in mind, Claiborne knew, but anything was better than sitting on the bluffs day after day, waiting for news.

"Need a hand?"

"Not just yet. I'm going alone for now."

"Hear that Ben? He's goin' alone. Our Gov'nuh boy here is aimin' to take New Orleans from the dons all by hisself. My, my, ain't we brave. How's you figurin' on gettin' yousself settled on the landing, Gov'nuh?"

His companion knew. "I reckon he'll fall back on his looks."

This time both were howling with delight, slapping their tattered buckskins and pounding each other's back, jostling a trio of colleagues coming out of the shack across. "Hey, boys: This here's the man aimin' to take on the dons all by his lonesome."

The sudden thunder of pounding hoofs mercifully put an end to the exchange, as all afoot scrambled to run for cover. Claiborne legged it along with everyone else, approaching the safety of a lumberyard in time to see a tribe of Choctaws descending on Silver Street, the feet of their wild-maned Opelousas red from the juice of wild strawberries through which they had stormed.

"Whiskey! Whiskey!"

Willing to give up one of their handsome, wiry little horses if need be to procure themselves with the desired liquor, Choctaws holding doubloons, dollars, halves, quarters, bits, pistareens, and picayunes didn't wait for the bargained-for barrel to materialize, and poured inside the grogshops and shanties, gulping down at breakneck speed the rye and whiskey their bodies had no tolerance for. This was the invariable *introitus* of Moskhagean descent into town. At some point during his climb to Upper Natchez, the Governor knew, a kind of hell would break loose, when the band would turn violent with whiskey rage, at which time only a certain old Frenchman living in a cave could whip them back into a semblance of normalcy. Dauntless in the face of knife or gun, the Choctaws had an inordinate fear of Baptiste's whip.

When he arrived on the bluffs, the gentility had gathered under the chinaberry trees on Main Street to watch the mayhem below. Baptiste had been dragged from his cave and, hair flying, was brandishing his whip. Claiborne walked on. He had seen the show before.

Aside from a table of card players not to be distracted from their wagers, the King's Tavern was empty, which suited him just fine. All he wanted was to drink his Monongahela rye in peace. The clock was chiming twelve, leaving half a day to arrange for transportation downriver. He would go down to New Orleans first thing in the morning.

As any American with relatives in the Old Country knows, an entire season can come and pass before acknowledgement of one's letter is received from overseas. Or, in the words of Mrs. Hagedoorn, "Life is nothing but waiting for something."

Even though Mrs. H.'s voice struggles under the weight of various sum totals when it delivers this verity, I am quoting it here for the benefit of the reader apprehensive at being abandoned outside the flagstoned, Gouvernatorial Mansion in Upper Natchez (while inside Bill Claiborne is shouting for dried beef and biscuits, his shaving box, musket, a change of shirt, and whatever else a gentleman of his station is likely to carry on the two- or three-week-float — dependent on the currents — down the Mississippi to the Iberville), only to be propelled across the Atlantic and deposited amongst strangers in more unfamiliar territory still.

It isn't that, free myself of the vicissitudes of travel, I revel in hurtling the unwary across vast distances at unnatural speeds, but, rather, that a rear sight of several months delivers one from the constraints of time imposed upon the participants.

In Washington City, President Jefferson and his Secretary of State are anxiously awaiting news from Paris and Madrid. In Paris, Chancellor Livingston is waiting to hear from Talleyrand while Bonaparte is impatient to hear from the SpanishCourt. In New Orleans, Governor de Salcedo is likewise eager for word to reach him from Madrid. And in Madrid, the whole Court is waiting for the King.

November 1802

H is Majesty, Carlos IV, King of Spain, couldn't put his finger on it. The behavior of his grandson Luis was baffling. He and the Queen had had twelve children, only half of whom had reached maturity, it was true, yet wasn't six a sufficient number to inform oneself of what was customary behavior in a child? The King was aware that children lost their charm when they acquired speech, but what child, at four, spoke about affairs of state? This was all the more painful because the boy was Pépita's, Their Majesties most beloved daughter. Was this the punishment for selecting a favorite from amongst one's own offspring? As a God-fearing Monarch, he must repent this parental transgression.

The King's confessor claimed that God had blessed rather than punished him in Luis, but it was in the nature of Jesuits to delight in clever words. They encouraged the boy to formulate sentences in the fashion of adults and replied to his questions as though they were pertinent.

This saddened Carlos, for Luis wasn't destined to enter the Church, and meanwhile his childhood — that precious time in the life of a prince when he was free to do as he pleased — was being frittered away in speech. Those things providing the deepest satisfaction — the forge, the hunt, bookbinding, shoemaking, carpentry, playing the violin — were not dependent on language. Simply opening the back of a pocket watch and observing its intricate mechanism filled one with a joy unequaled by any verbal address, including divine (may the Lord forgive him).

"The Contino is here, Your Majesty," the valet announced.

The King hastily gathered the watches on the heavy table into the pockets of his breeches and waistcoat and whistled for his confessor whom he had forgotten was already in the room. Two giant hounds emerged from their torpor near the smoldering fire to run alongside the Jesuit at the summons, then raced toward the opening door to welcome the slight visitor, knocking him over in their enthusiasm.

The Contino squealed with pleasure. "Good morning, Grandpapa!"

he shouted from the floor.

Carlos's sluggish face brightened. In spite of his odd ways, it was very difficult not to love the boy. "Good morning, Luis. Did you remember to say a prayer for your poor papa?"

"Yes, Sire," the accompanying governess bowed.

"When Papa dies I shall be king!" Luis cried at the dogs.

"You mustn't say such things." The governess pulled her young charge upright. "Look at you. You're full of dog hair."

"Why not? Everybody says he is dying."

"You won't be king until you are of age, even if your father dies," Carlos admonished sternly, lowering a fleshy jowl for his grandson to plant on a kiss.

The boy's intelligent dark eyes took in the bulging grandfatherly pockets. "Why do you carry so many watches, Grandpapa?"

"Because it spoils pocket watches not to be worn."

"When I am king, I will buy you better clothes. With bigger pockets," Luis promised. "Maybe even a uniform like General Bonaparte."

"Gracious heavens!" The King stared at his old nankin breeches caked with horse dung and the hairs of various animals. "I'm glad you reminded me. You'd better leave now. Grandpapa must prepare himself to meet the Queen and Don Manuél."

"I know! You have to sign the Treaty."

Grasping the boy's hand, the governess hurriedly bowed out of the chamber. "Your Majesty."

"Everybody's waiting for you to sign it, Grandpapa!"

The valet quickly shut the door, proceeding toward an armoire dark with age to retrieve clothes suitable for the occasion.

Carlos sighed deeply. "I can see no Christian charity in that boy, no humility, no concern for his desperately ill father. His thoughts are fastened solely upon receiving a throne. He flatters, he cajoles, he listens at doors, and addresses me like a minister who forgets himself. 'Where is my kingdom, Grandpapa?' he asks me roundly every other day. Are these the concerns of a four-year-old, Father?" The King looked imploringly at the plump Jesuit priest.

The confessor's voice was sympathetic. "The boy is intelligent beyond his years, Sire."

"So I am told. But if this be true, why then does he endeavor to spoil his own childhood? Would not a child as intelligent as you say be reluctant to toss away his precious youth for mere political intrigue? I have tried to reason with him, only to have him look at me with contempt."

The Jesuit smiled. "I doubt whether the Contino understands the meaning of contempt, Your Majesty."

"Do you doubt the King's ability to recognize contempt when he sees it? It is my punishment for confiscating papal lands, I tell you. I should never have let myself be persuaded to become a party to this ugly business. Not even for the sake of Pépita."

"Perhaps it isn't too late to make amends, Sire."

"And offend Pépita? And the Queen? And Manuél? And those rascally Frenchmen beating at the gates? Concessions! Concessions! How many more of them must I make before I am left in peace? Strife! Strife! Strife! I cannot bear it. Why do I have ministers if not to lift these burdens from me? Am I not a peaceful man? Don't I have the best of intentions for Spain? Is it the lot of a king to be unhappier than his subjects? I am told the people are poor, hungry, that they lead a hard life. I ask you, is it a hard life to be free to ply a trade? Can you say as much for your king? Am I free to enter the royal forge at my leisure? To bind my books? Repair my clocks?"

"What on earth is the matter? Why are you so animated, Carlos?"

Queen Maria Luisa and Prime Minister Don Manuél de Godoy had entered unannounced, sending the confessor creeping into a corner. The bony, beringed hand of the Queen tapped one of the hounds on the head. "Surely, sir, you would like to see this matter done with? Pépita needs a kingdom to go with her title."

"A title every royal house in Europe refuses to recognize."

"Because you refuse to sign the Treaty and make it legitimate. Could you possibly not want to see your daughter reigning Queen of Etruria?" Maria Luisa smiled incredulously at the thought, displaying a set of wooden teeth ranging in color from beige to auburn.

"You ask me to sign away a vast domain in the New World in exchange for a few Tuscan provinces that aren't Bonaparte's to cede?"

"A wilderness in exchange for a kingdom for Pépita. Don't pretend you don't know that Louisiana is a losing proposition. And the First Consul promised to indemnify the Holy Father for the confiscation of his lands."

The King turned to the lazily-sensual former Royal Bodyguard catapulted to Prime Minister by the Queen, who was dozing handsomely erect in his dazzling uniform of generalissimo — a rank invented by him for the purpose. "Do you trust that man to deliver on his promises, Manuél?"

"Bonaparte is a great soldier, Your Majesty."

"Soldiers have scant respect for property."

The Queen flared her several antiquated robes about in a gesture windy with anger. 'Are you a Bourbon, sir, or a Moor, who haggles over trifles?"

"I am the King of Spain, Madam."

"A king who prefers the company of hounds, horses, and Jesuits to that of the human species. A king who defiles his hands performing tasks the lowest hidalgo would consider beneath his dignity. If you are the King, sir, then perform a kingly task — sign!"

Accepting the papers from Godoy, Carlos sagged into his chair before the massive table, scrawling his signature wherever the Prime Minister pointed, after which he fled to the door, only to find the Contino lurking behind it.

"Did you sign, Grandpapa? Is it mine?" Questions which instantly earned him a royal slap on the cheek by an exasperated Carlos.

The King whistled and, with his hounds and confessor in tow, paced through the gleaming corridor of the Royal Palace in the direction of the forge.

I can't help feeling a certain affection for this King, who exhibits a logic all his own. Like any true believer defending his faith, there is not a question put to him for which he cannot furnish a reply.

This being said, one does well to keep in mind that the reign of Carlos IV seems determined on sundering the great empire that is Spain — with considerable assistance from the Queen and Godoy, true. To say nothing of Bonaparte, whose imagination, abundantly fertile though it is, could not have devised a trio more willing to fit into his designs.

November 1802

ne million two hundred thousand francs!" Bonaparte's voice boomed off the palatial ceilings of the Tuileries as he stormed down the staircase and burst into his wife's yellow drawing room. "A million two hundred thousand francs!"

Diminutive in layers of white Indian muslin, Josephine shrank further within the confines of the striped satin *causeuse*, awash in tears, vainly holding on to the voluminous skirt of one of two ladies in the room, both of whom had jumped up at the First Consul's sight and darted toward the door at which he pointed. Félicité stood yapping furiously at the intruder's boots, hairs on end in beribboned indignation. A moment later the pint-sized canine landed in the corridor, courtesy of those same boots.

"Have you gone mad completely?!" Looking about for an appropriate object to express his rage, Bonaparte grabbed ahold of the gilt-lidded Sèvres vase on the chimney mantle and sent it crashing against the silk-papered wall behind the *causeuse*. "One million two hundred thousand francs! I can finance my Louisiana expedition for one million two hundred thousandd francs! Who can pay debts of this magnitude?" The unlidded porcelain companion to the vase at the other end of the mantle followed the same fate of the first.

Talleyrand entered the drawing room and gently closed the door, allowing the servants outside to desert their niches and corners and take up closer listening posts. Prevented from keeping up with the First Consul less by his limp than by his lack of enthusiasm for the impending scene, the Foreign Minister's cool grey eyes marked the debris as being concentrated left of center and, consequently, repaired to the right. Conditioned by rules of breeding rooted eight hundred years in the past, Charles Maurice de Talleyrand-Périgord remained fixedly upright near the marble chimney-piece, unable to do otherwise until someone bade him be seated.

"I keep urging the country to be thrifty, trying to practice what I preach by adopting a policy of economy, setting a good example, and all the while my wife is throwing millions out of windows and doors! Millions she doesn't have! Millions *I* don't have! Money means nothing to her. When I earned a hundred, she spent a thousand. When I made a thousand she squandered twenty thousand. There's no end to it! She'll never change. It doesn't occur to her that bills have to be paid. Practical considerations don't enter her head. That would be facing up to reality, which is another subject that means nothing to her . . . "

Bonaparte sank into a mahogany chair near the fireplace, his sallow-skinned Roman face flushed with anger. Finding the temperature in the room as unbearable as his wife's debts, he ripped off the green coat of his uniform and threw it at the door behind which Félicité, recovered from her unexpected exit, was yapping with renewed fury.

Josephine continued weeping silently into a scented lace hanky at the extreme end of the pale yellow couch—a tableau of grief cloaked in white. Talleyrand wasn't moved. He had admired the tableau before and had no particular desire to be drawn into it. The other reason for his presence at the Tuileries was hardly more inspiring, he thought, prompted as it was by the United States Minister, who, in his single-minded harping on the subject of New Orleans was beginning to present a tediously predictable portrait of his own, but at least it had the virtue of being in the line of duty. Madame Bonaparte could do well to weep, it being one of the few functions at which she excelled. Together with a flair for instant improvisation.

Incapable of telling the truth, her lying had no purpose other than immediate extrication from the predicament at hand, at which time some inner instinct would prompt a response harmonious with the temperament of the person demanding whatever explanation of whatever indiscretion, resulting in more variations on any one theme than the most baroque of musical inventions. But, unlike the composer of such an invention, who would at least have noted down his efforts for future reference, Mme Bonaparte's mind refused to consider complications beyond the moment's. Not lying for either pleasure or gain, she could neither laugh nor reason her way out when caught, meeting the inevitable final confrontation behind a flood of tears.

Mme Bonaparte was no exception in resorting to this classically female weapon to disarm men, certainly, but to hold a sword didn't necessarily mean one was a skillful duelist, Talleyrand thought. His own wife, possessed of a brain similar in density to Josephine's, understood this very well. Rather than waste her energy, sobbing at random when faced with the vagaries of existence, Catherine reserved her own, not inconsiderable, supply of tears for the arrival of the first gallant rescuer (He ought to know. It was in this capacity that he had found his way into her bed, displacing the previous gallant). That, more than her beauty, was Catherine's redeeming feature. Beauty, once memorized, no longer fascinated.

"Did I ever tell you about the first time I saw her house at Croissy? It was a charming house. Full of lovely things, vases . . . " Bonaparte kicked one of the Sèvres chards on the Turkish carpet to illustrate his point. " . . . paintings, statuettes, elegant furniture, soft carpets, flowers everywhere . . . Very charming. Well, Citizen Minister, during the night I happened to wake up hungry and ventured into the kitchen. There was nothing in it. No pots, no pans, no cups; not a coffeepot, not a plate — pretty plates all over the walls of the house, but in the kitchen not a saucer — nothing that could serve a practical purpose. And of course not a morsel of food. That, Citizen Talleyrand, is my wife. The woman everyone in France tells me is my lucky star. 'Ha, General Bonaparte, what a lucky man you are!' they say. 'Madame Bonaparte is so kind, so sweet, so compassionate. An angel who gives us the jewels off her back because she can't stand to see a sad face.'

"On our return trip from my Italian campaign, a bunch of peasants stopped the coach to congratulate me. They were a wretched looking bunch — barefoot, dirty, probably starving. One look at them and my wife was weeping her heart out. 'Oh, Bonaparte, these poor people,' she cried, and immediately proceeded to make them into millionaires, taking off her jewelry and stuffing it in their grimy hands. I remember, there was a screaming baby she handed a diamond broach. He stopped screaming just long enough to try to eat it. This act the peasants interpreted as an omen the child would grow up to become a jeweler and get rich. Why else would he bite a diamond, correct?

"The whole miserable lot fell on their knees, and kiss, kiss, kiss" — Bonaparte kissed his shirt sleeve in several spots — "all over my wife, who beamed at me! 'Bonaparte, look how happy they are.' I told her, I, too, would be happy if I'd just been handed a fortune in diamonds. Diamonds which weren't paid for, needless to say. The crimes my wife has committed in the face of sadness, Citizen Minister, are simply innumerable. What she fails to understand is that all a hungry man needs to be happy is a bowl of soup. Only excess will satisfy her . . . "

Talleyrand kept standing patiently, philosophically, waiting for the Bonapartian monologue to play itself out. Experience had shown that interruption at this point would only needlessly jeopardize the remaining Sèvres. If only he was offered a chair.

"She tells me she loves animals." The First Consul rose to pace the carpet with his hands folded in back, a mannerism he couldn't control and which indicated a return to normal. "So do we have a passel of dogs? No, we must also have Merino sheep, Swiss cows, Arabian horses, Carolina ducks, ponies, kangaroos, chamois, gazelles, monkeys, parrots, cockatoos, West Indian birds, storks, and God knows what else of which I don't know the name. The same with flowers. Is she content with the myriads of flowers growing on French soil? No, she must have 250 varieties of roses alone, and introduce nearly as many new exotic flowers to the country. I am constantly tripping over strangers at Malmaison she tells me are botanical or zoological experts, cleaners, and keepers of paddocks and hothouses, and so on. When I ask what good these things are locked behind grilles and glass, the question astonishes her into tears.

"If it were my intention, Citizen Minister, to invade the botanical gardens of this earth, the world would be mine because my wife could point the way to every single one of them. To hold a pen tires her out, except when it comes to acquiring bulbs and seed. Nothing can stop her then. Not even war. When I was in the middle of my campaign against

Britain, my wife was writing the curator of the London botanic gardens asking for tulip bulbs."

Josephine, who seemed to have settled down a bit, shook her dark head behind the lace hanky to lisp feebly in protest: "Not tulip bulbs, Bonaparte. Tulips come from Holland."

"That isn't the point. The point is France was at war with England. The wife of General Bonaparte does not write the enemy her husband is fighting. It isn't done! Don't you *understand* that?" Bonaparte sighed in exasperation, shaking his head at Talleyrand, who smiled, asking:

"Did the curator reply?"

"He did better than that. He sent her the tulips. All while I am trying to sink England into the ocean. Can you imagine? You see what I am up against here?"

"We all have our cross to bear, Citizen First Consul."

Bonaparte nodded, his sallow face suddenly aglow with cherubic mirth. At least Josephine didn't commit the enormous gaffes of a Catherine Talleyrand, the latest of which still had the whole of Paris tittering. Last week at one of Talleyrand's *soirées*, the dunce had mistaken a famous author for Daniel Defoe, pestering him during dinner with questions about Friday. To save his hostess any embarrassment, the author had answered these inquiries as best he could; and the blunder would probably not have been discovered if she hadn't insisted on introducing him to other guests as Daniel Defoe, something to which the fellow took umbrage. As Bonaparte saw it, the fault was entirely Talleyrand's. If he didn't force his wife to read books, she wouldn't have known about Friday, and he wouldn't now be the laughingstock of Paris. "I married a spendthrift, Citizen Minister, and you married a fool."

"A clever woman often compromises her husband, a fool only compromises herself."

"And a spendthrift ruins both. Your wife may not be able to tell one writer from the next, but her instinct for recognizing a gold coin is infallible. In that respect at least she does you honor, Citizen. You have trained her well." The First Consul could never resist an opportunity to refer to his Foreign Minister's love of money. Talleyrand graciously bowed his elegant, lavishly-wigged head, as if accepting a dazzling compliment. "You overestimate my influence, Citizen First Consul," he offered in a low, pleasant voice. "Madame Talleyrand's instinct is a natural gift."

"In a Creole? Impossible!" Bonaparte pointed at Josephine. "All a Creole knows about money is how to lose it. I don't know what happens to an ordinary Frenchman when he becomes a colonist in the New World, but here before you sits the result."

Talleyrand could have reminded him that Josephine was born at Martinique whereas Catherine had grown up in India, which might have accounted for the difference. Instead he decided the moment propitious to ask: "Citizen First Consul, what shall I tell the American Minister with regard to Louisiana? He is becoming very insistent in his demands for official confirmation of the cession."

"I thought the American Minister was deaf. Is he blind as well that he can't see for himself what's in the newspapers?"

"It is precisely the conjecture in the papers which Mr. Livingston is anxious to see dispelled or affirmed by the Consulate. As I told you, his government is interested in acquiring New Orleans."

"As is everybody else. Mr. Livingston isn't the only one to be anxious. Where, Citizen Minister, is the Treaty?" The First Consul stopped pacing to pause before Talleyrand. "Didn't you assure me four weeks ago that it would shortly be in my possession, properly ratified?"

"The mails are slow, Citizen First Consul. In the meantime what shall I tell the American? I don't suppose you want me to be candid?"

"No need to tax yourself, Citizen Minister," Bonaparte smiled (Talleyrand resorted to truth the way other men resorted to lies — in an emergency). "What have you told him thus far?"

"Nothing of consequence."

"Fine. Keep it up."

"He has presented two memorandums addressed to you."

"What do they say?"

"As I said, they are addressed to you."

"Yes, yes, I heard. What do they say?"

"Not much that he hasn't said before."

"Very well. Then there isn't much for you to add to your replies. My concern is for the Treaty, Citizen Minister. Why hasn't it arrived? What is preventing those miserable Bourbons in Madrid from keeping their end of the bargain?"

"Reason perhaps?" Talleyrand couldn't help himself. Fortunately for France (and unfortunately for Spain) reason was a capacity the Spanish Bourbons lacked in abundance.

Quick to interpret a remark to be at his expense, the First Consul shouted, piqued: "While you are amusing yourself, Citizen Minister, my wife's debts are mounting! How do you propose to discharge this enormous sum? Since you and Fouché were so good to bring this matter to my attention, I assume you have in mind a solution?"

"I propose we do what we did the last time and offer the merchants half of the amount charged. They will be happy to comply. They were last time."

"You paid the merchants half of the amount charged the last time? What, pray tell, became of the other half? Isn't this being a trifle greedy, even for you?" Bonaparte walked over to Josephine, who had fallen to weeping desperately once again. "Enough of this!" His voice softened. "Why didn't you tell me right away this capital sum could be reduced by half? You know I haven't the kind of heart to see tears flowing unmoved." He turned to Talleyrand. "One can't be a man without being weak."

Josephine didn't reply. What her husband didn't realize and she realized all too well was that the given sum was the reduced one. Talleyrand had misunderstood, else he wouldn't have mentioned it.

"May I point out, Citizen First Consul, that Bourrienne dealt with the tradesmen the last time, not I." Talleyrand never made a secret of his taking bribes, only of their amount. However, he refused to stand suspected of a scheme he had neither implemented nor profited from.

"My secretary? I don't believe it." Already Bonaparte's baritone was reverberating through the hall. "Bourrienne?! Bourrienne?!"

Félicité stood growling cautiously in the open doorway, waiting for the arrival of the panting secretary to make her entrance in his wake. Bourrienne picked up the military coat at his feet, then, not knowing what to do with it, held it in his ink-stained hands. "Yes, General?"

"You've been skimming, have you? Pocketing half the money I gave you to pay off my wife's debts. My own secretary! I am surrounded by liars and thieves. Get out of my sight! You are dismissed as of this moment."

"General Bonaparte, please, listen to me. What you gave me was only half the amount due. We never dared tell you the entire amount. The merchants rob Madame. One of them was given thirty-five thousand francs instead of eighty thousand and still had the impudence to say he was making a profit."

As it began to dawn on Bonaparte that the 1,200,000 francs were not 600,000, but in effect half of a resounding 2,400,000, even the pugnacious mutt elected silence as the wisest procedure.

Talleyrand used the hiatus of calm to make good his escape, velvet-voiced and silken-ruffled, in a display of exquisite manners. All during his walk amidst the marble, gilt, and satin of the spacious corridor, his ears were treated to the sounds of shattering china and glass.

Anyone questioning the veracity of a Bonaparte leaving behind a trail of broken crockery ought to have a word with one of his household retinue. Any random selection will do, for it is a rare bird indeed which has not, at one time or another, been contacted by some flying projectile, human not excluded, Mme Bonaparte's hairdresser being foremost among these (as he assured me personally, not without a certain pride).

Parisians are amused at these tales of wreckage and rage coursing at irregular intervals into their city. Americans visiting the Chancellor would marvel at this, but American weights and measures are useless when it comes to sizing up the French. A good case in point is Jean Jacques Régis Cambacérès, whose passion for food is surpassed only by his passion for boys. In any other country a man like this would, at best, have been elected taster — not to pronounce on the quality of the food, but to be the first to fall silent should it be poisoned. In

France Cambacérès is appointed Second Consul and his first passion dismissed as "a little failing." The French can't decide on what is shameful and so they are ashamed of nothing.

But I am digressing. By this time Governor Claiborne is done battling cottonmouth water moccasins and other Mississippi terrors and has arrived in New Orleans, anxious to get a hearing from one of the Spanish officials and find out what is behind the closure of the port.

November 1802

Governor Claiborne hesitated before shifting position in the cypress chair, aware that every time the corn-shuck seat creaked, the Capuchin monk, reading his breviary by the window near the loggia, would turn his dark, penetrating gaze from the black leather-bound prayer book to coat him with disapproval for this wanton mobility.

Sitting in Governor de Salcedo's receiving room, trapped in his Sunday best, Claiborne knew he was in for a long wait. The fact that his visit to the Gouvernatorial Hotel was unexpected and that de Salcedo was a man long past his prime, who took ten minutes to cross the street and would probably need half a day to step into his uniform of brigadier-general, were not likely to shorten the waiting period.

The fireplace was dead, and the brick-floored room unreceptive to the mild fall weather outside. Suspended on the whitewashed wall above the hearth were the portraits of what seemed to be the King and Queen of Spain. The King was a hearty type with a double chin, the Queen looked slightly drunk or slightly crazy (it was hard to say which), with vivid, arresting eyes and a chin resembling her spouse's.

Immediately above the royal pair hung a black wooden cross with a bronze Christ, who looked balefully down at the gold framing His Catholic Majesty's likeness. A branch of dried out palm was stuck behind the crucifix. To the monk's right, between the window and the glass double door, was the picture of a Madonna cradling a Spanish-looking infant Jesus whose right hand was clasped affectionately under his mother's cheek. *La Virgen Blanca* it said at the bottom. The Virgin, however, was gold rather than white, from her multi-pointed crown and smiling face down to the richly decorated garment covering her feet, as was her Son. A rosary was draped around the glassed-in image, reminders all that this was papist territory, a place where saints and sinners, nuns and whores, gamblers and priests walked together in peculiar harmony.

The Spanish colonials rushed from church to gaming hall in their gold-epauletted uniforms and flashing medals, unburdening their souls and pockets with equal dedication. Severe Capuchins would shout at them from the pulpit in the morning and glare over their fringed epaulettes at night, staining their austere cassocks with the better goods of this world while publicizing the advent of the next one. A difficult lot for an Anglo-Saxon and Protestant to understand, and not just because of the difference in language, which was a barrier in its own right.

General Wilkinson had promised to act as translator, claiming to be fluent in Spanish as well as French. A claim not easily verified, Claiborne realized, since he himself was a stranger to both tongues, but which he found hard to accept at face value, for he was no stranger to the General.

There was no denying General Wilkinson was on cozy terms with every Spanish official of note, running to partake of their generous hospitality at every turn. Governor Claiborne hadn't been surprised to see him that morning working the Wilkinson magic on a planter's wife in Chartres Street instead of laboring with his men to broaden the Natchez Trail into a passable road. The General wasn't too keen on toiling in the wilderness, his nature inclining him more towards the delights of New Orleans. It was a preference he shared with most men, and hardly one you could blame him for, Claiborne thought. Even his knack for striking up intimate friendships with the dons wouldn't have troubled the Governor, if it weren't that General Wilkinson, Commander-in-Chief of the United States Army, had not, somewhere along building these intimacies, become a spy in the service of Spain.

The General, of course, tossed aside these charges with the same grand flourish of arm deployed in kissing a lady's hand. Invention, fabrication, gossip of the jealous and the malicious-minded, suggested he. When Claiborne wondered why first President Adams, and now President Jefferson, kept as head of the country's army an individual publicly known as Number Thirteen, his questions were dismissed by the veteran politicos as being inspired by the idealism of youth.

Idealism?

He was young, yes, yes, but wasn't idealism perfection? Was it demanding perfection to want a U.S. Commander-in-Chief who *wasn't* a spy for a foreign country? The thinking in Washington seemed to be that a known spy was preferable to a secret one, for then important information could be withheld from him, or . . .

A smattering of voices in the loggia interrupted Claiborne's reflections. A black valet in a white wig threw open both panels of the French door in a gesture supposing an eminent or voluminous entrant. It was the latter.

With a grin as broad as his carcass, General Wilkinson advanced on the Spanish monk, who dropped his breviary in the excitement of recognition. *"Muy general mío!"* His triangular face bloomed on reaching to embrace the General.

"My dear père Antoine."

Claiborne was on the side of Andrew Ellicott, who, having been the recipient of various Spanish embraces on Spain's official transferal to the U.S. of the Mississippi Territory, had pronounced men's kissing a most abominable custom.

Wilkinson seemed to the custom born, smacking back every kiss on the monk's bony cheeks. "Hello, my boy," he greeted Claiborne. "Sorry I'm late. Père Antoine, my dear amigo, this is Governor Claiborne, a compatriot and dear friend, who has asked for my assistance in his dealings with His Honor, Governor de Salcedo."

The Capuchin nodded, to the manner rather than the incomprehensible English, extending a stringy hand to Claiborne. *"Me alegre."*

"Pleased to meet you, Father." Claiborne picked up the prayer book and was in the process of returning it to its owner when the valet returned, bearing a silver tray with steaming coffee, hot milk, sugar, chocolate-covered sweets, and a bottle of Armagnac. He deposited the tray on the table before the hearth, staring expectantly at Wilkinson *"Vous désirez autre chose, mon général?"*

"No, this'll do nicely. *Merci*, Florentin." The General sat down, inviting Claiborne and père Antoine to do likewise. "This, Governor, is the best coffee in the world. Only the Spanish know how to make good coffee," he explained, drinking his cup like a man who had tasted the brew in every corner of the globe and had found it wanting. Silence ensued as the monk said grace.

When the pastries were consumed, the General leaned back in his *empire* armchair and, a cognac at arm's length, asked Claiborne: "You didn't stop at the Intendancy, did you?"

"Why, yes, General, I did. Seeing as it was on my way and the Intendant being the one who clamped down on trade, I thought I ought to."

"A tactical error, my boy. You should know by now the Governor and the Intendant aren't on speaking terms. What did he say?"

"He wasn't at home for me."

"Lucky for you. The Governor is plenty upset as it is without you going behind his back, consulting with his enemies. He's lived too long to have his authority trampled on at this point by a civilian. This whole business is getting to him. He's coming apart just hearing Morales mentioned."

Wilkinson's handsome features struggled valiantly for recognition under his bloated, florid face. When successful (not too often nowadays), it was possible to discern in it a certain resemblance to those angelic, winged infants with which papists liked to decorate their buildings, Claiborne mused. "I sympathize, General, but if the Governor really is the authority around here, then why doesn't he simply ignore the Intendant's proclamation and reopen the port?"

"The purse is an office independent of the sword. The Governor can't meddle in the affairs of the Intendant without orders from Spain. Don't worry, Governor. I'll put in a good word for you."

"It's not for *me*, General, it's for the country."

"Of course it's for the country, my boy, but countries don't run themselves. Good words are put in by and for the people who run the countries, otherwise what good do you think they'd be?" Wilkinson paused to take a sulphur-tipped splint from the chimney mantle and drew it through the fold of glass paper nearby to light one of the small cigars he favored, puffing furiously to erase the foul smell of the sulphur with that of the cigar. "I single-handedly opened the River to

American trade. When Jay and all the rest of Washington's boys were throwing up their arms, resigned to leaving the Mississippi to Spain for all time, *I* showed them up for the ninnies they were."

Claiborne nodded, accepting one of the small cigars. He was only a boy at the time, but the General's initial descent into New Orleans was a tale people loved repeating. There had been a few others before him who had attempted the trip. When a man saw a river he was bound to try it out. The Spanish at the other end, though, hadn't been too enthusiastic; without official guidelines, they acted as the mood moved them. Until, in 1787, General Wilkinson loaded two flatboats with tobacco, salted meats, beaver pelts and the like, and, loading his own person in a separate vessel, took to the Mississippi in style, staying in Natchez just long enough for the news to reach New Orleans that an illustrious personage was on the way.

Unsure as to the identity of the illustrious personage and unable to contact Madrid in time to find out, Spanish colonial officialdom frantically took steps to accord the distinguished traveler a reception worthy of his elevated station.

Carpets were rolled out, fanfares assembled, the people informed. The military stood waiting in gala dress and the notables in their finery to welcome the visiting eminency, who was no less splendidly arraigned for the occasion, with shining sash and silver sabre rattling over his general's uniform. After he had been duly embraced, Wilkinson addressed the crowd in English, a language that nobody there spoke and was, perhaps therefore, wildly applauded. The illustrious guest was dined and feted, and allowed to sell his goods, making a hefty profit.

Governor Claiborne didn't hold with those who begrudged the General that profit. Was he to have floated downriver in empty boats, when the very object of the venture was to open up New Orleans for business with the U.S.? What nonsense. With the bravura and bluster that were his stock-in-trade, Wilkinson had accomplished in one stroke what pints of ink spread over official paper by government luminaries hadn't managed. All of it without speaking a word of Spanish or French (he still didn't). Maybe there was something to the General's claim that success depended on the person doing the talking rather than the country he was doing the talking for.

"You think I am going to stand by and let my achievements of the past be wiped out by some conniving civilian? I've got a reputation to protect, you know."

Claiborne smiled. "I understand, General." Wilkinson's reputation was on the tattered side, Agent Number Thirteen plastered on it once too often. Yet the word traitor carried a connotation of grandeur not fitting the man. It was a matter of dollars and cents to the General. His endless adventures in search of riches and his undeniable flair for getting himself invited to the best tables notwithstanding, General Wilkinson was perpetually in debt and looking for ways to get out of it. How could anybody so given to overstatement possibly be an effective spy? That wasn't to say he shouldn't be closely watched. His penchant for Wilkinsonian deviations from an established line demanded constant vigilance.

The Capuchin blew a puff of smoke in Wilkinson's face, tilting his grey-bordered, bald monk's crown and rolling his black eyes to communicate his enjoyment of the cigar. "Why do you call him père Antoine if he's Spanish?"

"The French Creoles have nicknamed him that; they like him now that he's come to his senses. Years ago he came into New Orleans like a shot, talking of nothing but bringing on the Inquisition to get the sinners cleared out. Don Miró — a dear friend of mine — was governor then, so when our padre here demanded an army to set his Inquisition scheme in motion, Miró had him arrested and packed off on a boat going back to Cadiz . . . " A sudden commotion in the loggia made the men look up.

Governor de Salcedo, uniformed and booted, and accompanied by half a dozen subalterns, including his personal valet, his surgeon, and two female servants, all chattering at once, made his way through the gallery, squinting in the open doorway to distinguish the visitors through the cigar smoke in the room. Wilkinson was the only one he seemed happy to recognize. A barrage of Spanish words directed the monk elsewhere.

The Governor refused a chair, saying they should all repair to the drawing room, which was soft, beautiful, and hot, "and where we can stay until three hours." Noticing Claiborne's surprise on hearing him speak English, he explained: "I am going to school in England."

An event undoubtedly many a summer in the past, Claiborne thought. As he stood in his boots, the Governor could be anywhere from seventy to eighty. "I am very grateful, Your Honor, for according me your time," he started. "Any personal assurance from you concerning the imminent resumption of trade between the U.S. and Spain would only increase my gratitude."

Governor de Salcedo slowly moved his nobly wrinkled face from side to side. "I am deeply pained by your affair with the Intendant," he told Claiborne. "Like all the world, Morales is a servant of the King." He motioned toward the portrait on the wall, prompting one of the underlings to straighten it. "Are you thinking *I* don't suffer? This is much more than *your* affair. It is me, the army, attacked by peoples without uniform. *Intrigantes*, who want to take me away for . . . for . . . to . . . " Unable to adequately express his distress in English, the Governor reverted to his native tongue, pouring out a torrent of sentences soaked in anger and emotion, gradually working himself into such a frenzy even Wilkinson joined his voice to those in the entourage, trying to calm him down. Then, suddenly, the chorus of voices fell silent.

Claiborne watched in amazement as Governor de Salcedo's left eyelid drooped to cover his eye (the right remained open) while his body keeled backward, prevented from crashing against the brick floor by the personal valet who jumped to shield his master's fall. The surgeon opened the window facing Toulouse Street.

A mulatto woman in calico dress, a multi-colored *tignon* covering her hair under the basket filled with figs, nuts, preserves, and sweets she balanced on her head, swayed past the window, wailing: *"Belle de figues! Bons petits calas! Tout chaud! Tout chaud! Barataria! Pralines! Pistaches! Confitures coco! Pacanes! Barataria!"*

This casual intrusion of daily life on the seriousness of the moment disturbed Claiborne. The behavior of the people surrounding the Governor was equally unfitting. The colored woman fanning the Governor's bloodless face was chatting idly with père Antoine, who had reappeared to make the sign of the cross over the prostrate figure, followed by a spray of water from a palm branch drenched in a silver vial.

"We'd better clear out now, before he revives," Wilkinson whispered. "No need to trouble yourself, my boy. It's only a fainting spell the old fellow falls to when he gets himself worked up. Our staying around will only remind him of Morales and aggravate his condition. He's obsessed with the idea that Morales is trying to oust him as governor and replace him with somebody younger."

"Considering the shape he's in, I can't see it as such a bad idea."

"The old boy may be overdue for retirement, Governor, but keep in mind that he's determined to reopen the port, if it's the last thing he does. Never mind his motives. What counts is that he's planted firmly on our side. There is nothing you can think of which hasn't already crossed his mind with respect to putting an end to . . . "

"My affair with the Intendant?"

"He's coming to. Don't let him see you." Remarkably light-footed for his bulk, the General tiptoed to the door, his index pressed to his mouth, signaling to Claiborne to follow. Père Antoine nodded approval over this unceremonious exit. The air outside felt pleasantly warm.

"Where are you staying, Governor?"

"Here, on the levee."

"In a public house?" Wilkinson stopped walking in surprise. "Why? Any planter in the vicinity would be delighted to put you up. We can't have dinner in a public house."

"We can if we pay for it."

"Pay for it?" The General looked stunned, as if presented with a totally new concept.

"Where are *you* staying, General?"

"The place is too far away," he said pensively, gesturing his chin over the water. "Across the River. What time is it?"

"I don't know. Three o'clock?"

"Perfect." General Wilkinson had recovered his former confident self. "I know a Catalan who cooks a good teal duck. Not far from the French market. Come on, my boy. It will be a treat."

Yes, mine, Claiborne thought.

"Unless you prefer roasted pigeons at the Café Royal, which offers the additional treat of excellent card tables?"

Claiborne smiled. "I think I'd rather have the duck." One Wilkinson treat would do nicely for one day.

As representatives of the various States filed into the House and Senate, the mood in the nation's capital became one of anger . . .

December

December 1802

Meriwether Lewis thought the time had come to set his quarters in order. He had idle hours on his hands now with the Jefferson daughters relieving him of some of his household duties (Martha anyway. Maria wasn't much use). Another good batch of rain and the Lowestoft finger bowl would overrun its chipped brim. The bowl was no match for the leak overhead, but there were more serious cracks in the ceiling of the east room and only so many damaged containers to be had from the proprietary-minded Frenchmen lording it over the crockery.

Lewis emptied the rainwater collected in the various receptacles into a bucket, promising himself to take down the bucket later. First he must get rid of the stack of newspapers near the fireplace (drawing fairly for a change) before Martha got an eyeful of the stories about the President and Sally Hemings. Lewis had already stored two months' worth of this ongoing press saga, which was swelling with hyperbole and invective with every reprint ever since that ungrateful wretch of a Callender had originated it last summer. None of it would offer much in the way of revelation to Martha, who was familiar since birth with the peculiar relationship often existing between master and slave on the plantation, but who, like many a female in her position, chose to stay blind where a beloved member of the family was involved. To see her father's liaison exposed to the country at large would constitute a forcible removal of the blinders that kept her vision pure.

The door to the room was pushed open slowly, hesitantly, the way one would open the door to an empty house belonging to somebody else. A flaxen head and clear hazel eyes revealed the handsome face of John Randolph. At least from this distance it looked handsome. A few steps into the room, Lewis knew, and Johnny's youthful face would disappear behind a mask of evil lines. Evil, because he hadn't come by them naturally. In his late teens, Randolph had fallen victim to a mysterious illness that left him unable to grow further, only age. A decade later he remained a beardless youth, trapped in the skin of an older man. His mental faculties hadn't been affected, though, and neither had his vituperate tongue. That he should be staring in stupefied wonder at the sight confronting him, the inevitable riding crop motionless in his overlong fingers, was something of a wonder in itself.

Lewis's eyes followed Randolph's astounded gaze as it took in bowls, basins, the chamber pot, and the dark patches on the ceiling, settling on the army blankets strung halfway across the room to hide the bed. Lewis smiled. "Would you care to have a look behind the partition, Johnny?"

"My God!" Randolph piped in his soprano voice (His voice likewise had remained stuck in adolescence), "when I think that I envied you for living here."

Johnny envied anyone who was in Jefferson's confidence, Lewis thought, whether they lived at the President's House, as he did, or elsewhere, as did Madison. "I'm used to the outdoors."

"I'm used to horses. That doesn't induce me to sleep in a stable." Johnny's traveling eye encountered the bottle of brandy in the recess of the window. "I suppose it has its compensations."

"I get to eat well, too. Feel like a dram, Johnny?"

"I can't stay, Captain. The Gallatins are expecting me. I take it Mr. Jefferson is still out riding?"

"Yes and I don't see him coming back before dinner. He's had a fierce headache all day."

"Where are the ladies?"

"Out visiting."

"Are you aware, Captain, that the porter's lodge is unattended? Anybody with a mind to can just walk inside."

"If they find their way here I will do my best to keep them entertained."

"In that case you'd be well advised to rely on your liquor supply."

"Is that why you came up here, Johnny? To point out my failings as a host?" Lewis was surprised at his own patience. Barely younger than

Randolph, he felt, if not smarter, wiser somehow. Or maybe he just plain felt lucky that the rumors about lost manhood were being whispered about Johnny and not himself. Fate wasn't one to discriminate. It might have happened to him instead of Johnny. Considerations of that kind were bound to keep your reaction in check.

"A host can be no better than his guest," Randolph relented. He had been up half the night nursing the hideous pains in his stomach. "I came by to inform the President that the House is asking to look at all the correspondence pertaining to the New Orleans matter. Tell him he oughtn't to see it as a hostile act. It isn't. Never mind those delegates who are wetting their horse-lips in anticipation of cracking down on something sweet. As long as *I* am speaker, I'll whip . . . " Johnny's riding crop suddenly cleaved the air, setting the newspapers fluttering wildly. " . . . the sugar clear off their tongues." Seeing Lewis had jumped back during this demonstration, Randolph smiled — the white-toothed, arrogant smile of a charming youth. "I'll take you up on that brandy later, Captain." He stalked out of the room and down the stairs. Awkwardly long-limbed, Johnny was a graceful figure only when riding his horse.

When Lewis clambered down the staircase with the piles of newspapers, Randolph's shrill tones were still piping in front of the house. Sitting grandly on his horse, he was gesticulating to another Randolph: Tom, Martha's husband and first cousin. Johnny was cousin to both, as well as to Mr. Jefferson, whose mother had been a Randolph.

Virginia was overrun with Randolphs, all of whom were entangled in an inextricable web of kinship stretching from the Tidewater to Piedmont. Their predilection for marrying cousins (like her sister, Maria's husband was also a first cousin) kept weaving ever more curious twists in the web, not to mention the minds of some of this Randolph offspring.

Johnny lived in Southside in a house called Bizarre — alone since the age of 23 with the care of two small nephews (one deaf-and-dumb, one ill), legacy of his admired older brother Richard, who had died under suspicious circumstances in 1796. His father, mother and a younger brother had died earlier. Before his death Richard had been implicated with his wife's sister in a fantastic scandal of infanticide and incest. His acquittal had been due partly to the combined brilliance of Patrick Henry, John Marshall, and Alexander Campbell who served as his defense. It was not surprising that Johnny galloped on his horse in the dead of night through Southside, shouting: "Macbeth hath murdered Sleep! Macbeth hath murdered Sleep!"

At this moment he was laughing loudly, looking back from his leaping mare at Tom Randolph, who stood on the gravel shaking his fist.

"Of course he keeps doing it, Tom. He knows he can depend on your getting upset every time." Martha's eyes were on the rapidly diminishing contents of the brandy bottle before her husband on the table. "Do you see Jack getting upset? Or Meriwether? I'm sure Johnny speaks just as villainously to them."

"Indeed," Jack Eppes agreed.

Dinner had been consumed *en famille*, without unexpected or invited guests, as the Jefferson daughters preferred. The common dining room was pleasantly warm in the waning afternoon. Exactly the sort of intimate atmosphere Martha had been looking forward to enjoying on this visit. Her husband knew this better than anyone else present, yet he persisted in spoiling the moment by playing injured party to John Randolph, as if he were Johnny's only target. "How's your headache, Father?"

"He said I was riding your coattails," Tom complained to the President. "That I could've never gotten into Congress on my own."

Eppes smiled. "What do you think he tells *me*?"

"Oh, Tom," Martha sighed. "How can you take Johnny seriously?"

"All good and dandy for you to say. He calls *you* a saint."

Jefferson shook his head, sighing. "Johnny deals only in extremes. His praise matches his abuse in extravagance. I no more like the idea of having a saint among my daughters than I do having a son-in-law without talent. Fortunately, I needn't be concerned on either account."

Why are you smiling, Meriwether?"

"Well said, sir. If he was smiling, Lewis thought, it had to be in amazement at Jefferson's eternal willingness to excuse one of his own. A man of occasional charm and wit, Tom Randolph seemed the seventh child in his own brood of six. Or five — one had died in infancy, Lewis remembered. Anyway, it would soon again be six, judging from Martha's belly. Very soon.

Fathering children appeared to be what Tom Randolph was best at. That and getting his father-in-law to square his gambling and other debts. In spite of a continuous battle to settle his own (inherited) debts, Jefferson invariably obliged, refraining from criticism and lectures, moved by an unfailing spirit of reconciliation when it concerned one of his family. This was all the more amazing because the President was implacable toward his political enemies — Patrick Henry, John Adams, Alexander Hamilton, etc. In Henry's case, Jefferson had gone so far as to claim that "we must devoutly pray for his death" (Heaven had answered in 1799). But Tom Randolph could beat his wife and be absolved by the same Jefferson.

The trouble was, it was hard not to feel sorry for Tom Randolph, who hadn't been too set on marrying Martha in the first place. Tom liked girls with ruffles, literally and figuratively. Martha was about as unruffled as they came. Five years in France had taught her nothing of feminine dress or coquetry. She stalked through life looking like a young Thomas Jefferson got up like his grandmother. Petit had tried to work her over once. Years ago, on the occasion of some do at Monticello — a wedding, Lewis thought. He remembered it was summer.

The French cook had approached Martha as if she were a cake that hadn't turned out right and whose imperfections would have to be hidden by a great deal of frosting. He talked a lot about rose and pistache and *couleurs bonbons* (Bohn-bóhn, he pronounced it). Petit was an experienced hand in the kitchen. His desserts especially often looked too beautiful to eat. But Martha wasn't a piece of cake. Pistachio decorations did little for her. Lewis would have been hard put to say just what it was she had on. He seemed to recall pink rosettes and a greenish-yellow dress with flower buds much like the butter cream ones Petit so cleverly twisted from his pastry tube.

Jefferson's eyes that day must have stretched one-eighth of an inch all around. Whenever his elder daughter came within sight he was taken anew with surprise. Even Dolley Madison grew speechless. Sporting a gown with a comestible theme herself — Lewis recalled ears of corn and grapes — she couldn't begin to compete with Martha's bonbon frosting.

Martha politely accepted the compliments of the company, and on their retiring, retired the bonbon outfit in turn. Between her looking glass and her father's guests, she elected her looking glass the more reliable observer.

Remarkably lucid in reading her own reflection, Martha's perception clouded when Mr. Jefferson stepped into the mirror. Looming larger than any other mortal, the paternal image left no space for a mere husband to make an impression. Tom consoled himself with liquor and cards, and creating such disturbances as might annoy his wife.

It occurred to Lewis that the fellow could do with a more enthusiastic partner, if only for the duration of a meal. He would seat him next to Anna Payne, Dolley Madison's younger sister, at the New Year dinner, Lewis decided. Miss Payne would satisfy Randolph's craving for ruffles. And if he were flanked at the other end by Thomas Paine, Martha's husband would look a teetotaler by comparison. Maria was half asleep, her delicate, beautiful face nodding toward a plate of leftover applecake. Tom was sulking over his glass of brandy. Maria's husband was rearranging the burning logs in the fireplace. "How can you be sure?" Eppes was asking, ostensibly in reply to something the President had said.

"It's clear from private accounts from New Orleans that the Governor doesn't agree with the Intendant," Jefferson answered. "We expect the Spanish Government won't waste a minute in countermanding the order. At least, that's what Yrujo says. The question is one of time, Jack. The time necessary for the countermanding order to get to New Orleans from Madrid."

"Yes, and there it is we're going to run into trouble, I have a feeling, going by the mood in Congress today."

"Talking about Yrujo," Lewis interjected. "Are the Yrujos coming to the dinner?"

Martha stopped pushing the dishes toward the end of the table where George, a middle-aged house slave imported from Monticello, was stacking them on a tray. George's tan brow knotted in unison with Martha's. "What dinner?"

"The dinner in honor of you and Maria on January first," Lewis reminded her.

"Oh that." Martha's face relaxed. That was still two weeks in the future. "I don't know."

"No. Leave that, George." The President retrieved his uneaten portion of apple-cake. "I expect the Yrujos will spend Christmas in Philadelphia. The Spanish make a great fuss over Christmas."

Martha nodded. "As do the French. Remember all the wonderful lights and decorations in the shop windows at the Palais Royal, Father? The sugar confections and glazed chestnuts at Berthelot's? You should have seen it, Meriwether. It was just beautiful, wasn't it, Father? Why can't we celebrate Christmas in America, too?"

"I doubt the French are doing much Christmas celebrating these days," Jefferson said. "Their Revolution did away with religious holidays. Christmas isn't a part of the Revolutionary Calendar. If your heart is set on sugar confections and glazed chestnuts, Martha, have a talk with Petit."

"By Christmas . . . " Tom Randolph came alive to wave his index finger like a menacing baton. " . . . we will be at war. I realize war is not what you have in mind, sir," he told the President, "but you won't be able to stop it anyhow."

"You're putting the cart before the horse, Tom," Eppes disagreed. "Congress has barely assembled."

"Leaving no doubt as to where it's headed, though."

"The opposition, well . . . " Eppes shrugged. "What did you expect? It won't matter. We're in the majority."

"Wait till all the representatives of the West get here," Randolph promised.

"The West on the whole is on the side of the President, Tom, you know that."

Randolph wasn't to be shaken. "Representatives are on the side of their constituents, as I see it, in the West or any place else. They'd better be unless they aim to retire."

"Tom is right." Jefferson rose to cool his throbbing head against the cold pane of the window. "All we can hope is that reason will prevail. Taking New Orleans would mean seven years of war, at the cost of a thousand lives and a hundred million in additional debt. I can imagine no . . . " His knuckles rapped the glass to draw the attention of a servant outside. "Take away that wheelbarrow! Somebody may trip over it in the dark . . . I can imagine no thinking man, whatever his politics, wishing such a calamity on his country. I won't be swayed from my course. If the House wants to see the New Orleans correspondence, it shall see it. This administration has nothing to hide. If Spain ordered the closure, Yrujo's assurances to the contrary notwithstanding, we have left her a way out by assuming that Morales acted independently."

"Mr. Yrujo wouldn't lie to you, Father." It was thanks to her father that the Spanish Minister had remained in his post. Sally Yrujo herself had told Martha so. Sally was the daughter of Governor McKean of Pennsylvania, one of President Jefferson's staunchest supporters. Madame Yrujo, as Sally liked to be called nowadays—a strange form of address, it struck Martha, seeing Yrujo was Spanish—had said that "certain elements in the Adams Cabinet had tried to remove Carlos."

"I wouldn't bet on it, my dear." Tom Randolph poured himself another brandy. "Obligations are not the surest way to a man's loyalty, as I see it."

"Oh Tom." Martha sighed deeply. If he wasn't whining, he was being nasty. Why couldn't Tom be like Jack and enjoy having an uncle and father-in-law who was President of the United States?

When Chancellor Livingston went to the Hotel Gallifet to meet with Talleyrand that December morning, he had yet to hear of the closing of the port . . .

December 1802

France has ever inspired the people of the United States with sentiments of attachment and confidence, Mr. Livingston." Dressed in a burgundy camlet peignoir, a blonde morning wig replacing the customary nightcap, Talleyrand was civility personified. The hooded grey eyes cool, the entire countenance exuding a polished warmth, he moved about in a way as to suggest that elegance and refinement were not to be had without a limp.

Livingston, ensconced in the copper velvet of a Louis XV chair, nodded, unable to mouth the expected reply. Like a fly that kept on escaping the flat of your hand, Bonaparte's Foreign Minister simply wasn't to be cornered. Any inquiry into the ownership of Louisiana bounced across an empty wall of courteous phrases. This man, who advised his subordinates, "Above all, don't be zealous", remained unzealously ahead of your every move, your every question, subtle or direct.

Three platinum-wigged manservants in embroidered livery slid silently across the carpeted parquet, setting up the serving of the eleven o'clock cup of hot chocolate with ritualistic precision. Not an early riser, Talleyrand was still sipping his coffee. He seemed absorbed in the balletic movements of his staff, waiting for Livingston to be presented with a silver cup of chocolate to dismiss the liveried trio with a languorous gesture of his beringed hand. "Has the French Republic ever shown a desire to impede the prosperity of the United States? To lessen her influence? Weaken her security? Or pose any obstacle to the progress of her commerce?"

Livingston smiled. The French Republic, under the Directory, certainly had done her utmost to undermine U.S. commerce, seizing American ships and their cargoes — estimated at a value of nearly four million dollars. Paris was full of ship owners and merchants come to seek restitution from the Consulate for their losses. Bonaparte steadfastly refused to accept responsibility for the actions of the regime he had overthrown, even though he held the Jefferson administration accountable for President Adams sending arms to the rebels in St. Domingue. If the French treasury was bare, the United States was still burdened by an enormous war debt, a situation which had not improved with Hamilton's unholy schemes of Federal assumption of state debts, Livingston thought. It was hoped in Washington that these legitimate American claims could be applied against the purchase of the Island of New Orleans, or an equivalent port in the Floridas — if the Floridas were included in the cession.

The United States had a right to the use of rivers passing from her territory into New Orleans and both Floridas, but she was prepared to pay for it in the interest of peace. "For a nation to have to depend in perpetuity on the goodwill of another nation is unrealistic at best, I think you will agree, Mr. Talleyrand. Peace, under these circumstances, becomes precarious. It is of vast importance for the U.S. to get jurisdiction over a space large enough for a commercial town on the bank of the Mississippi, as near the mouth of the River as possible."

"I understand, Mr. Livingston." Talleyrand turned from the stack of papers before him on the gold-inlaid bureau to feed a piece of sugar to the effete miniature canine reclining in a fur-lined basket at his feet. With the lack of zeal prevalent in the house, the canine scrutinized the offer, without committing herself one way or the other. Aware that the U.S. Minister was hard of hearing, Talleyrand repeated: "I understand your position, Mr. Livingston. Be assured that your diligence in pursuing the aims of your country commands my deepest respect. I regret that it is not within my power to assist you in achieving them."

Flattery, flattery. The man was a master at it, as he was in the art of evasion. Livingston sat down his cup on the silver tray with a sigh. "I am sensitive to your opinion, Mr. Talleyrand, and it is to that opinion that I address myself at the moment: Has Spain ceded the Louisiana colony to France?"

"As I have told you, the information that has been received is not sufficient to authorize a detailed explanation."

"I am not asking for details. Only for your personal confirmation of the cession."

"I cannot confirm that of which I am ignorant."

"Am I to conclude then, sir, that the newspapers in France have access to information denied the Minister of Foreign Affairs?"

"The newspapers, like the theatre, must cater to the hunger of the public for improbable tales." Talleyrand smiled. "Another cup of hot chocolate, Mr. Livingston?"

Mrs. Livingston's destination was the courtyard of Saint Eustache, but instead of seeing the stalls, booths, and colorful umbrellas of the Saint Eustache market, she suddenly found herself lost in a maze of narrow streets. Two horrendously dirty children, shivering in their frayed coats, accosted her for money. Men with the angry eyes of those out of work glared threateningly from stoops. Women with greasy hair and skin stopped their shouting at one another to stare from windows and doorways in common hostility.

Dropping a few *sous* in the sticky hand of a little girl, Mrs. Livingston hastened along, praying that the glutinous mud wouldn't drag her down into the open sewer, trying to give her walk some of the determination which characterized that of Madame Tranche, her cook. Mme Tranche's step had a quality that discouraged approach. Paris was a city of pedestrians. Vehicles of any kind were extremely scarce. And the pedestrians were of two kinds: those who stepped aside and those who passed. Mme Tranche passed.

Nothing in her natural appearance had appointed Mme Tranche to take up this role of authority. Short and squat (She had stopped growing at eleven on her father's orders, she said, because "tall girls eat more than their share"), she brought to mind a feisty little dog. One of those tiny, tightly packed creatures with a pushed-in face, who yapped fearlessly at dogs ten times their own size. This was not an uncommon sight, yet Mrs. Livingston couldn't recall one instance where the bigger dog—who could have swallowed the belligerent nipper whole—had made any attempt to demonstrate his superior jaws and teeth. A befuddled look was about all these giant dogs were able to muster under the circumstances. Mme Tranche had a somewhat similar effect on people.

Her engagement as the Livingston cook had been a temporary measure. She refused to sleep in, which was terribly inconvenient. Cleanliness was a condition she avoided with the argument that water cost a *sou* per pail. As unpleasant as the prospect of having to dismiss someone was, one of these days Mme Tranche simply would have to be let go. Mrs. Livingston remembered that she had said this before — every time another new maid could not get on with Mme Tranche and left. Four maids had come and gone in as many months. One girl from Dieppe had lasted only half a day. "Your cook has locked me out of the kitchen," the girl had cried.

When asked for the reason, Mme Tranche came straightaway to the point: "I will not consort with somebody from Dieppe."

"But why?" Mrs. Livingston was near tears herself.

"You don't know Dieppe, Madame." The words were ominous with implication, delivered in that resolved way which precluded any further questions.

Mrs. Livingston didn't know Dieppe, it was true. And ever since then, she had harbored an unusual curiosity about the town, wondering what it might be that had so set Mme Tranche against it.

The alleyways and passages now were jammed with carts, vendors, shoppers, dogs, cats, children, idlers, beggars, butchers — and suddenly, making the congestion total — a slaughtered ox.

The pool of still-warm blood around the dead animal was gently steaming in the cold air, trickling down his hind legs which had slipped into the sewer — that foul-smelling trench taking up the center or sides of every Parisian back street. Mrs. Livingston hugged her beaver-lined coat, as if to shield the body within it from contamination.

This must be the butcher's *quartier* she had heard about. Paris had no abattoirs. Every morning two dozen oxen were herded in from the country by a man and a pair of dogs, to be butchered in front of whatever shop was to sell the meat.

In imitation of those around her, Mrs. Livingston held on to the sooty walls of the houses, stepping gingerly on the blood-soaked soil and offal, in order to get through. Only to come across a second slaughtered ox, and piles of refuse obstructing all further passage.

A shopkeeper, in a canvas apron of undetermined color, who had followed Mrs. Livingston's despairing gaze at the mount of rubbish before his door, smiled philosophically: "We need a good thunderstorm, Madame, to wash away this glut." He pointed to a band of small boys busy constructing a makeshift bridge over the sewer with wooden boards. "There! The Savoyards have come to the rescue."

"*Passez! Payez!*"

The boys obviously made their living in this way, Mrs. Livingston thought, as they were extremely agile in collecting toll and in ganging up on anyone trying to cheat them out of it, advertising their service, shouting: "*Payez! Passez!*" She hoped she would negotiate the rickety planks without sliding or being jostled into the black, verminous muck underneath by citizens attempting to cross without paying.

Mrs. Livingston rather admired the enterprising spirit of the Savoyard boys, and that of their counterparts, the Auvergnats, who traveled the city, pushing their water-butts mounted on wheels, or carrying buckets hooked to a wooden ring, to provide those of the 600,000 Parisians not residing near a public pump with drinking water. Her admiration had suffered a setback when both Robert and she had been confined to bed, a chamber pot nearby, as a result of drinking this water drawn from the Seine — a river in which floated every conceivable form of waste.

It was against the law for the Auvergne boys to do this, said Mme Tranche, but river water was free whereas the water drawn from the public fountains had to be paid for. The scarcity and cost of water made the populace think twice before using it for matters not related to cooking. When Mrs. Livingston had offered Mme Tranche a bucket of it free of charge in order to scrub herself, Mme Tranche had voiced concern over using the precious liquid for so superficial a purpose.

Sliding through oxen blood and other dark, slimy substances in the bowels of Paris, Mrs. Livingston recognized the value of her concern. One couldn't enter these streets without taking on their appearance. It would take the better part of the day just to discard their smell, and this was possible only because, unlike Mme Tranche, she could afford not to return to them.

"Maybe it would be best if *you* did the marketing in future, Madame Tranche," a chastened Mrs. Livingston told her cook when she finally had found her way home.

"I shall not go to *your* baker," Mme Tranche immediately countered. "His wife is full of the depravity of maids."

Mrs. Livingston nodded, prey to a desire to be agreeable. Perhaps the baker's wife *was* full of the depravity of maids. Mrs. Livingston wasn't sure how one identified such a failing in a baker's wife. She handed her coat to Zoé (from Toulouse, a locale inspiring only indifference in Mme Tranche), who stood staring with intense fascination at her dirt-spattered mistress.

"You have soot on your face, Madame," she said at last. "And yours will have my hand on it if you don't get moving," Mme Tranche promised. "Take off your apron and put it on the *causeuse* for Madame."

"I only have two hands," Zoé complained, holding up the coat to illustrate that these extremities were already engaged. The expression on the cook's face swiftly induced her to greater dexterity.

Mme Tranche spread the apron on the sofa, so Mrs. Livingston could rest her abused limbs without risking to soil the velvet. "Take off your shoes, Madame, and I will put them by the stove to dry."

Mrs. Livingston looked at the black-and-white flagged floor, delineating in mud her every step into the parlor. What a comfort it was to be here. Even that iron monstrosity called a stove seemed to give off a warmth which was more than mere heat. "Thank you, Madame Tranche." The words were in response to the reception rather than for the glass of port the cook insisted on placing in her employer's hands (Mrs. Livingston would have preferred a cup of hot chocolate this early in the day). Mme Tranche meant well. And it wouldn't do to offend anyone who meant well. Indeed, one ought to make some effort at reciprocation.

"How is your condition today, Madame Tranche?"

Mme Tranche suffered from an ailment diagnosed by a doctor as "an abdomen full of air" and referred to by the cook as "my condition." The doctor had prescribed omelets fried in oil and sprinkled with fennel to be applied to the affected area. Mme Tranche followed her own version of this prescription by "applying it internally" and eating the omelets.

"Unfortunately still the same, Madame."

"I am sorry to hear it. And how is Monsieur Tranche?"

"Ah Madame . . . " Mme Tranche sighed deeply. Monsieur Tranche couldn't be so readily explained as the rest of mankind. "No matter how I shower attentions on that man, embroider waistcoats for him, or buy him caps and cravats, nothing will prevent him from being himself."

Mrs. Livingston smiled. She couldn't understand why Robert refused to remain in a room which also held Mme Tranche, a fact of life both women were reminded of when a key was heard turning in the lock. In the fashion of most local houses, the front door led smack into the parlor. Mme Tranche made for the drawing room door, trotting toward the outer regions of the house where the kitchen was located. Mrs. Livingston swallowed a bit of port, surprised to find it tasted no different in the morning.

"Good morning, Robert."

"Good morning, Mary."

Livingston's greeting was automatic—a reaction triggered by the familiar gentle voice—his thinking embroiled in the fabrication of new entryways into the unreceptive Consular camp. His eyes had noted an ill-groomed female of uncertain age and unkempt coiffure, sitting in her stockinged feet on his *causeuse*, drinking port before midday. Then, his mind caught up with his eyes.

"Mary! What happened to you?!"

After dinner and a nap, Mrs. Livingston felt the morning's adventure obligingly beginning to recede into memory. She changed into the silk lilac gown, created by none other than the great Leroy himself (Mme

Bonaparte's couturier) looking at her reflection in the glass above the *lavabo* with a mixture of trepidation and pride.

Fashion in the French capital dictated that ladies showed themselves *au naturel*, under pseudo-classical style coverings of muslin and gauze, which was all good and well for the Thérèse Cabarrus' and the Juliette Récamiers of this world, Mrs. Livingston thought, but which it would be folly for a woman nearing fifty to blindly obey. In this respect she found herself on the side of the First Consul, who veered from the motherly approach (draping shawls and capes over the ladies' shoulders) to insults ("Either buy yourself a new dress or get another body") in his determination to make the Consulate respectable.

Though the lilac silk was on the daring side, Mrs. Livingston felt confident it would pass the Bonapartian criteria for modesty. Anyway, she and Robert were going to the theatre this evening, not to the Tuileries.

She left the bedroom for the drawing room where Zoé had lit a fire and was filling decanters with brandy and wine. Mrs. Livingston didn't share her husband's enthusiasm for the stove in the parlor, preferring the pleasant dusk of this adjacent room where the light of fire and candles cast intriguing designs on the wood paneling.

"Where is Mr. Livingston'?" she asked Zoé.

"I don't know, Madame."

"Have you looked in the study? Mr. Livingston tends to forget the time when he's working."

"He's not there, Madame."

"Not there . . . " Mrs. Livingston was surprised. "Has Monsieur Tranche arrived yet?"

"I don't know, Madame."

Mme Tranche's husband was a cabriolet driver. The very reason, Mrs. Livingston was certain, why Robert didn't put his foot down about dismissing the cook. Carriages for hire were no more numerous than private coaches. To have a cabriolet at one's disposal when one was needed was an unexpected bonus. That Jules Tranche drove his horses through Paris like a madman hardly diminished the advantage, for in this he was no different from other drivers, public or private. Having the city all to themselves, drivers vied with one another in terrorizing pedestrians. Tranche lost nothing in favoring the Livingstons, whose largesse exceeded that of the random passenger and included free access to their (kitchen) table.

"Would you like port, Madame, or Madeira?"

"Yes, Zoé. Thank you." Mrs. Livingston sat down near the hearth, pondering the cause of her husband's delay.

"Would you like port, Madame, or Madeira?" Zoé repeated, requiring a more definite answer before she could proceed. She held the decanter of Madeira above a glass to encourage her employer in a specific direction.

"Fine, Zoé." Mrs. Livingston accepted the glass of Madeira. "Go and see if Monsieur Tranche's cabriolet is in back. And check the study again, too, would you?"

"Yes, Madame."

The hammer strokes preceding the rise of the curtain would be heard at six o'clock sharp. This was the rule at every one of the many theatres in Paris, allowing the play to end at an early hour and patrons lacking transportation or a lantern-bearer to find their way home in the dimly-lit, treacherous streets with minimum damage to limbs and pocketbook (In addition to the sewers and ruts, the streets at night offered the presence of perfidious individuals). Except, of course, for the Ambigu where mayhem and murder raged indefinitely on the stage, to a point where, one supposed, the audience considered possible assault or robbery outside a bagatelle by comparison. One visit to the Ambigu had cured Mrs. Livingston of all curiosity. In the space of half-an-hour she had been forced to witness a fatal stabbing, one bloody ax murder and two gory decapitations. A minor player had succumbed to poison.

This gruesome fare, fortunately, was not representative of the Paris stage, though the theatre here was very different from the theatre in New York. In New York the entire play was explained beforehand; bills or newspapers informing prospective attendants as to the denouement. A curious practice, it struck Mrs. Livingston, in view of the fact that the audience in the main consisted of the better classes, who might be ascribed certain powers of observation. Was it really necessary, for instance, in the case of Richard III, to say that: "In this play is contained the death of King Henry VI; the artful acquisition of the Crown by Richard III; the landing at Milford Haven of Henry VII, and the battle of Bosworth Field"?

In Paris, where even beggars went to the theatre — due to a "Right of the Poor" forcing theatre managers to give out free tickets to those who couldn't afford to pay for them — nothing was explained. It would have been difficult, in any event, since the play often shifted in directions unenvisioned by its author, dependent upon the instructions being shouted from the gallery.

Mme Tranche personally had had a hand in transforming El Cid into a Frenchman, she and her fellow connoisseurs in the top balcony not disposed to grant to Spain heroes of that magnitude.

In a country where two out of three children nowadays were born out of wedlock, without anyone raising an eyebrow, the populace wouldn't tolerate any illegitimate doings on stage. Cuckolded husbands and deceived wives, abounding everywhere in daily life, were hooted and booed off the boards, without mercy for the poor actor or actress playing the part of the lover or mistress, whose villainy, after all, was not of their own making. This was no concern of the gallery, who demanded the guilty party reform on the spot and continue in a virtuous vein or else be relegated to the wings. Mrs. Livingston felt so deeply for the plight of the Parisian actor that she had felt compelled to comment on it to a theatre manager met at a dinner party.

"What a hard life it is to be an actor," she had commiserated. "Those poor people . . . "

The manager smiled like a man who told his correspondents to write symbols on the outside of their letters so he could guess the contents without having to pay postage. "Actors are not people, Madame."

"If they are not people, Monsieur, then what, pray tell, are they?"

"Ha Madame . . . " The manager kept on smiling. "That is the mystery. Nobody knows."

Zoé poked her head about the drawing room door. "Madame

Tranche says Jules is coming around the front to pick you up. Shall I get your pelisse, Madame?"

"But Mr. Livingston isn't home yet."

"Monsieur won't be home. Madame Tranche says he received a very important letter from America and had to go see Monsieur Talleyrand immediately. He will join you at the Français as soon as he can, Madame Tranche says."

All during the bumpy ride and the progression of the first act of Timoléon, Mrs. Livingston wondered as to the nature of the very important letter. Her initial fear that something had happened to someone in the family having quickly subsided on hearing Talleyrand's name, which seemed to place the sender in Washington.

The gallery was on its best behavior tonight, unwilling to quarrel with any thespian so magnificent as their beloved and revered Talma, allowing Timoléon the assassination of his brother Timophane, a would-be tyrant of Corinth no different from the one they themselves had eliminated nearly a decade ago. Pit and balcony sat in rapt attention as Timoléon expounded on his love of liberty. In a box across from Mrs. Livingston's, a lady was moved to draw the red draperies before her face to weep in private. A friend of Bonaparte's from the days when he lived in a dirty little cubicle in the Rue de la Huchette, Talma turned to the First Consul's box as he concluded his speech, and the house responded with thundering applause.

In the second act Timoléon had gone to Sicily to establish democracy, and the stage was left to Mademoiselle Montansier, who had come out of retirement to interpret the role of Timoléon's mother, at Talma's urging. Mlle Montansier had seen better days both as an actress and a woman. Dotty and feeble-voiced, she insisted on cursing Timoléon for the slaying of his brother. This pleased nobody, including, seemingly, Timoléon, who returned from Sicily prematurely to step on his mother's lines.

This, in turn, upset Mlle Montansier, who departed from the text to elaborate on the lack of professionalism rampant on the Paris stage today, foolishly reminding everyone that she had been a protégée of

Queen Marie Antoinette and expected better treatment. A reference which infuriated the upper regions of the theatre into an uproar of shouting voices and stamping feet, clamoring for her exit.

Livingston, who had been waiting behind the rows of seats downstairs, took advantage of the disruption to join his wife in their box.

"Oh Robert, I've been worried about you. What was so important that you had to run to the Foreign Ministry when you were there just this morning?"

"Don't concern yourself, Mary. I'll tell you later. It's about New Orleans."

"New Orleans?" Mrs. Livingston sighed. New Orleans was all Robert ever talked about these days. "What about New Orleans?"

"It has been closed to the U.S. — the port that is. The Spanish closed it."

"Oh, dear." Mrs. Livingston sighed deeply. What next? Mlle Montansier retreated and Talma reprised his love of liberty speech to the roaring approval of the crowd.

I was a witness to Mrs. L.'s (or Mrs. Chancellor, as she is called here in New York) muddy homecoming and escorted her to the Français *in Tranche's cabriolet later that same day. If I am keeping my presence out of the proceedings, it is so as not to further clutter a tale already too abundant in personae. The same consideration prompts me to circumvent the Chancellor's daughters (cum spouses) and trim to manageable size a veritable litter of domestics.*

The Livingstons, as no one in New York needs reminding, are powerful and wealthy landowners; whether belonging to the old manor clan or to the Chancellor's Clermont, so long as it spells Livingston it is going to read landlord. And no landlord is bound to leave his realm and set up house in Paris without the accoutrements to show for it. In any event, the Chancellor didn't.

The retinue that poured onto the frigate Boston *behind Chancellor Livingston fairly struck terror in the hearts of Captain McNeill and his crew. In addition to the aforementioned daughters and their husbands and, of course, Mrs. L., there was Colonel Burr's little protégée, Mademoiselle Delarge, whose safe passage had been entrusted to the Livingstons, a gaggle of French*

*acquaintances, Thomas Sumter, the secretary of the Legation, and myself, all —
or nearly all — accompanied by maids, governesses, slaves, valets, cooks, and
what have you, toting stores and trunks and numerous conveniences including
the Chancellor's carriage, and hoarding aboard chickens, pigs, sheep, and a cow
complete with calf.*

*Whether profusion of this sort would endear an American republican to
post-revolutionary France was a question readily answered by the French expa-
triates aboard, all of whom, at last, were able to return home without fearing for
their noble necks. There was a fresh wind blowing through the Tuileries at present. Bonaparte was now in charge — a Bonaparte who, in the unflappable esti-
mation of Talleyrand, had "everything." And what he didn't have, one might
add, he was going to make it his business to get.*

"What is all this nonsense you keep writing me in these petitions?
Do you believe persistence is a virtue, Citizen Laussat?"

Bonaparte paced the carpet, a long army coat slung over his night-
shirt and a handkerchief sitting on his head, which was his own version
of the prevailing morning wear of peignoir and nightcap (Rooms took
their time to warm up, particularly rooms in a palace like the Tuileries).
Bourrienne, engaged with quill and ink at a desk near one of the high,
narrow windows, kept an open ear to the conversation, occasionally
supplemented by a furtive glance.

"Who told you I might need a prefect for Louisiana?" The First Consul's penetrating gaze searched the cherubic face of Pierre Laussat, who
stretched his 5'1" frame to tall effect.

"The Frankfurt *Gazette*."

"The Frankfurt *Gazette* doesn't know what it is talking about."

"General Bernadotte told me . . .

"Ha-ha! You hear that, Bourrienne? I thought as much. You are a Béarnais, like Bernadotte?"

"Yes, Citizen First Consul."

"I am seeking to secure the affection of the Louisianians, Citizen, not
incur their damnation by letting loose a horde of Béarnais on them."

"It is my understanding, Citizen First Consul, that the command of the fleet has passed from General Bernadotte to General Victor."

"And with good reason. Since you are on such tender footing with Bernadotte, you must be aware of the man's incapacity to be satisfied. Why are you so set on becoming colonial prefect? You have no experience in that line. What does Madame Laussat say of all this?"

"Madame Laussat supports me in whatever I do."

"A good woman. I am glad to hear it. Do you have children?"

"Yes, sir. Three girls."

"Excellent. I like families. This determination of yours to go to Louisiana, is it a decision you have made with sufficient deliberation?"

"Absolutely, Citizen First Consul. I wouldn't take such a step lightly."

"Well, since you are set on it, you shall go to Louisiana."

Laussat's plump little face lit up. "You won't regret it, Citizen First Consul," he said passionately.

"That remains to be seen." Bonaparte pointed to a striped taffeta-covered mahogany chair near the fireplace. "Sit down, Citizen." He added a few chunks of wood to the fire, leaning his back against the chimney piece to soak up the warmth. "We must take possession of Louisiana as quickly as possible. If the English get wind of French ownership, they will descend on the colony before *we* can, and claim it theirs. A takeover for them would be child's play. They have ships of war in the Gulf of Mexico and everywhere else. Admiral Decrès is organizing the expedition as if it were directed toward Saint Domingue. Our true intent must, of necessity, remain a secret. About 3,000 infantry and artillery troops are being assembled on the River Scheldt, to depart from Antwerp as soon as feasible. You will sail ahead of the fleet on the *Surveillant*, with the necessary personnel. Captain Girardais has been informed and is awaiting further orders. Tomorrow you shall have your official nomination. How much time do you estimate you will need to prepare yourself and your family for the departure?"

"I would say about a week at the very most."

"A week at the very most. Well, well . . . " Bonaparte tapped Laussat on the shoulder as he walked him to the door. "It seems your decision to be Colonial Prefect was formed way ahead of mine." He turned to Bourrienne on closing the door behind Laussat. "Confident, isn't he, for such a little fellow?"

Bourrienne smiled. "Did I tell you, General, that the new map detailing the Floridas has arrived?"

"The new map, ah yes . . . " The First Consul resumed his pacing of the carpet in his unusual costume, hands in back and thoughts on the Floridas. "I am going to write the King of Etruria to get him to induce his father-in-law to give me the Floridas. I'll tell him I will add his ancestral duchy of Parma to Etruria in exchange for the Floridas. It will be easy — write this down, Bourrienne —"

As always when one of his ideas struck him as inspired, Bonaparte's pale face took on a glow of mischievousness. "It will be easy for you to induce the King of Spain to make a treaty by which Spain will reunite Florida to Louisiana and retrocede to France the River and port of Mobile and the territory which belonged to her before 1763 to the west of the River. In addition Spain shall cede to France the other parts of West Florida and all of East Florida . . . " Noticing the look of disbelief on his secretary's face, Bonaparte stopped to ask: "You are skeptical, Bourrienne? Do you think this Etrurian travesty of a king has the wits to question my proposal?"

"Anything but, General." Bourrienne remembered all too well the Etrurian couple's visit to Paris earlier in the year. The "King" had made his entrance into the Consular company, tumbling out of his ancient coach before the waiting ladies and gentlemen, victim to a seizure of grand mal epilepsy. On being upright, his speech and behavior had been that of a child. He was enchanted by General Bonaparte's uniform and, at the theatre, had jumped up and down the seat of his chair at some private delight. The couple's child, by contrast, had behaved like an adult. "I was thinking of the reports listing the King of Etruria as seriously ill and not likely to last much longer. The fact that their child has been packed off to the court of Madrid would seem to support these reports."

"Then we had better get on with the proposal at once. Where was I?"

It is Laussat's peculiar achievement that he has managed to antagonize more people than Bonaparte without ever going to war. Madame Laussat, on the other hand, has in common with Madame Bonaparte that she is liked even by her husband's enemies.

I was introduced to the Laussats by a mutual acquaintance, a lady who recently took up residence along the Hudson (a circumstance nobody could have foreseen when she prepared to sail on the Surveillant *to Saint Domingue where she was to marry one of General Leclerc's aide-de-camps). Were it not for this beautiful and dear lady – whose identity I cannot reveal – and her eternal willingness to indulge my curiosity with respect to Louisiana and related matters, I would have to rely for my information on one Duke Biggs, illegitimate son of Florentin Delpasse, valet to Governor de Salcedo, and one Leoncette Biggs, laundry mistress in that same household, or so Duke keeps assuring me, after swallowing great quantities of rum (prerequisite remuneration for his services) at the* Queen's Head.

Not that I doubt Duke's word. Not entirely. Or that I begrudge him his rum. The difficulty is, rather, that those at the Queen's Head *(where I often take my meals) who informed Duke Biggs of my interest in New Orleans misinformed him of my situation. Begging continually for credit as I must, I am assumed to be rich; consequently Duke does not heed me when I explain that rum is my best offer and he ought to look elsewhere for an income.*

And while I am on the subject of sources, I neglected to mention that, as regards Natchez, I am conversant (through the mails) with Governor Claiborne, thanks due the intermediary offices of my good friend Captain Lewis.

Where Madrid is concerned, though, I have waited purposely until now, when my "informant" personally steps upon the local scene, for he is not a character to be forced. His name is Charles Alquier, French representative at the Spanish Court. Unlike Duke Biggs, who has less to say than he says, and Meriwether Lewis, who could say more, Alquier's speech runs a natural course. As he says himself: "The creation of favorable impressions I leave to the miniaturists."

MADRID

December 1802

ife here is debauchery of the most revolting kind," the French Ambassador told Graham. "Urbanity, delicacy, public or private decency are utterly lacking. No veil is thrown to hide this appalling spectacle from the masses.. . " Alquier waved his arm to encompass the entire Plaza Mayor, which at this morning hour was a hotbed of shouting hawkers and vendors, squealing pigs, cackling parrots, hens and turkeys, chanting beggars, oranges from Valencia, vats of olives, dried peppers, cabbages, onions, and other local winter produce.

A harsh judgment, John Graham was thinking, of what made for a rather colorful scene, when he realized the Frenchman was referring to a scene of royal colors.

"There isn't a peasant in Spain who doesn't know that to appease the Queen's unnatural sensuality, the complacency of the King, the ministrations of the Prime Minister, and the virility of the entire Royal Bodyguard corps are all required. The King knows nothing, sees nothing, suspects nothing of the irregularities that have been going on for over thirty years. Warnings in writing, the intrigues brewing about him, even the existence of two children who bear a striking resemblance to Godoy — none of this has availed to open the King's eyes . . . "

A fanatical republican, who classified any monarch a despot by definition, Alquier poured his opinions before the young Secretary of the Legation, not bothering to filter words falling on the ears of an American — a fellow-republican hailing from a country which had successfully fought off the yoke of a royal tyrant. Since Charles Pinckney, the U.S. Minister in Madrid, followed a policy of *laisser-aller*, Graham welcomed this chance meeting with the French Ambassador, whose regicidal rage often carried with it grains of intelligence not to be gleaned elsewhere.

"Don't think this blindness is the result of his being stupid. The King is not wanting in the normal amount of sense, as kings go. His conversation is markedly more fluent than that of Louis XVI, believe me. But, prevented by piety to think ill of another, he has reached such a pitch of purity he no longer believes in the possibility of adultery where princesses are concerned."

Graham smiled as they made their way through a narrow passage between a crate of oranges and cages of pigeons. He, too, once had believed in the superiority of princesses, if not on the moral level, surely on the esthetical one. The Spanish princesses had been a grave disappointment on both counts. Queen Maria Luisa's skin was green and her few remaining teeth yellow, in contrast to the false wooden ones, which were brown.

Pépita, the royal couple's favorite daughter, looked as though she'd been left soaking overnight in a tub of hot water and had dried that way. The eldest daughter, Carlota, married to the Regent of Portugal and called the Princess of Brazil, limped grotesquely and was also hunchbacked. Carlota had inherited the Queen's sexual temperament and, like her mother, took to her bed grooms, coachmen, and palace guards. In the face of all this esthetic injury, Graham couldn't help feeling grateful to the Prime Minister, who, while no political visionary or intellectual light, at least possessed a certain physical radiance which had assured the Spanish Crown of some nominal Bourbons committing no violence on the esthetically sensitive eye.

"The King means well I think," he offered to Alquier.

The Frenchman wasn't to be soothed. "The harm done the world by people who mean well is inestimable, Mr. Graham. Just think of the missionaries. We can rejoice that this abhorrent royal line is, quite fitfully, doomed to extinction; minds and bodies exhausted by inbreeding, it is now able to produce only idiots and epileptics."

"What of the little count of Etruria? He is deemed very clever by all accounts."

Alquier shrugged, sniffing an orange. "A last gasp of sanity. A dying man's final lucid moment before the inevitable collapse. By the time he is twenty, the boy will be an irrepressible imbecile like his father, and as physically repulsive as any Bourbon seen in the light of day."

"Maybe we should appreciate Godoy's contribution to the line then?"

"These children are of bearable appearance, I grant you, Mr. Graham, but have you noted any improvement in their mental faculties? I daresay you haven't, and how could you, when their father has a brain inferior to that of Caligula's horse. I understand that you are unhappy with Mr. Pinckney, and I agree that the United States hasn't shown the greatest judiciousness in his selection as minister; however, the courts of Europe are filled with ambassadors who are unqualified for their posts. Mr. Pinckney is perhaps just a little more unqualified than most. This isn't very important. Mr. Pinckney's lack of talent will not destroy America. It is when an individual of Godoy's staggering incompetence rises to a position of absolute power that he is a threat to his country and that the people are to be pitied. I have no love for this land. On a December morning like today the sun here shines with a brazenness it daren't assume in my country in summer. There is too much light here. The people cannot think for all the light, else they would long have plotted the destruction of their oppressors. They cannot see that everything in Spain is theirs for the taking."

"So the French will do the taking in their stead, is that it?" Graham was surprised at his own daring, but Alquier seemed to take no offense, encouraging him to add: "Starting with her colonies. Louisiana, say?"

Alquier smiled. "We are trying."

"And are you succeeding?"

"According to rumor, yes."

"Is this your best offer, Mr. Alquier, rumor? I had hoped for something a bit more definite from one republican to another."

"Do you consider it proper to intrude on Mr. Pinckney's terrain, Mr. Graham?"

"*Someone* ought to, since Mr. Pinckney obviously prefers walking around it."

"Don't worry over Mr. Pinckney.

A sudden disturbance amongst the pens of squalling chickens and the counters of pickled peppers and cured pork attracted the men's attention. After some elbowing, they discovered the cause to be a dog wearing a collar around his neck with the inscription: "*I belong to Godoy. I fear nothing.*"

Within moments the police arrived and, failing to turn up the responsible party, promptly arrested the dog. Never having been arrested, the dog failed to grasp the gravity of the situation, barking in a happily excited way at the huddle of shouting humans surrounding him. Only the patrons of the *botellería* across the square, who had come out to watch the commotion between the stalls, inspired him to growl for some reason.

Alquier and Graham stood looking with the rest of the market crowd as the dog was carted off to prison.

"*Voilà*, Mr. Graham, why you mustn't worry over Mr. Pinckney. In a republic, too, a dull or despotic mind may rise to the top, but only at the pleasure of the people; never is it imposed on them by divine right.

Friends have scolded me for allowing the obviously biased Alquier's point of view to prevail unchallenged; however, I feel that an obvious bias is difficult to overlook, and therefore easily sidestepped. The dangerous account is the one insidiously crafted to manipulate reaction, for it requires an insidiously crafted mind to unmask. Who, but Alquier would ask Bonaparte to please "send me to a reasonable country"? The First Consul, by the way, obliged, though how "reasonable" Naples — the "country" to which he was sent — appears to the regicidal Charles is an open question, seeing as how the King of Naples is brother to Carlos IV and cast in much the same mold, and Queen Caroline, a sister to the unfortunate Marie Antoinette, loathes all things French and republican.

It was during the pause between Madrid and Naples late last winter that Alquier arrived at the Chancellor's for dinner one afternoon and, as luck arranged it, I was among the invited. But I am running ahead of myself. Before this happened, at about the time Christmas festivities came to a close at the Spanish Court, preparations got underway at the President's House in Washington City to celebrate the New Year.

JANUARY

I borrowed a kilo of cocoa from Madame Pichon," Petit told Martha, preceding her down the musty-smelling stairs to the basement.

"Then you can make the soufflés. That's wonderful, Petit. You know father loves chocolate soufflé."

"Yes, but I cannot do the chateau potatoes. I see the potatoes we have are shooting."

He meant sprouting. Martha had no trouble interpreting the cook's English, as well she should after seventeen years. She and her father had met the Frenchman at Sèvres while on their way from Le Havre to Paris where her father was to succeed Mr. Franklin as minister. Petit had been cooking in his mother's pension and spoke a little English even then, on account of his having fought in the American Revolutionary War — a war that had returned him to France a virtual cripple. Her father had arranged to have him operated on — her father was always like that, helping people — and Pierre Gerville, alias Petit, had been with the Jeffersons ever since. First in Paris, then in Monticello, and now in Washington City. January first was awfully early for potatoes to start sprouting, Martha thought. "You must have stored them in the wrong place."

"Ah-a-ah!" What was she telling him? That he didn't know how to winter potatoes? "There *is* no place." Petit gestured toward the walls, glistening with moisture wherever daylight caught the smoky sandstone. "This is not Monticello, Madame Martha. We are in the swamps here. I have no sheds, no outbuildings, no nothing. The dry spots I must keep for the wine."

"Of course, Petit. Of course you must," Martha was quick to agree. She didn't want him to change his mind about the soufflés.

"You shouldn't be down here with a baby coming any minute, in the first place," admonished Petit, who had no use for Martha on his trek to the wine cellar. If it had been her sister beside him on the stairs, his concern would have been genuine, but he felt confident that Martha could be abandoned in the flooded catacombs of Rome and she still would manage to bring forth any number of healthy infants at the appointed time. At least she could be trusted not to steal. Anything belonging to Mr. Jefferson, his eldest daughter would guard with her life. Only the President and he had a key to the wine cellar door, yet, even with this precaution, bottles had a way of disappearing out of dark corners, perhaps right while he was making his selection, Petit suspected. She would make a good sentinel, if nothing else.

Petit unlocked the door, holding up his hand in a demand for silence or respect, Martha couldn't guess. She kept herself at a safe distance from the temperamental chef, inhaling the slightly sour, darkly-pleasant smell hovering over the bricked compartments in which reds and whites, champagnes, ports, Madeiras, and brandies were resting in cool isolation from one another and from the small, grilled window, whose circle of light modestly confined itself to illuminating a few empty crates and a stack of discarded newspapers on the floor beneath it.

No sounds from above penetrated here. The house upstairs might have been deserted, Martha thought. Half of it was, actually, as most everyone had gone off to church, or rather to the Hall of Representatives where a service was being held. The kitchen, though, she knew, was bustling with activity, the slaves washing, cleaving and chopping the provisions hauled in from Georgetown with the wagon early that morning. Martha watched Petit bounce from niche to niche, sniffing, grumbling, asking his own advice, gently arranging his choices into one of the empty crates. She was about to ask how he proposed to lug the case upstairs when her eye fell on the Richmond *Recorder*.

"*By this wench Sally,*" she read at random, "*our President has had several children . . .*"

"Could you keep your eyes open here while I go find Julien to help me?" Not hearing a reply, Petit looked up to see Martha hide the newspaper behind her back. A useless move, for anyone able to read was aware by now of the ceaseless attacks on Mr. Jefferson flowing from the pen of James Thomson Callender. Even more useless in the case of Petit, to whom the continuous newspaper saga about the President's liaison with one of his slaves was an affair only Americans could get excited about. "Your father has a mistress? So what?" It could hardly be news to Martha.

"What are you talking about? Keep your vile tongue!"

Petit smiled. People considered Martha intelligent because she had no interest in clothes or jewelry, or the husbands of other women, as if intelligence were the inescapable result of this lack of interest. She had been taught Latin and Greek and read Diderot in French, but she couldn't take in the simple English of a Virginian newspaper. "Life is not so serious as you make it, Madame Martha."

What Petit failed to understand was that years of plantation life had trained Martha's eyesight not to perceive those aspects of it not conforming to the ideal, the way a doting courtier failed to notice the excrement on a king's mantle. A perception not likely to be understood by outsiders. That Petit had had ample opportunity to exercise his own eyesight mattered not a whit. Never would she stoop to acknowledge to a French cook the existence of this slander. "Go ahead. Get Julien."

When Petit's steps were no longer audible, Martha scooped up the rest of the newspapers and, resting them on her heavily pregnant stomach, bounded out of the wine cellar, too disturbed to bother about closing the door. What were a few bottles of Madeira when her father's honor was at stake?

Martha rushed upstairs seeking the privacy of her bedroom to look at the papers. Children's voices heard within sent her scurrying back down (eleven-year-old Anne and ten-year-old Tom, the two eldest, had accompanied their mother to Washington). Since guests were expected to dine at the President's House this afternoon, the servants were laying fires in the rooms on the ground floor, to bring up the temperature to a tolerable degree, driving Martha back up the stairs. By the time she hit upon the East Room, her knees were buckling.

Slamming the door shut with her foot, she dropped her burden to the floor, desperate for a place to sit and get her bearings. The only chair visible in the barn-like space was way at the other end, near the brownish blanket behind which Meriwether Lewis slept — fortunately not at the moment. Aside from a wobbly table, the furnishings consisted of an odd number of containers and an iron bucket in which the few inches of water had frozen. Martha turned the bucket upside down to make a footstool and, sagging onto it, grasped at the nearest newspaper:

> It is well known that the man, whom it delighted the people to honor, keeps and for many years has kept, as his concubine, one of his slaves. Her name is Sally. The name of the eldest son is Tom. His features are said to bear a striking though sable resemblance to those of the President himself. The boy is ten or twelve years of age. There is not an individual in Charlottesville who does not believe the story, and not a few who know it. Mute! Mute! Mute! Yes very mute! – will all those Republican printers of biographical information be upon this point . . .

As she was reading, the ice, loosened by the warmth of her body, thumped out of the bucket. Martha retrieved it and threw it in a basin, pressing a piece of it against her forehead.

Behind the partition, Lewis woke up, believing himself still in 1802. The next minute his head was reeling and his mouth tasted like glue, perverse reality telling him that 1802 and the party were past and that the thumping in his head and room were in the unavoidable, wretched present. What was going on? Lifting the blanket to find out, he fell back on his bed, groaning out loud. Martha!? His pain suddenly intensified. Where had she gotten those newspapers? Who had given them to her? And why, in a house with some thirty rooms, must she read them here? Why wasn't she at the service, hearing the Reverend Manasseh Cutler expound on the evils of drink?

The thought of an entire congregation holding their heads while the furious Yankee lashed out at them from behind rolls of preacher's fat, made Lewis feel a little better. He should have gone to the Hall and endured Cutler's maledictions like any other man. There was consolation in finding oneself amongst fellow-sufferers. Nobody listened to these guest preachers anyway. So long as Washington City would be without a real church, the services held at the Hall of Representatives would remain little more than an opportunity for the men to talk politics and the women to giggle and gossip. To escape the Reverend Manasseh Cutler only to find Martha Jefferson Randolph on the tender threshold of 1803 didn't bode too well for the rest of the year, Lewis thought.

"Is that you, Meriwether? Are you there?" With a step as resolute as her character, Martha lost no time in securing the answer. "I thought you were in church."

Lewis groaned some more. Wished he had been. Wrenching his tongue from the roof of his mouth, his voice to his own ears sounded disgraced by supplication. "I'd give my eyeteeth for some of that ice."

Years of tending to Tom Randolph in similar situations had given Martha a keen understanding of what was required. Always the mother, she was back in a minute with a lump of ice wrapped around her not-so-white kerchief and had placed it on the patient's head, while stuffing another lump into his mouth, talking of coffee and of lighting a fire, shouting orders out the door at passing slaves and promising imminent recovery from the ailment without any reference to its cause.

Something within the secret folds of Lewis's being responded to the treatment. Already the blood in his temples seemed to be bound on a less violent course. Not a sight to soothe the eyes at the best of times, Martha today looked more haggard than ever. Being pregnant didn't round her out the way it did other women, in spite of a front trying to bulge through her stuff dress. But beyond that appearance forever in disarray, those pinched looks, there lurked something noble, he thought. Exactly like Jefferson, from whom she had inherited it, as she had her unnerving good health.

Lewis lay perfectly still in his cocoon of woolen covers so as not to dislodge the ice, listening to the scraping and sweeping about the fireplace, watching the fine cloud of ash-dust rising to the space above the sagging army blanket and the ceiling. Critta brought in a pot of smoldering embers from downstairs.

"No, not the oak," Martha ordered. "Pine burns much faster. Where is the coffee?" Already she was back at Lewis's side, displacing the cold air by her rapid passage, and bringing along the piquant smells of burning wood and freshly brewed coffee. "There!" She sat down at the edge of the bed. "Are you wondering what I was doing in your room?"

"I could see well enough what you were doing. What I'm wondering is, where did you get your reading material?" Lewis handed Martha back her kerchief, barely wet even now with pine blazing up the chimney. "Turn around for a minute, will you, Martha. I can't drink coffee lying in bed." He hurried his legs into his breeches so he could run to the fire and continue dressing there.

"Oh Meriwether . . . " The discovery in the wine cellar suddenly became too much for Martha. "Why are such libels allowed?"

"I can only tell you what Mr. Jefferson said to the Baron von Humboldt when he asked the same question. Put that paper in your pocket, Baron, he told him, and if you hear the freedom of our press questioned, show them the paper and tell them where you found it."

"Freedom indeed. License I call it. License to slander, to destroy a person's good name."

"What do you expect in a country with so many newspapers? They have to come up with *something* to entertain their readers. Do you think Mr. Adams or Mr. Washington were spared?" Adams had reacted with the Alien and Sedition Act, an Act to which Callender had been one of the first to fall victim for Callender was on the Republican side then. It was Mr. Jefferson who had bailed Callender out. Lewis himself had carried the $50.00 needed to assure his release. Callender had switched sides when all further attempts to secure favors from Mr. Jefferson failed. But there was no point in telling Martha all this. "You should see what's being written about Vice President Burr. And by a Republican editor yet. At least your father can depend on the Republican press to take up his defense."

"My father doesn't need defending against vile, personal attacks. You, of all people, ought to know that."

Lewis was of no mind to argue. A man's private life was his own, after all. What difference did it make whom the President, whose wife was long dead, invited into his bedroom? Planters all over the south had been taking up with their slaves ever since their arrival on these shores. It was custom by now. If this were the yardstick for measuring merit in public office, half the country's elected officials would be found wanting. Martha's grandfather, John Wayles, had died, leaving a whole nest of octoroons possessed of the natural right to call him father. A fact of life Martha was well acquainted with but which she chose to ignore. Just as she chose to ignore her father's determination to take up where Wayles had left off. Well, that was her privilege. The only sticky part, as Lewis saw it, was that Wayles hadn't gone up to Philadelphia to claim equality for all. No wonder the President was plagued by debilitating headaches.

"Poor father . . . I shudder to think what he must be going through. Coming at the same time as that New Orleans trouble, too. How long has this been going on? Some of this trash is dated August . . . " She kicked one of the papers in the fire with her slipper. Seeing it go up in flames prompted her to kick in a second. And a third.

"Stop that! You'll clog up the flue, burning so much paper."

She didn't hear. Not until the last copy was smoking and everything in and around the fireplace was a flying mass of black particles, did she regain her customary sensibility. "I will personally call on a sweep for you tomorrow. No, tomorrow is Sunday. Monday, first thing."

Lewis was struck by the brightness in her face. She nearly looked a natural woman, by God. "I expect you will."

Martha smiled, pointing at the windowsill. "Is that brandy you have there? I sure could use a drop."

Lewis went to get the bottle. I don't have glasses," he warned, aiming the remains of his coffee cup at a crisped snippet of paper persistently dancing toward his face. "Say when."

"I feel so much better, Meriwether."

"Wait till you taste it before making pronouncements. Be careful now. Don't gulp it. This is not your Piedmont persimmon flip, you know."

"You talk as if I'd never tasted brandy."

"*Cognac*, Martha. *French* cognac. Personally, I feel our American brandy is every bit as good. Even Tom Paine says so and he ought to know." Lewis shook his head. "Talking about being hounded by the press . . . Now there's a man who could tell you a tale on the subject."

Martha wasn't impressed. "Mr. Paine invites criticism. You can't write what he writes and expect the American people to approve. I wish father wouldn't ask him here so often. It reflects badly on him."

"On the contrary, I would say that Mr. Jefferson's loyalty reflects well on him. I, for one, admire him for it."

"*You* hid those newspapers in the wine cellar, didn't you, Meriwether?" Consulting with herself, Martha nodded. "It eases my mind to know that you are here to look after things." She took a sip of the cognac. "You're right, this brandy *does* stand up to the best of French cognac."

"It *is* French cognac, Martha."

The headache was going into its second week, always an encouraging prospect to Jefferson, for it meant that any day now the weight would be lifted. Not suddenly or unexpectedly, but slowly and deliberately—a reluctant loosening of the vise. It wouldn't be today.

It wouldn't be this morning, he corrected himself. Negative suggestions discouraged positive results. If he were able to believe that the tincture of valerian, or another of the remedies on the cherry washstand, could dull the pain, however briefly, then perhaps it would do so, however briefly. Instead he accepted as fact the view that the effectiveness of medicine decreased with its frequent use because it was a view supported by evidence. Yet there was evidence as well supporting the side of faith. He had witnessed it first hand. On a French country road while on his way to visiting the great cities of Italy.

At some undetermined spot, a group of peasants had denied passage to the carriage. This was highly unusual, Jefferson remembered thinking. Centuries of living under the heel of royal tyrants had so ingrained subservience within the rural French that the mere sight of a man dressed in a suit of whole cloth made them step aside and bare their heads in tribute. They scattered like chickens at the approach of a coach, making way for the traveling stranger as if he were Louis XVI himself (which, for all they knew, he might have been). Only as a corpse did the peasant proceed at his own pleasure—or at that of his bearers. A dead man could go before a rich one.

But this was no group on its way to the cemetery. Nothing passing for a coffin was to be seen. Curious, Jefferson had followed Marius, his driver, out of the carriage to find a very young girl—a mere child—convulsing on the trampled grey dirt before a priest in a cassock shining green with age and a haggard-looking woman undoubtedly the girl's mother. There was a cautious distance between the trio in the center and the onlookers.

Two of the sturdier peasants were standing guard before the door to a miserable dwelling just off the road "to prevent the demon from entering the house and hiding up the chimney from where he could climb down in the night and repossess the girl's body," Marius explained.

Demon, my foot, Jefferson thought. The child was possessed of nothing more extraordinary than the disease of epilepsy. He had seen it before. Jemmy Madison used to fall prey to seizures exactly like this. In a few moments it would all be over, whether or not the priest, who had more flesh on him than the girl and her mother combined, beseeched the heavens in Latin. And so it happened.

Suddenly the girl stopped shaking and that was that, except for the expression of utter trust with which she beheld the fat priest, making perfectly plain that she considered him and his incantations the sole reason for her deliverance. It was an expression mirrored in the eyes of the others.

When she began to convulse again, the priest commanded her to be still, saying the demon had been expelled from her being and could torment her no more. And if there had been anything extraordinary about the girl's condition, it was her belief in these words. No sooner had her mind absorbed the message than her body obeyed. Such was the power of faith. And because it was so powerful, it wasn't given to all. Lucky the man who could blame his visiting ills on the devil, who dared call his enemy by name and chase him off. "Be ye gone, Satan!"

Personally, he didn't have the voice for it. His own enemies were of this earth and wouldn't be intimidated. "Be ye gone, Federalists!"

Jefferson shook his head as he lifted his feet from the basin of ice cold water, his hand grappling behind him on the high bed for the towel he knew to be there. Here he was, elected to the highest office in the land, wishing he were back at Monticello, selecting crops for the spring planting. What was the matter with him? It wasn't as though the opposition had already won. The fight had barely started.

But he was not the man to relish a fight. Like Madison, he enjoyed the strategy of the game, not the action — an inclination not congenial to the Westerners, who demanded instant restitution of their rights at whatever cost, and very convenient to the Federalists, who fanned this demand with belligerent rhetoric.

The inhabitants of the West, heretofore considered filthy democrats and dabbling would-be rivals by the New England seafaring states (if considered at all) all of a sudden had become dear brethren in a common cause. An alliance so unnatural it must strike even the indifferent observer as suspicious. Surely, the West wasn't fooled? Of course, a man who thought himself on the verge of drowning didn't question the motives of those he saw as his rescuers. Strategy meant nothing to him.

The Western Representatives, however willing to support the Administration's policy of restraint, were under great pressure from home "to do something." A situation that would not improve in the coming days when Congress met, and the calls for war would turn official.

Except for John Randolph, whose scathing tirades had a way of striking terror on both sides, the Republican majority in the House would be hard put to hold its own in a verbal confrontation with the opposition, who outnumbered it in speakers of talent. But Johnny was erratic. Like the drunk who praised you beyond reason one moment and accused you of disloyalty the next, Randolph was given to taking strange turns. To be sure, nothing more kindled his rage for debate than finding himself alone in the face of an advancing hostile horde. If anyone could stop this lot in its tracks, it was Johnny.

Before it was that far along, though, weeks would pass, and meanwhile the Senate would have taken up where the House had left off, and there was no John Randolph in the Senate. And, as time was wasted in endless debate, the discontent out West would mount, the cries of "yellow" and "coward" at his own address increase, while the Federalists basked in their self-appointed halo of defenders and rescuers. Other than a reversal by Spain, the only way to forestall this turn of events was for the Administration to make a surprise move and appropriate to itself the shining role of rescuer.

Monroe.

The longer he thought on it, the more Jefferson became convinced that Monroe was his man. If appointed to assist Livingston in securing the desired port from the French, heated tempers would cool down. James Monroe had credentials in Western eyes, having acted on their behalf in the past. With Monroe as their spokesman, the West would turn its back on the Federalists, whose portfolio contained nothing to recommend them as an ally. The advocates of war would suffer a setback. It wasn't likely to shut them up, but it would take down the noble timbre in their voices.

Jefferson nodded pensively at the washstand, above which the oval, cherry-framed mirror was tilted in such a way as to reflect only his eyes. The eyes moved up and down in agreement, then frowned at his selection of leg wear. Woolen hose? On a day when the President was holding open house and the rooms would be overrun with Federalists in their finest bib and tucker? Doing away with levees, those pompous receptions held by the Washingtons and Adamses, was one thing, "but don't overdo it, Long Tom," the reflection, now tilting into full view by the pressure of Jefferson's index finger, warned. "Even a democratic President has obligations as a host."

"Open house and then a dinner . . . I won't be able to go out riding," he sighed.

"It's going to be a long day," the reflection sighed back.

"And with a headache, too."

"Not to mention the Reverend Cutler."

"A preacher should keep politics out of his sermons."

"Especially a Federalist preacher."

"At the rate you're moving this morning, you'll arrive at the Hall when the service is over."

"Not a bad idea."

If it were going to be a long day, Jefferson thought, he might as well get dressed for it. Exchanging the thick woolen hose for a pair of white silk ones, he closed the drawer suddenly in a hurry. Maybe Madison had gone to the Hall. He'd be curious to see what his Secretary of State thought of the idea of appointing Monroe Minister Plenipotentiary. No, that wasn't true. He could fairly well predict Madison's reaction. The reason for his sudden haste was to let his old and good friend in on the move. Sometimes long days were not without their compensations.

Carlos Martinez, Marqués de la Casa Yrujo, and Sally McKean, Marquesa de la Casa Yrujo, needn't fall back on swirling staircases and swept-open French doors to make a grand entrance. That indefinable something in the Yrujo walk made an impression all its own, Sally knew. The walk owed to good breeding and bearing, and to being at all times aware of your rank (which was nearly at all times above that of everyone else). Born a Spanish grandee, Carlos had come by it naturally. Born an American Republican, Sally had adopted it and, with a singularity of purpose known only to the truly dedicated, improved and perfected it.

It was a point of honor with the Yrujos not to arrive on time for any social affair. Never so late, of course, as to miss dinner at the President's House. That would not only be rude but would cheat them out one of the best meals served in Washington City, if not in the entire United States. That Sally and Carlos had arrived at the Palace just in time for the chocolate soufflés was due entirely to circumstances beyond their control, as Carlos was explaining the President and his guests.

"You would not believe me, if I would not believe it myself," said

Carlos, arranging the English words into one of those peculiar sentences he came up with when excited. "We have been traveling for five days."

"Five perfectly horrible days," Sally confirmed.

The trip from Philadelphia, Sally's hometown and the residence of her father, Governor McKean of Pennsylvania, had been fraught with misadventure, their coach being nearly overturned, their driver injured, and the Yrujos themselves the victims of endless delays and vexations, including a forced stay in a filthy hovel pretending to be an inn. They had left Philadelphia two days after Christmas, meaning their bones had rattled over the ruts and gulches of the abominable winter roads a full five days for a journey that ought to take only two. A journey filled with horrors of every description, not the least of which was having to spend the year's end in the company of hawkers, tooth-drawers, bleeders, and other traveling rabble.

That she and Carlos, after their excruciating ordeal, could still manage an entrance in accordance with their station impressed even Mr. Jefferson, Sally noted. Dolley Madison was so stunned she forgot to wipe the snuff off her nose and started sneezing into Tom Paine's inevitable brandy, with the snuff from the platinum, lava-tinted box in her hand flying in all directions. Sally smiled. Nothing could rival true class. Muddy shoes, soiled garments, wrinkled foulards, and undone hair disappeared before it. Silken shirts and linen waistcoats alone did not a gentleman make.

Few members of this fine company understood the art of elegance, she thought. Mr. Jefferson's overlong body was wrapped in a suit of black silk and a frilled cambric shirt with cravat, distinguished but for his ruddy farmer's face. Madison was, as usual, invisible behind the mass of nodding feathers in his wife's turban. Dolley had on a satin print gown imposing more scenery onto the weary travelers' eyes than they had encountered during the wretched five-day-excursion from Philadelphia to Washington. Looking at Dolley Madison you had the feeling her greatest regret in life was that she could only wear one dress at a time (no doubt she made up for it by dressing for two). Compared with Dolley, the eldest Jefferson daughter looked like a refugee from a parsonage. Martha was hopeless, something which became more apparent the harder she tried. Awkward in a silk navy shift, Martha sat under her reddish wig the way Dolley sat under a light—afraid to move lest it be lost.

That glorified errand boy, Meriwether Lewis, whose tailor-made captain's uniform couldn't hide his bowleggedness, had a certain flair for seating arrangements, Sally decided, noticing the pair of unused table settings between the impeccable Colonel Burr and the stylish Hannah Gallatin near the President.

Mr. Jefferson, gracious as always, insisted the Yrujos sit down and have dinner. Before they could protest (from the looks of it the meal was over), the President instructed Lemaire, the French steward, to that end. Handsome in his livery, Lemaire was already on his way.

Carlos smiled gratefully, adjusting his jewel-studded small-sword as he took the seat next to his spouse. "It is true, Madame Yrujo and I have not had a palatable meal since leaving Philadelphia."

"I can imagine," sighed Dolley Madison. "Travel is nothing but hardship." Colonel Burr nodded. "The road from Baltimore is sheer persecution."

"We will do our best to make up for it," Mr. Jefferson promised.

Everyone at table seemed either of buoyant spirits or on the verge of dozing off, Martha's husband having passed the verge, obviously, which was just as well. Snoring quietly at his sagging chocolate soufflé and unfinished brandy, Tom Randolph gave the impression of a man at peace with the world, an illusion that would be shattered the moment he opened his mouth. Beside him, the younger Jefferson daughter didn't look much livelier. At the other end of the large round table, John Randolph, in white top boots, buckskin small clothes, and other eccentric attire, was piping a monologue for the benefit of Jack Eppes, mistaking Eppes glass for his own in the process. Eppes was too tired or too indifferent to notice.

While Carlos and she appreciated the excellent rice soup and tender saddle of veal, Sally pondered the inebriated status of some of the guests. Mr. Jefferson was well known to dislike excess of any kind. No toasts were drunk at his table for precisely that reason. Federalists were not invited to dine with Republicans, and vice versa, in order to avoid clashes. Open house! Of course. The President had open house on the first day of the year. That explained everything. No wonder Maria was exhausted. It was no picnic to stand for hours on end and invite all comers to partake of one's food and drink. A pity that a beautiful young woman like Maria, who had everything needed to shine in society, should be too shy and delicate to take on the task, while an incorrigible frump like Martha played the indefatigable hostess.

Even now, after the demands of open house and looking pregnant beyond endurance, Martha couldn't keep to her seat, everything on the move except her head under that copper fright of a wig; meddling with Lemaire's rounds of beef and oyster pie; providing a fresh bottle of brandy for a Tom Paine receding into his glassy-eyed stage; talking Piedmont Virginian to a liveried slave and chasing after him to the kitchen. Instead of enjoying her delayed segregation from the men, as did the other women!

But for the Yrujos' untimely arrival, the tablecloth would have been removed and the ladies relegated to their own company in the oval room, where they would comment on each other's gowns and play Loo, while the gentlemen indulged in their social glass and favorite topic — politics. Rumblings of that topic were beginning to be heard around the President.

Sally didn't understand it. If a man dug graves all day to earn his bread, he was relieved to have done with the dead at night and return to the living. Not so politicians. Fascinated with their own doings, they dragged themselves elsewhere only to describe them to their cronies, who were likewise obsessed. Politesse and deference toward the opposite sex would contain this obsession for a prescribed time and, that time having elapsed presently, it was churning in their insides like bad wine in a bottle, due to burst through the conversation at any moment, to the disaffection of the women who were barred from it (at least in public).

"Monroe! That's a brilliant idea!" Randolph squeaked, leaping from his chair in his blinding boots to congratulate Mr. Jefferson.

All the men were of the same opinion, including Tom Paine, who vigorously nodded agreement, than asked Madison what he had agreed to. Sally decided to agree with the *Columbian Centinel*, which saw in Paine the indubitable marks of a confessed sot, who was somehow able to stand and talk after he had swallowed great quantities of brandy. As for Monroe, his one redeeming feature was his wife, Elizabeth Monroe being that rare American female who knew how to enter a room. With Monroe clumping beside her, she was greatly handicapped, however. A curious choice for the President to make. Monroe no more knew how to talk than how to walk. How was such an inelegant clumper to glide into a French salon and seduce it into relinquishing New Orleans to the United States? A far more appropriate candidate for the post would be Colonel Burr.

Burr's deep, mellow voice could persuade the most reluctant words into sounding like promising language. "An excellent choice," he was saying now, mixing his mellifluous tones amongst the general sentiment. Sally couldn't contain a smile.

"You don't agree, Madame Yrujo?" The Colonel returned her smile. He was a keen interpreter of the unsaid. Especially so with women. His notions about women were quaint to start with, out of step with the rest of the band.

Disappointed by the birth of a daughter, he had set about educating her as if she were a son, claiming there was nothing she couldn't learn as well as a boy. The girl believed him. At ten Theodosia was quoting Horace, Lucian, and Terence, frightening America with her knowledge. Burr never stopped feeding her information. She had turned out pretty and, after her mother's untimely death, grew into a cultured and accomplished hostess when barely in her teens. The world was astonished, most notably an Indian Mohawk Chief by the name of Thayendanegea and the scores of French nobles in the country at the time (No less a connoisseur than Talleyrand had sung Theodosia's praises). The Colonel's entourage — men and women of polished exterior and with the tortuous mentality disposed to deny convention, à la Burr himself —

applauded furiously. But nature could not be tricked without her responding in kind. The astonishing Theodosia, erudite on all subjects, disliked politics, refusing to discuss the topic nearest and dearest to her father's heart. The Colonel took it well, as he did all adversity, including Theodosia's marrying Joseph Allston at seventeen and her removal to his plantation in far away Charleston, the noble side of his nature somehow rising to the occasion.

Carlos was repeating for the benefit of the company what he had told the President and Madison from the beginning: that the Intendant had acted on his own advice in closing New Orleans to the Americans; that he had promptly notified his government in Madrid of the situation and harbored no doubts the Spanish Court would at once dispatch orders to restore the deposit and deal severely with Morales . . .

Sally had heard the story several times in the past weeks. That it was true didn't add to its fascination at this count. "How is your little grandson, Colonel Burr?"

The Colonel's dark hazel eyes lit up, New Orleans and Monroe obliterated for the time being. "Very soon now, he beamed at Sally, "little Aaron will know his letters. I told Theo to put a pen in his hand and set him to the task. There is no reason why the boy shouldn't read and write before he is three. This, with speaking French, would make him a tolerably accomplished lad of that age."

Sally smiled. The boy was all of seven months old. "You missed your calling, Colonel. You should have been an educator."

"My views as a pedagogue are not widely sought."

"Could it be that your standards are too high?"

"Not too high, Madame Yrujo. Never too high. It is merely that they don't vary for either sex."

"Not every woman is a Theodosia Burr, Colonel."

"Nor every man a Benjamin Franklin, Madame Yrujo. But every gentleman has at his disposal the opportunity to find out. The rarity of genius in women can easily be traced to the errors of education, prejudice, and habit. When these errors are corrected, a Mary Wollstonecraft, even a Phyllis Wheatley, will cease to be regarded as curious phenomena . . .

" Burr paused to watch Lemaire pour coffee for Sally, savoring a sip of cognac.

Sally nodded indulgently, the wisest course when the Colonel expounded on his pet theory. She hadn't read Miss Wollstonecraft's *Vindication of the Rights of Woman* and could only hope it in no way resembled the poems of Phyllis Wheatley that she *had* read. A slave who had been educated by her Boston owner, Phyllis had rewarded Wheatley by penning bundles of verse bursting with New Englandian religious and moral fervor, the likes of which would have put to sleep Calvin himself. They certainly had Sally, and with her every American south of Massachusetts excepting President Washington, who, never on target, pronounced Phyllis a genius.

"Your mind is a legal morass," the soprano voice of John Randolph was heard piping to Madison, then, as if the name Wheatley had just penetrated his awareness, Randolph turned to Burr: "Phyllis Wheatley?!"

He sat his spindly body down next to the Colonel, on the chair vacated by Carlos, who had moved on to the seat left by Mrs. Gallatin near the President. Whenever politics reared its dictatorial head over a dining cloth, separation of the sexes automatically followed.

Hannah Gallatin had joined Maria Jefferson Eppes and Dolley Madison at one end of the table, where Dolley was explaining the Roman tableaux in her sapphire necklace. Dolley's much-younger sister Anna Payne seemed reluctant to follow, feeling it her duty to stealthily keep pushing the bottle of brandy out of Tom Paine's reach. A foolish and even dangerous exercise, for if there was anything grating to a drunk, it was the deliberate withholding of his liquor. Sally was surprised Martha's all-encompassing hostess' eye hadn't caught on to this detail and retouched it. Hospitality, as Miss Payne well knew, being a perpetual lodger at the Madisons, didn't mean denying guests, unless they resorted to verbal or physical abuse, which Paine was far too hardened a drinker to fall to. But Martha had not been seen since her Piedmontese exit with the liveried slave. No doubt exhaustion had finally overtaken her and she lay amongst the ruins of the dinner's flat- and silverware in the kitchen, a collapsed ruin herself. Carlos, Gallatin, Madison, Eppes, and the inescapable Meriwether Lewis were huddled about Mr. Jefferson, who was lounging on one hip, speaking in a soft voice.

Dissatisfied with his poor share of the audience, Randolph's deceptively clear gaze stalked the length and breath of the table accompanied by his best I-am-going-to-say-something manner. "Phyllis Wheatley?!" he reprised, squeaking at top volume.

Burr smiled good-naturedly. "I heard you the first time, Johnny."

Yes, thought Sally, and this time so had everyone else. All conferred on Randolph that fleeting attention accorded a predictably obnoxious child. Dolley Madison momentarily abandoned her Roman tableaux to cast a protective glance at her undersized spouse, often the butt of Randolph's bile. Yet even she joined the majority in extending to the obnoxious child the indulgence of a misguided parent. The President interrupted his talk to nod absentminded consent (He, too, had dozed with Phyllis Wheatley) "Religion indeed has produced a Phyllis Wheatley, it could not produce a poet," he offered before resuming his discourse.

Randolph smiled triumphantly at Burr. "Your turn, Colonel."

Burr shrugged. He had been speaking in favor of Wheatley's education, not her work. Even so, it was hard to pass up a chance to tease Johnny. "England made a great show of Miss Wheatley."

Randolph didn't think twice. "England makes a great show of dogs, too."

His answer moved Paine, who was born in England, to a crooked grin and memories of Martha Jefferson Randolph bearing gifts of brandy, presently dissimulated by the ruches and furbelows of a feminine sleeve. "My dear Miss Payne," he started, gently rescuing the bottle from Anna's grasp, "I would think your time could be better employed. Or is it you fear I will prove the *Centinel* wrong and fall in your lap?"

The dutiful Miss Payne jumped to her feet in fright (Why? Sally wondered – at the sensibility of the advice?) – fair-haired beauty menaced by the aquiline-nosed Paine's sarcasm.

John Randolph, his mind bogged somewhere in the ancient Court of Chivalry or glad to have his fight at last, sprang to his boots and to Miss Payne's rescue. "Mr. Paine, sir, you are not a gentleman!"

Paine smiled his crooked smile. Aside from seeing in him "the indubitable marks of a confessed sot", the Federalist press had found Paine to be "that disgrace and opprobrium of human nature, offensive to decency, smitten with the leprosy of scorn, the natural enemy of virtue, the most infamous and depraved character of this or any age." For anyone to tell him at this point that he was not a gentleman was like branding a man a murderer and then telling him that he was not polite. "Ah, Johnny, and how do you propose to support your charge? Don't I live above my means as befits a gentleman? Am I not contracting debts with the best of you?"

"A child can contract debts, sir! A man of honor does not exhibit himself at Lowell's for the distraction of the curious in exchange for a meal."

The company gasped at Randolph's cruelty, the President rising to position himself near his quarrelsome relative—"Now, Johnny"—but Paine seemed undisturbed. "Why, Johnny, I thought you admired me?"

"I admire your writing, sir, not your person."

Paine spread out his arms, hitting Meriwether Lewis, who had followed the President's example and was standing guard next to Paine. "This coat was fashioned to fit Mr. Jefferson. You think it fair to blame Mr. Jefferson's poor selection of a tailor on me?"

"I wasn't referring to your clothing, Mr. Paine."

"Good! Then I shall not refer to yours."

Everyone smiled at Paine's retort, though none enjoyed it more than the pipestem-queued Madison, who returned Randolph's hatred of him with all the seething passion of the introvert and nearly choked on his Madeira, coughing out candles and blowing wax on Gallatin's ruffled shirt in his merriment, drawing attention to his schoolmasterly person in a way to which Randolph himself would never stoop.

Her husband's uncommon exhibition prompted Dolley to some unusual behavior of her own. "Mr. Madison, please!" she cried in a voice loud enough to disturb a corpse, though not, ostensibly, Martha's husband, who kept on snoring peacefully.

"Mr. Jefferson, please, listen to me?" begged Petit, sounding as if he were weary of repeating the question.

"Petit?" The President turned to look at his cook, who was not given to making unannounced appearances in the public dining room. "What's the matter? Anything wrong?"

"It is Madame Martha, Mr. Jefferson. She has been delivered of the new baby."

"What?" The President sagged onto Randolph's chair, amidst the delighted yelps of the ladies. "When did this happen? Is everything all right?"

"Oh yes, very all right. Madame Martha and the little girl are healthy and tired now."

"Can we go see her?" Dolley chanted.

"And *very* tired now," Petit emphasized.

Mr. Jefferson looked stunned. "A girl, is it? When did this happen?" he repeated. "Why wasn't I told?"

"Madame Martha said it would spoil the party."

"My God'. She might have died."

"What of Mr. Randolph?" Petit wanted to know.

"What of Mr. Randolph indeed?" the President sighed.

"Shall I try to wake him?"

Eternal meddler that he was, John Randolph was already shaking the crumpled form of his namesake into life, piping shrill encouragement.

"Johnny . . . ?" A joyful glow of childlike surprise slowly supplanted the initial look of distrust on Tom Randolph's face. He sat up, eager to absolve his angelic-faced tormentor for the offering of a grin. 'What happened?" he voiced his surprise at his eccentric cousin's unexpected civility.

"Rejoice, my friend," Randolph chirped. "You are a father! Mrs. Randolph has been delivered of a baby,"

Tom Randolph's face fell. "Oh." Here he was, entertaining the notion of a *rapprochement*, when Johnny's sole purpose in rousing him was to announce the birth of yet another child destined to be weaned a Jefferson worshipper by its mother. He had been awakened under false pretenses. Was that his drink?

"It's a girl."

"I suspected as much." Girls made better worshippers. Martha's husband picked up his unfinished glass of brandy: "You are a cheat, Johnny."

Lewis tells me I should take Sally's version of events with a pinch of salt, that she tends to lack charity and has an exalted sense of her own rank. Perhaps, but then, who in a democracy can remain immune to the lure of a title? Didn't John Adams propose to bestow upon an unsuspecting George Washington "His Highness the President of the United States of America and Protector of the Liberties of Same?" — as baroque an address as was ever bandied about any royal court, certainly. And, as Mrs. Hagedoorn has it, "Charity isn't an article that springs to the surface like sweat, when called for."

I have no intention of quarreling with Mrs. Hagedoorn, even in these pages, especially at this stage, when a modest lack of charity may lend a sorely needed touch of levity to the proceedings, which are everywhere mired in frustration, depression, anger, resentment, powerlessness, and variants of these, due to the absence of news, understanding or cooperation from superiors, colleagues, underlings, the elements, the opposition, the gods.

In Paris, Bonaparte is being checkmated by the Dutch winter; all the while, in the Bay of Biscay, Colonial Prefect Laussat and his entourage prepare to sail for Louisiana. In Washington City, Jefferson anxiously awaits word from abroad, and the arrival of some startling piece of news only increases the suspense. In New Orleans, Governor de Salcedo's patience is severely tested by the incomprehension of the Spanish Court, while, in Madrid, Carlos IV is being forcibly detained to deliver decisions.

But it is Chancellor Livingston who, indisputably, is bearing the worse of it

January 1803

The valet, in silken wig and brocade livery, was waiting discreetly for Talleyrand to look up from the papers on the exquisitely carved desk and notice him. At last, the Foreign Minister's indifferent grey eyes became visible below the heavy lids. The eyebrows rose questioningly as he gazed at the servant. "Yes?"

"Mr. Livingston is here again, sir."

"Tell Mr. Livingston I am not in."

"Very well, sir."

As he turned to execute the order the old valet hesitated, pursing his mouth as if he were about to say something. Talleyrand's eyebrows repeated their upward motion. "Anything else, Firmin?"

"That is what I told the gentleman last time, Monsieur.

Talleyrand smiled. "And what you will continue to tell the gentleman if he persists in coming here." His voice was soft and impersonal, devoid of irritation or impatience.

The servant's manner was likewise detached as he bowed his silken-queued head. "I understand, Monsieur."

The cat had made one of his rare appearances in the parlor. Sitting on the warm black-and-white tiles near the chimney, he glared angrily at Mrs. Livingston, as though he begrudged her the cozy corner near the snoozing stove. Mustafa didn't know he was Mrs. Livingston's cat. Recognizing Mme Tranche as the human who fed him, he viewed both Livingstons with distrust when he didn't ignore them. He had no use for Zoé either because, like Mme Tranche, he was a Parisian and contemptuous of provincials.

Mrs. Livingston smiled on hearing her husband at the door. "Robert is back early today, isn't he, Mustafa? I wonder what it means?" The answer came immediately.

"There never was a government more opposed to negotiation than this wretched Consulate!" Livingston cried at the sight of his wife. "There are no people, no legislators, no counselors. Bonaparte is everything! He never asks advice and so never hears any. Every thinking Frenchman is against this wild expedition to Louisiana, but not a single one dares tell him so." Overflowing with anger and disgust, he threw his topcoat at the nearest chair and sank on top of it, too depressed to return Mustafa's furious glare. "Ministers are mere puppets doing his bidding. They well know that by grasping at New Orleans, he is forcing the United States to side with Britain. Don't they realize that, if we go with England, France will be raising her arch enemy to world supremacy? Isn't there one man of character in the Tuileries to pound this fact into Bonaparte's megalomaniacal head?"

Mrs. Livingston gently pulled the coat free of her husband's weight. "Not likely, Robert." To point out the error of his ways to a man as overbearing as the First Consul would only reinforce his decision to proceed along the chosen route, with the ill-inspired advisor probably losing his position for his trouble. Mrs. Livingston sighed.

Robert's appointment as minister to France, which had so delighted him a few years back, was turning out a disappointment. No representative exerted himself more on behalf of his country than did he, yet none had less to show for his efforts, leaving an already distrustful Jefferson in Washington free to further improvise suspicion with regard to his appointee.

The President had not tossed this post Robert's way out of the goodness of his Republican heart. Free gifts did not exist in the world of politics so far as Mrs. Livingston had seen during nearly thirty-three years of being the wife of a politician. That her husband happened to be the best man for the job was sheer coincidence, little to do with his selection. But talent wasn't enough when you were up against the combined maneuvers of a Bonaparte and a Talleyrand bent on frustrating every American approach. Talleyrand made for the more obstinate part of this joined stumbling block, in her opinion.

"The First Consul is a sorry excuse for a head of state, I grant you,

Robert." A man with the manners of a foot soldier, blurting out inappropriate remarks at every turn, Bonaparte was totally unsuitable for public life. Talleyrand was civility in the flesh. Nothing escaped his mouth, which had not been polished for smooth consumption. "But Talleyrand is devious beyond human comprehension. A lifetime of lying has brought him to a point where he can no longer recognize the truth, entirely unlike the First Consul, whose natural impulse is to say what is on his mind."

"If that's the case, he is doing a splendid job of stifling his natural impulses."

"I'm not saying he can't be as devious as the situation requires, only that he isn't inclined that way by nature. Whatever his reasons for excluding you at present, they are not Talleyrand's. Talleyrand takes pleasure from seeing you humiliated. He hates America. He is taking out on you his dislike of the country. He wasn't exactly well received when he was an *émigré*."

"He received the reception he deserved. Where did he think he was? Did he fancy himself on one of the Islands, sporting through the streets of Philadelphia with a female of dark complexion hanging from his arm?" Recollecting the resulting scandal brought a smile to Livingston's face.

Talleyrand, that tireless schemer, certainly had miscalculated in thinking the Philadelphians racially tolerant simply because they made a great to-do about not holding slaves. She was a handsome woman, he kept saying, as if that fact somehow transcended her color, unable to comprehend that he should have contained the object of his admiration somewhere within the secret confines of an attic instead of flaunting it before the upper layers of the Philadelphia citizenry, whose doors were slammed shut in his face at once as a consequence.

Society elsewhere in the country followed suit. President Washington refused to receive him. Jefferson, who had an eye for color himself, albeit a discreet eye, would have no truck with anyone so publicly exhibiting his private tastes. A sprinkling of would-be abolitionists and other rowdies read in Talleyrand's *faux pas* a statement conforming to their own opinions and proclaimed him their champion. Talleyrand refused the honor, claiming he had seen a beautiful woman and had treated her as such, thereby alienating his few remaining sympathizers.

Some people, of course, found the incident amusing — Aaron Burr, for one, and with him not a few other New Yorkers, most of whom were awed by the noble *émigré*'s ancient lineage — and invited him to their tables and beds despite the brouhaha. "It wasn't as though he were left to languish in the gutter. Many a prominent New York family welcomed him."

"*We* didn't."

"Because I happened to be in Albany at the time he arrived in New York, Mary, not because of his taste in women. I have made that quite clear to the Foreign Minister."

"As the Foreign Minister is making quite clear to you that his not happening to be at home when you call is not because of his distaste for America."

"Nonsense. In this government only Bonaparte has any say. If I am not received at the Rue du Bac, it is on Bonaparte's orders. That, precisely, is the problem here!" Livingston's anger, temporarily relaxed by contemplating Talleyrand's plight in the United States, flared back to its original intensity. "You are not *listening*, Mary. I don't care if Talleyrand hates America. I don't care if the entire Consulate hates America! All I want is to negotiate. Dissuade that Corsican dictator from embarking upon his mad expedition to New Orleans before it plunges us into war."

"Then you should be happy to know that the fleet of French ships preparing to sail for Louisiana is sitting knee-deep in ice on the Scheldt River."

Livingston jumped to his feet, remarkably supple at the sound of the intelligence reaching his ears. "Where did you hear that?"

"The American Consul stopped by this morning. He is coming back this afternoon to tell you all about it. According to him, the ships are likely to be icebound for weeks to come."

"Why didn't you tell me right away?"

"The Consul is reserving for himself the pleasure of telling you the good news, Robert. He expressed his implicit trust in my leaving him the pleasure, too."

"A man of the Consul's experience ought to know better than to place his implicit trust in women. Don't worry, Mary. I won't give you away. I'll pretend ignorance."

Mrs. Livingston smiled. "With a face dripping satisfaction?" If she had known to what extent her husband would perk up at the news, she would not have waited this long to break her promise to the American Consul.

"I'll do my best to look properly dejected," Livingston vowed, forgetting in his joy that the grey feline lounging under his stove did not take to the Livingston touch. "Ouch!" He rubbed his clawed hand. "I never saw a more temperamental cat."

"He's a French cat, Robert."

"And well he shows it."

In New Orleans, Governor de Salcedo's patience is severely tested by the incomprehension of the Spanish Court . . .

overnor de Salcedo returned the dispatch to his son. "*You* read it, Manuél. I don't have my spectacles."

Father Sedella, who was in attendance, made a movement toward the spectacle case on the chimney mantle, then bethought himself, watching Manuél's eyes scan the contents of the message from Madrid. The son wore his captain's uniform with a panache reminiscent of the father in his younger days, he thought.

The Governor leaned forward in his spoon-back chair. "Is the news good or bad, tell me?"

"Neither, father. The Royal Court has appointed Brigadier-General de la Casa Calvo your assistant in transferring Louisiana to the French." Manuél spoke rapidly, as if in so doing the meaning would escape the old man. It did — for a moment.

Governor de Salcedo nodded benevolently — "I see . . . " — before stamping a booted foot on the cypress floor in shocked surprise. "An assistant?! Another intriguer, you mean, trying to undermine my position! De la Casa Calvo . . . Let me see that!" He snatched the communiqué with one quivering hand while with the other tried to put on his spectacles, whisked there by an ever-attentive Sedella. "*Yo el rey* . . . The King himself. . . I am undone! Even His Most Catholic Majesty now is siding with my enemies . . . "

"You are behaving unreasonably, father. I should think you would be pleased at the Court's consideration in assigning you a workhorse. There will be no end of official ceremonies and receptions at which Calvo can replace you."

"I don't *want* to be replaced at official ceremonies and receptions! They are the only rewards attached to this post. Why not replace me altogether while you are at it? Do you want this job? Do you think you can do better? Have you any idea what it is to govern a colony this size, peopled by the most undisciplined subjects in the realm?"

"My interest if for a military career, father, as you well know."

"If you hope to rely on your military training to carry the day, you'll be sorely disappointed. These colonists are not soldiers, you know. They will read your proclamations the way they read stories of passion, to while away the time. You are not dealing with Spaniards here. Not even with Frenchmen. The Louisianians are unlike any race the world has ever seen. Their sole object in life is the pursuit of pleasure, and nothing you can say or do will keep them from that pursuit. They will nod and smile at your orders and edicts, and disregard them with the utmost courtesy — no people are more graceful in the flouting of authority. The Governor stopped, arrested by a prior thought. "Is it my son who speaks to me in this way?" he cried at the monk. "I am not close enough to the grave for him; he is determined to be the nail in his father's coffin."

"Father, please, try to be reasonable. You are upsetting yourself over nothing. No one wants to replace you, least of all me. What would be the point? The colony is no longer ours. In a few months' time we will all of us have to make way for the French. You see enemies and intrigue where they don't exist."

"Manuél is right, Your Honor."

"Be quiet, Padre Antonio. This is nothing to do with the Church. I suppose . . . " The Governor turned to his son. "Morales doesn't exist, in your view? I suppose it was *I* who closed the port to the Americans?"

"I didn't say that, father."

"And I suppose I have no enemies intriguing against me in Madrid either, according to you?"

"I wouldn't know to what purpose."

"Then why do I receive dispatches from the Royal Court assigning me assistants instead of orders to reopen the port?"

"I'm sure I don't knew, father."

"Aha! You're sure of your ignorance — you admit it — yet you have an opinion on every subject under the sun. You claim you know nothing but you talk on everything. In how many wars have you fought, tell me? How many of the enemy have you killed? Do you even know how a soldier survives in peacetime? Ah, opinions come easily when one is young and a captain, don't they, Padre?" The Governor stretched to accept the cigar being lighted by the monk at a candle flame. "Let me confide to you, Manuél, I will be glad to have done with Louisiana . . . " He paused to puff at the cigar, pondering its aftertaste, which seemed to disappoint him. "This is New Orleans tobacco. Where are the cigars General Wilkinson brought me?"

"You smoked them all, Your Honor."

"There!" The Governor nodded to his son. "Another reason why I will not regret Louisiana. The climate here corrodes the tobacco as well as the bones. I would be a much younger man if it weren't for serving in this humid country. Do you remember Spain at all, my boy?" The old man's eyes filled with the tears of homesickness and cigar smoke.

"I always thought you felt a deep affection for this colony and its people, father."

"I feel a deep affection for you too, Manuél, but that doesn't blind me to your faults. I know them so well, in fact, I can list them in a moment without their altering my affection, which, believe me, my boy, is the ultimate test."

Moved by his father's words, the son responded with a military salute, not knowing what else to do. He looked expectantly at Sedella, who understood his role at once.

"Exactly what Manuél would say to *you*, Your Honor, if he had your talent for words."

"Exactly, father, if I had your talent for words."

In Washington City, Jefferson anxiously awaits word from abroad, and the arrival of a startling piece of news only increases the suspense . . .

I haven't had a chance to thank you, Johnny, for a job well done," said the President, looking up at Randolph who sat astride his trotting horse, a pistol stuck in his belt, and a riding crop dangling from his wrist. Two dogs tagged closely at the horse's heels. "You've made mincemeat of the opposition," Jefferson grinned, relishing the Republican victory in the House.

"Don't pretend you're surprised," quipped Randolph, laughing uproariously at his own lack of modesty. Acute barometers of their master's mood, the dogs jumped at Johnny's boots, barking wildly to express their delight at his joy, one chasing a squirrel until it disappeared into the bushes and returning to leap and bark with renewed excitement. Randolph flashed his crop at the air and shouted for silence, firing his pistol at a random treetop to underline his command. The mare trotted on peacefully through the cabal, wise to her company's ways.

Jefferson smiled to himself. He pulled his hat deeper over his eyes in anticipation of riding his own horse. They were arriving at the stable where Wildair was stalled and where he was headed when Randolph had come tearing down the street with his canine following. "If the Senate confirms Mr. Monroe's appointment as envoy tomorrow we'll be out of the woods for the time being. How is your health, Johnny? Lewis told me you haven't been feeling fit."

"My health is as good as yours," snapped Randolph, who refused to be sicker than the next man.

"I'm happy to hear it."

"You'll be happier to hear what I have to say next." Johnny pulled in the reins, bringing the horse to a standstill. He waited for the dogs to stop wagging their tails and understand this was nothing to do with them before leaning over to the President, who was staring at him in suspense. "Bonaparte's brother-in-law is dead." Randolph smiled, satisfied his information had made the proper impression.

"General Leclerc — dead?"

"Of yellow fever. His troops are being wiped out by it. And those who aren't nabbed by the fever are being murdered by the slaves. Saint Domingue is in a state of anarchy."

"Dear Jesus! Where did you hear this?"

"At the Union Tavern. A brig arrived in Alexandria with the news. Georgetown is buzzing with it. The ship had to make a quick getaway because the waters around Cape Francis were crawling with French deserters trying to climb aboard. All we need is to carry those plagues over here." Yellow fever wasn't the only epidemic feared to wash from Saint Domingue onto American shores. The contagion of insurrection was equally dreaded by the slave-holding states. "The French are finished in Saint Domingue, Mr. Jefferson. How often can they keep sending reinforcements? It's a wonder there are any soldiers left."

"France is a populous country. There are more Frenchmen than Englishmen."

"There won't be after Saint Domingue. I hear the number of casualties runs to fifty-thousand. That's not counting this last batch headed by Leclerc which is supposed to come to another twenty-thousand."

"I think I'll ride over to Alexandria and have a look at that brig." Jefferson was already striding toward the stable door. "How are the roads, Johnny?"

"Frozen, mostly!" Randolph shouted at the closing door as Jefferson disappeared inside. He tightened the reins. "We've seen worse, haven't we, boys?"

The dogs barked assent, then stood waiting with ears perked for the clicking noise in Johnny's cheek, which sent them dashing through G Street after the galloping mare.

In Paris, Bonaparte is being checkmated by the Dutch winter . . .

W hat do you mean, the ships are stuck in the ice?" Bonaparte shouted. He dropped the knife with which he had been carving random designs in his chair and fell to pacing the floor in his habitual manner. "Who is responsible for this?"

Admiral Decrès smiled. "The weather, most likely." As the valiant defender of Malta and a veteran of other battles, he could afford to tease a fellow soldier.

"Excellent, Denis! When I need a jester I won't fail to call on you. In the meantime, try to apply your wits to the navy. How long do you estimate my expedition will be immobilized?"

"It's difficult to say. The reports I received are not encouraging. The Dutch sailors and farmers are all predicting a severe winter for Holland, apparently. Barring an unexpected warm spell, I would say indefinitely, for now."

"Three-thousand French soldiers are sitting idle on a flotilla of frozen ships in Helvoetsluys while the *Surveillant*, which depends on the fleet for backup, is at this moment setting sail for Louisiana from a Spanish harbor? Bonaparte's voice was dripping irony. "Am I leaving something out, Admiral? Maybe there are a few footnotes you'd like to add?"

"The news is no easier for me to tell than it is for you to hear, General, believe me."

"I ought to have you shot for bringing it."

"If I could believe the situation would be reversed as a result, I might be inclined not to protest."

The First Consul stopped pacing to nod pensively, as if he were considering the offer and was forced to reject it. "As it is, some of the regiments in Saint Domingue just will have to be diverted to Louisiana. On the high seas the *Surveillant* will look no different from any other French merchant vessel. Once it arrives in New Orleans, though, there will be no way to keep from the English that the merchandise being traded is a colony. British spies are swarming everywhere in the neighborhood. They would be heard laughing all the way to London if they got wind of the cession and saw us going in for the takeover with a handful of functionaries. They got Carolina, remember, just by walking in, never even bothering to make a treaty."

"That territory, at least, I had the pleasure of seeing them lose to the United States." Decrès had put in his share to see that they did. No American soldier had reveled more than he at the British defeat. It hadn't been so in Canada where, not satisfied with the grasping of large portions of French-held territories, the British had pillaged and burned, uprooted and destroyed an entire settlement of people of French descent. "The English are the most perfidious race that ever walked the face of the earth," he said passionately. "They colonize the wilderness strictly in order to look down on the natives. They view foreign cultures, not with fear like the Spanish — who sincerely believed that if they eradicated the heretics all would be well—but with the insufferable smugness of an illusionary superiority and the hypocritical piety of a religion which supports that mentality."

A smile tugged at the corners of Bonaparte's mouth. "My dear Decrès, soon you'll have me convinced you were in earnest about throwing yourself in the fire for the good of France."

"You don't agree?"

"About the English? I could add a little powder of my own to spark up your litany. About throwing yourself before the gunners in a fit of patriotism? Come, come, my friend, let's leave patriotism to the masses who are in need of it."

"What of Toulon, Mondovi, and Marengo, where you put your own life on the line?"

"Do you believe it is patriotism responsible for my winning battles?" Bonaparte shrugged. "Do you suppose I triumphed in Italy to make great men of Directory lawyers? Do you suppose it was to establish a republic? What an idea . . . He smiled, his voice taking on a confidential tone. "A republic of thirty-million—with our morals and vices? It's an illusion with which the French are infatuated but it will fade like so many others. The French must have glory and the satisfaction of their vanity. They know nothing of liberty."

"What do you have in mind, if not a republic?"

"All I am saying, Denis, is, don't be in such a hurry to die out of your bed. Inform my brother-in-law in Saint Domingue about the change in plans, and . . . " He tapped Decrès on the shoulder in a gesture indicating affection and meant to convey comfort. "Why don't you come to dinner this afternoon? I'm sure my wife would be glad to see you."

"This afternoon?"

"Fine. Tomorrow then, if this is too short a notice for you."

"No, no, not at all. I'll be delighted to come this afternoon.

"Good! I'll tell Bourrienne."

In Madrid, Carlos IV is being forcibly detained to deliver decisions . . .

January 1803

T he King put aside the letter and moved his chair to avoid contact with the wet carpet area at his feet. (He had returned from the morning's hunt sopping wet). "This must be the sixth or seventh person troubling himself to writing me this slander . . . " Carlos sadly shook his head, causing his wig, already sagging due to an excess of water, to slide off his shoulder. "The malice that lies in some human hearts is quite beyond my comprehension."

The Confessor nodded, picking up the wig and handing it to the valet who was spreading his master's wet hunting garb before the fire to dry. "That is because Your Majesty's own heart is a stranger to malice." A slight dose of it might have eliminated the need for anonymous letters exposing the Queen's infidelity, the Jesuit thought. He himself had penned such a note once, long ago, when the affair between Queen Maria Luisa and Prime Minister Godoy was in its initial fiery stage and obvious to all but the poor, cuckolded husband, whose being ridiculed behind his back had prompted its writing. Today, when the bloom of the adulterous passion had withered to a peculiar affection, the chances of opening the King's eyes were slimmer than ever.

"This letter is by an educated hand," Carlos decided, slightly surprised. "I would have thought a man's petty sentiments decreased as he became enlightened. From the evidence before me it would appear this is not always the case." The discovery seemed to distress him.

The manservant turned from the steaming hunting clothes and the equally steaming hounds in time to sympathize with the Jesuit, who was casting an exasperated eye at the whitewashed ceiling. More intimate with the Spanish Monarch than anyone else in the Palace, both servant and priest were fiercely devoted to the King (who reciprocated in his own fashion), but there were times when their devotion suffered under the test of strain.

"It is a simple question of logic," advanced Carlos, who had given the question some thought and felt disposed to reveal his findings. "I know you think of your King as a man who prefers the woods to the salon, but I have, of necessity, spent sufficient time in the salon to know that adultery creates bad blood between the parties involved. I am not referring to the deceived husband, who has the right to his malevolence and, in fact, often is less mean-spirited than his deceivers, who are forever fixing one another with dark, suspicious eyes. Because an adulterer, as you are well aware, Father, is a sinner, and a sinner is concerned only with his own desires. It is not an adulteress who will seek to please her lover by selecting for him a bride younger and far lovelier than herself.

"Yet the Queen has chosen for Manuél the little Countess of Chinchon, who is all of those things and a Bourbon in addition! And what of Pépita Tudo? Admitted by everyone, including Manuél himself, to be his mistress. Why would the Queen elevate Pépita Tudo to the coveted post of lady-in-waiting?"

Noticing the expression of distaste which had descended on the Confessor's face like a cloud, the King felt constrained to explain: "I am not condoning Manuél's conduct, Father. I was using it to point up the logic in my reasoning. The benefits of adultery escape me entirely. Even if it were not a sin, I cannot conceive of committing it. In the case of ladies I can see why they might be tempted to abuse their time in this way, for their days at Court are filled with idle hours. But when a gentleman, who can select any of many pleasurable pursuits, engages in these illicit doings, I must wonder whether he does not do so *because* it is a sin. I have reflected on this and can't find another reason . . . "

The King paused to look inquiringly at his Confessor.

Having spent a lifetime surrounded by males, the Jesuit was unable to shed any light on the subject. "The very company of women is painful to me, Your Majesty," he confessed, not without pain.

The eyes of both King and Priest now turned to the valet, who had the solemnity of bearing that came with age and from being a king's personal servant these many years, but who was known, in Carlos's absence, to roam those corners of the Palace certain to harbor females, this in spite of his having a wife and grown children.

The valet hesitated. It was not his role to express opinions. Not until the King became impatient—"Speak up, man!"—did he see fit to venture: "Adultery has its compensations, Sire." Seeing his answer amused only himself, he quickly added: "A man gets bored with being cooped up." A reply Carlos pronounced more respectable, indicating to the servant with a move of his broad, kingly hand that he would not be called upon for further comment and could return to the hounds and clothing before the fire.

"It is true," the King mused, "that when I am confined to a room before a bureau covered with documents, I soon fall prey to restlessness. I ascribed this boredom to my elevated station, because everywhere below me I see men delighted to take up quill and parchment." He gestured toward the anonymous letter as a case in point. "Why would an obviously intelligent, educated man exert himself constructing this writing, which he *knows* will displease his King, unless the exercise were pleasurable to him?"

Considering his words for a moment, an appalling conclusion entered his mind. "The malice! The malice!" he cried, jumping to his slippered feet, oblivious to the soggy carpet, and tossing the malicious sheet at the fire, where one of the hounds got ahold of it and promptly returned it to him.

"Get away! I want it burned!" Consoled somewhat by his perfect aim the second tossing, Carlos watched as the paper went up in flames.

"I don't believe, Sire, that the malice is directed at Your Majesty." The Confessor was speaking from experience. "It is an attempt to discredit the Prime Minister." And the Queen, he would have liked to add, but felt it was safer not to.

"Discredit Manuél? Why? Manuél is a fine fellow."

"A fine fellow, certainly," the priest agreed. A fine Prime Minister, certainly not, he thought. The King refused to see this, as he refused to see his wife's dissipations, willing to sacrifice not only his own honor, but also Spain itself so long as he was left in peace. The King, too, was a fine fellow.

The Confessor suddenly became overwhelmed by an inexplicable longing for the deceased Carlos III. Not such a fine fellow that. Especially not from the viewpoint of a Jesuit, for the Jesuits had been expelled from Spain during the reign of Carlos III. And yet, and yet . . . "But if I may point out, Sire," he started, pausing to select his words. "Don Manuél's promotion of his relatives and friends to ranks and positions others feel they are entitled to has created great animosity in those who think themselves overlooked." At one sitting alone, Godoy had transformed no less than twenty-four of them into lieutenant generals and thirty-two into major generals, none of which could have been accomplished without the King's consent.

"If those who think themselves overlooked would have been promoted, others would have taken their place to feel themselves slighted. If God does not see fit to bestow His blessings equally on all His children, how can I, an earthly king, be expected to bless my subjects in equal measure? This being said, I confess that I have never known a Prime Minister to have as many relatives as Manuél."

"Yes, and I suspect that one of their number will share Your Majesty's dinner today."

"Not Ceballos again?"

"I saw him walking in the garden with Don Manuél."

"What does he want now?"

"I don't know, Sire."

"Well, he cannot bring affairs of state to the table. I will not have my orders disobeyed! And immediately after dinner I am returning to the hunt. No Ceballos will stop me."

The priest didn't doubt it. Once, when informed that one of his children was dying, the King had shrugged: "Well what can I do about it?" before setting out for the woods anyway. "You may be putting the cart before the horse, Your Majesty. Perhaps the Minister of State is here to pay a social call."

Carlos smiled. That a Jesuit could be so naive as to suppose a minister of state had come to pay a social call struck him as amazing "Never, in my twenty-four years of ruling Spain, have I known a minister to come to the Royal Palace without an ulterior motive."

"Where are you going, Carlos?" The Queen swiftly rose from the table in pursuit of her husband who was moving rapidly toward the door.

"I am going where I have been going, rain or shine, every afternoon after dinner these past forty years," the King replied with a certain dignity. "Your question, Madam, is superfluous. If you'll allow me ... " He grasped Maria Luisa's hand to pull her away from the door before which she had defiantly stationed herself.

"Go back to the table, sir! Dinner is not over," she ordered, her black eyes glowing to support her command.

"Then by all means return to your plate and company," Carlos advised, and with a resolve that surprised even himself, he pulled his spouse to the side and hurled his bulk through the opening passage, whistling for his Confessor, whose round form followed after him like a shot.

The Queen screamed — a long piercing scream that sent the servants running to the spot and the Confessor crouching behind a wooden armchair. Diners abandoned their food to have a closer view of this royal scène de ménage and of the King who stood staring incredulously, stunned at what he had wrought.

"Has he killed you, Grandmama?" the voice of Luis was heard shouting.

Had he? the King wondered. When the noise subsided there was no doubt that he had been surrounded. Maria Luisa, Manuél and Ceballos — two of them people he liked well enough when they kept their distance (the smooth, never-disturbed ways of Ceballos he found unnerving) — were glaring at him like generals after a successful coup. Carlos sagged onto a velvet-covered banquette beneath a Flemish diptych. A king was no match for a queen when it came to cleverness, he thought "What is it you want?"

"This will only take a moment," Manuél promised, genuinely concerned with the King's well-being. He smiled his lazy-sensual smile. "All that is required is Your Majesty's signature."

The King made an attempt to rise. "If that's all you want there's no point in detaining me. You can leave the paper on my bureau."

"To sit there till you can summon up the courage to read it?" the Queen cried.

"It is the King's duty to read the papers he must sign, Madam. It is the duty of the King's ministers to keep the papers to a tolerable number."

"Don Pedro can't wait that long! Sit down, Carlos. This is an emergency."

"Not another uprising?"

"No, no, Your Majesty." Ceballos smiled. "Nothing as serious as that. Just a little misunderstanding in the colonies which it is in the interest of Spain to clear up without delay."

A little misunderstanding in the colonies . . . Whenever there was news of disastrous proportions, they would feed it to him one small piece at a time, as if he were a child who could not digest it otherwise. He would save them the trouble, Carlos thought "We have lost Cuba to the English?"

The Queen smiled. "My dear . . . " Her voice was pervaded with uncommon warmth. "You are off and running on your horse before you are in the saddle. Explain the matter to His Majesty, Don Pedro."

"I strongly suggest that Your Majesty revoke his previous orders and reopen the port of New Orleans to foreign commerce," Ceballos said. "Our Ambassador in the United States and the Governor of Louisiana are both alarmed at the American reaction to the closure and are urging immediate countermeasures. I have drawn up the papers which, approved by Your Majesty's hand, will reopen the port . . . "

"What has New Orleans to do with me?" the King interrupted. "Louisiana belongs to Bonaparte. How much longer must we be responsible for this infernal colony before the French take up their duties?"

"I'm sure General Bonaparte is eagerly preparing for the event, Sire," Godoy, dressed in his generalissimo lustre, defended his idol from across the border.

"It would be unwise for Spain to risk a war with the United States in the interval, Your Majesty," the Minister of State continued. "Even if we disposed of an adequate military force in the area to withstand an American attack, the effort would not benefit Spain."

Carlos nodded. "These very thoughts occurred to me when you proposed closing the port. To what earthly purpose should the King take such a measure, I asked myself. To keep a few poachers from encroaching on the territory?"

"Smugglers, Carlos, not poachers," Maria Luisa corrected.

The King shrugged. "Smugglers, poachers . . . What is the difference? They are neither of them worthy of the King's time nor of his soldiers. The United States is not a monarchy, gentlemen. The rulers there cannot prevent the people from taking up arms if they are so inclined. I am told the American President is a man intent on keeping the peace, but what is the good of being a peaceful ruler when the people can do as they please? I, too, am a ruler intent on keeping the peace and, what is more, *I* can underwrite my intention . . . Give those papers here, Don Pedro."

Impressed by the King's speech, Godoy broke into spontaneous applause. Carlos's surly looks brightened as he scrawled his big copperplate signature on the paper and returned it to Godoy. Ceballos, standing fixed in diplomatic polish on the Flemish carpet, watched the King and his Prime Minister, wondering who was the greater of this pair of fools.

The Queen, remembering that dessert was waiting on the dining room table, gathered up her skirts for departure. "Perhaps His Majesty will join us?"

The King shook his head. With the rain still coming down in sheets and the light of day vanishing with the speed of winter, the pleasure of the hunt would be altogether lost if he did not get moving at once. "My grooms are waiting, Madam."

In the Bay of Biscay, Colonial Prefect Laussat and his entourage prepare to sail for Louisiana. They, at least, are happy . . .

January 1803

Captain Girardais scanned the heavens stretching beyond the mountainous Basque provinces, his blue eyes brimming with satisfaction. The clouds had just enough movement to them to guarantee continuance of the winds carrying the *Surveillant* out to sea.

"The weather is most cooperative, gentlemen!" It was a good omen, the Captain thought. He signaled to the stewards poised to uncork the champagne.

The small deck was crowded with colonial appointees, eager to be on their way. Aside from Prefect Laussat, there was a sub-prefect for Upper Louisiana, an administrative commissioner, a director of estates, a chief justice, two surveyors, a paymaster general and a botanical gardener, most of whom were accompanied on the voyage by their families. The ship's doctor was also on deck.

Some fishermen, returning with their catch of bream and anchovies, and a sprinkling of Aix locals either too young or too old to be useful elsewhere were watching the departing French brig from the stony shore, squinting at the glare of the white sails and pondering the reason for the extravagant number of corks being popped overboard.

The Captain waited till every hand had been furnished with a share of the celebratory liquid before speaking. "I wish for a safe crossing," he started humbly, "not only for us, the advance party, but for the thousands of French soldiers sailing with General Victor from the north." His voice was gaining momentum as he continued: "May our expedition to the New World be successful. Louisiana, gentlemen, is French once again!" He held up his glass. *"La Louisiane française!"*

"La Louisiane française!" all repeated.
"Vive la France!"
"Vive la France!"

FEBRUARY

February 1803

I don't know what you're complaining about." Lewis's hand dropped the fork on the remaining griddlecake on his plate to open both arms in support of his question as he looked at the President. "Whatever you ask for, the Congress seems hell-bent to grant you. You ask for two million to buy New Orleans, and they give it to you. 'Sure Mr. Jefferson. Anything else you can think of while we have our hands on the till?' 'As a matter of fact and just between us, gentlemen, how about twenty-five hundred so Captain Lewis can go looking for the source of the Missouri out west?'"

"If I had told them *that*, we wouldn¹t have gotten a cent."

"I think they would have given you dancing girls, sir, if you'd have asked."

Jefferson smiled. "I'm too old for dancing girls."

"I was thinking more in terms of my crew, who will all be healthy, able-bodied men whose morale is liable to suffer under the solitude and hardships of the trek."

"With all those barrels of whiskey to fall back on, I doubt their suffering will be extensive."

"If a barrel of whiskey a week is but a small allowance for a large family without any cow, then our poor little barrel a man is a puny allotment by comparison.

"If you would take the trouble to listen to yourself, Meriwether, you might understand why some people question the wisdom of my selecting you to head this expedition." The President nodded at his empty coffee cup.

"You selected me because I am eminently qualified to head it, I should tell them. I was an expert hunter and trapper before I was twelve. And when the Army, being the Army, ignored my skills as a frontiersman and made me regimental paymaster instead, it unwittingly did me a good turn by giving me free run of the country. Name me one American who has more uncharted miles under his belt than I do? Who else do you know who's gotten lost in the wilderness between Detroit and Pittsburgh — twice?"

"That is just what I mean, Meriwether. People hear you going on like that and they wonder at your seriousness."

"When I was a boy, I remember your saying that the man you had in mind had to be skilled in botany, natural history, mineralogy, and other subjects, and at the same time be a man of great firmness of mind and strength of body, expert in woodcraft and familiar with the Indians."

The President had long dreamed of exploring the vast unknown expanses to the west. And Lewis had dreamed with him. While still a twit of a boy he would listen, spellbound, to the tales of ferocious Indians and giant wild bears said to stalk the region (or was it giant wild Indians and ferocious bears?). Lewis had been no stranger to the woods even then. From his earliest days he had tagged after his mother, Lucy (a "yarb doctor" known throughout Virginia), crawling amongst the catalpas, pippins, maples, oaks, and mimosas of Albemarle County, holding her rifle while she gathered chokecherries, and chasing woodchucks and wild pigs bigger than himself.

No one was more delighted than Meriwether when Captain Marks, his stepfather, moved the family to Georgia and settled upstream at the very edge of the forest, far removed from the smattering of log cabins that made up the small colony along the Broad River. He left the family at the tender age of fourteen to return to Albemarle County and manage his father's estate, which he, as the eldest son, had inherited according to the English law of primogeniture, running over to Monticello whenever the master was at home.

There was always a rush of visitors when Mr. Jefferson was in residence. The civilized company would sit in a room lacking a wall or a roof, while Mr. Jefferson held forth on one of his favorite topics — law, government, history, architecture, mathematics, medicine, agriculture, languages, literature, education, philosophy, religion, and natural sciences stretching from astronomy to zoology — devastating the guests with his erudition and knowledge. Mr. Jefferson might not be in his element speaking from a public platform, but, seated around a dining room table, there was no stopping him. When he elaborated on his plans to one day reconnoiter the immense territory to the west, there existed no doubt in Lewis's mind that he was destined to be a part of the exciting venture.

Meriwether, Mr. Jefferson had claimed, was far too young and inexperienced to be involved in such a dangerous undertaking. "I couldn't face your mother if something untoward were to happen to you out there." Captain Marks having died in the meantime, the Lewis-Marks family was once again living at Locust Hill.

"My mother has other children," Lewis had reminded him. What could happen to him out west which couldn't have happened in Virginia or Georgia? He was going on seventeen. "Everybody says I am a man."

"The man I have in mind has to be skilled in botany, natural history, mineralogy, and other subjects, and at the same time be a man of great firmness of mind and strength of body, expert in woodcraft and familiar with the Indians," Mr. Jefferson had patiently explained. What choice did Lewis have after that but to try and become that man?

"I was speaking of the ideal man," the President said now, pushing back his chair to leave the breakfast table. He stopped, right hand on the back of the chair, an expression of pleasant surprise spreading over his freckly face. "You *remember* that?"

"That, and a good deal more," Lewis assured him.

"When are you planning on leaving?"

"As soon as the boats are built and the crew assembled. When I have my passports—British, Spanish and French."

The President made an impatient gesture. Lewis could never resist a temptation to inappropriate jesting. The expedition would not be ready to leave until early summer, as no one needed to remind Jefferson, who had been plotting it off and on for over a decade. "I mean leaving for *Philadelphia*, Captain?"

"Any time you say, sir."

It had been arranged for Lewis to receive final instruction in Philadelphia from a trio of distinguished scientists. These learned minds were among the few to know the main purpose of the voyage was not to buy land from the Indians and set up additional American trading posts in the wilderness in order to break the British fur monopoly – a proposition Congress had been expected to embrace unanimously and deliver the funds for, whereas if it had been told the President's intent was to discover the source of the Missouri (among other things), the waters of that venerable River would immediately have turned a suspicious Republican color, a phenomenon no self-respecting Federalist would have cared to investigate.

"The idea that you're going to explore the Mississippi must be generally given out," the President advised. "It will satisfy public curiosity and sufficiently mask the real destination."

Lewis nodded. When it came to walking up the garden path without being seen, few could equal Mr. Jefferson, he thought. You never saw him coming and when you did he had arrived. But the need for secrecy was not lost on Lewis. It wasn't only a question of deluding Congress. There were the Spanish, British, and French, none of whom would look kindly on American scrutiny of their respective territories, which, according to their own expansionist vision, they would interpret as being directed toward an eventual takeover.

In this case, the President's reputation as a philosopher and dreamer, established by the Federalists, stood him in good stead. If Mr. Jefferson, via Captain Lewis and Lieutenant Clark, wanted to sniff at a mountain of salt and collect exotic buttercups to press between the pages of his French encyclopedia, there was no reason to refuse the passports that would allow access to these treasures.

"It strikes me as ironic," said Lewis, following his train of thought, "that to Congress the scientific nature of the expedition must be denied while to the foreign attachés it must be *emphasized* to deny the charting of their country's territories."

"Have you a better suggestion, Captain?" Jefferson asked, striding toward the door of the common dining room.

"Not likely, no, sir. It just strikes me as ironic that nobody can be told the truth about what is, after all, a noble effort."

The serious undertone in his secretary's voice prompted Jefferson to retrace his steps. Beneath the annoying predilection to engage in pointless jest, there was the Lewis he had selected to head an important undertaking, the man he trusted above all others (including Madison), whose loyalty and courage it wouldn't occur to him to question, as it didn't occur to him to question the ultimate successful outcome of the dangerous mission with which he had entrusted him. The trouble when people admired you was that they sometimes lost track of reality, he thought. Better to attend to these lapses in perception with quick, incisive remedies. "You would have lied to your father's grave to set this scheme in motion, Meriwether."

Jefferson's unusually blunt language startled Lewis into setting his coffee cup down in his plate of sticky griddle cake when his aim had been an undesignated spot beside it. "True," he admitted readily, disarmed by the President's candidness. "If it meant my being a part of it."

"I suggest you keep it in mind the next time you get to feeling self-righteous."

Self-righteous? Was that what he had sounded like? The expedition fully intended to establish new trading posts and catalog any unknown wonders encountered on the journey. "I suppose we are lying only by omission," Lewis offered humbly. No mean trick in the world of politics.

"I suggest you keep it in mind," Jefferson repeated.

This past summer, Captain Lewis and a crew set out for Louisville from Pittsburgh in a boat built to Lewis's specifications by local craftsmen. In Louisville he means to meet up with his old chum Lieutenant Clark and the rest of the crew. If all has proceeded according to schedule, they are at the present time setting up winter quarters in Wood River, from whence they intend to embark upon the expedition proper early next spring.

People hereabouts, hearing of the proposed push into the uncharted western exterior, automatically assume the venture to be a natural consequence of our acquisition of Louisiana, but since these preparations began long before that development, this is obviously not the case — which is why I felt compelled to include them.

The continuation of the events of last February returns us to —

February 1803

Governor Claiborne looked on as two workmen, armed with a roll of posters and a bucket with paste and brush, glued one of the posters to a cypress tree:

$2,OOO REWARD
FOR THE CAPTURE, DEAD OR ALIVE, OF
SAMUEL MASON!

Claiborne nodded at the black numerical symbols screaming their presence on the white paper. "If a sum of that magnitude doesn't do it," he thought out loud, "nothing will."

Samuel Mason was one of the notorious bandits working the Natchez Trace. Like Joseph Thompson Hare and the Terrible Harpes, Mason somehow had procured himself a Spanish passport, which was one way of escaping American authorities. Mason was a late bloomer to the criminal life, discovering a talent for it when already into middle age, after having led a more or less respectable existence in Virginia and having accumulated a decent record as a fighter in the Revolutionary War. As a result, he became extremely sensitive to his reputation as an outlaw and was pained to the core when upstaged by Big Micajah Harpe and Little Wiley Harpe. Not content to rob and kill, this brotherly twosome tortured and mutilated their hapless victims and were more than deserving of the "terrible" attached to their name.

Once, when disturbed by the snoring of a fellow lodger in the dwelling where they had stopped for the night, Big Harpe quickly settled the matter by tomahawking the noisy sleeper, after which he did away with the woman who owned the house and with her baby. Mason despaired on hearing such tales, aware that he and son Tom were a long way from inspiring that kind of terror.

Hare was no problem in this respect. A dandy, who seemed to think a bandit should above all be well-dressed, Hare sneaked amongst the sumac and cane in crimson silk-lined coats and dashing cravats, killing only when he had to and often returning a few coins or a gold trinket to his prey. He was literate enough to keep a diary, an additional reason why Mason *père* considered him too eccentric to be much of a competitor. A host of criminal elements of lesser fame active on the Trace concerned him not at all.

Aside from Mason *père & fils*, the Mason gang consisted of one James Mays and his club-footed sister. The Harpes roamed with two sisters, both of whom were continually letting loose on the world a succession of newborn Harpes. When word reached Mason that Big Harpe had smashed to death one of those infants against the wall of a cave, Mason decided to take drastic measures. From now on he would advertise — **"DONE BY MASON OF THE WOODS"** was scrawled beside the mutilated body of a planter — and expand his career to include the River, heretofore left fairly untouched.

The indignant outcry of the fourteen-hundred-odd Natchez inhabitants prompted Governor Claiborne to take some drastic measures of his own. Nobody cared how many of their own kind the Harpes saw fit to send to the other world. What mattered was the protection of the law-abiding citizenry, and nothing but the prospect of an enormous amount of cash could bring about Samuel Mason's capture. There wasn't much else to be done in Natchez anyway, with the port of New Orleans closed.

Lower Natchez, always a hotbed of activity, looked deserted these days. Since only goods consumed or used locally were being deposited on the landing, traffic on the Mississippi had come to a virtual standstill and, consequently, so had that in the grogshops on Silver Street. Claiborne noticed two lumberyard men, a medicine peddler, a boy working in the brick kiln, and a few idle whores gossiping out the windows of their smelly hovels while their snot-nosed offspring rolled about in the dirt with a mangy-looking cur. A mud-covered wild hog was snorting under a magnolia, and a lone chicken marched defiantly on the sunken flagstones.

Claiborne returned his attention to the workmen, who were pasting on a second poster facing the River, when a flatboatman swaggered out a grogshop in their direction. The boatman — a straggler, from the looks of his torn, filthy clothes and two-weeks-worth of greasy beard growth — stationed his muscled body before the poster, his eyes narrowing and his face contracting, as if by applying physical force the black letters would reveal their meaning. "Two-thousand for what?" he asked finally. He could read numbers.

"The Gov'nuh here is offerin' it to anybody what can catch Mason," one of the workmen told him.

The boatman whistled, nostalgically rubbing the area of his empty pockets. "I seen Mason once," he informed the trio. "They ain't many that had the privilege and lived to tell about it." The refined dress and manner of Claiborne irritated him. "You ain't no *gov'nuh*. You're Annie Christmas's pimp'."

Claiborne smiled, amused at being thought the protector of a female who towered high above any male, who personally tossed into the River any troublemakers from her floating cat house. "I don't think Annie needs protection."

"If you ain't no pimp, you sure ain't no gov'nuh neither! Instead of settin' in your fancy mansion on the bluffs, figurin' up ways to waste the people's cash, why ain't you marchin' on New Orleans? Or cain't you see folks ain't floatin' downriver no more?"

Bodily confrontation was avoided by the two workmen, who waited for the flatboatman to stagger down to one of the calling whores before continuing on their way, putting up the remaining posters.

Claiborne, still ignorant of Monroe's appointment, felt no less frustrated than the riverman by his government's failure to act. He chided himself for nearly hitting a man robbed of his livelihood, a man who didn't realize that to march on New Orleans wasn't the governor's decision to make. The Mississippi Territory might not be part of the Union as yet, but it was United States property all the same.

Unhappy with Washington's seeming indifference to the West and displeased with his own behavior, Claiborne climbed the bluffs toward the chinaberry trees of Upper Natchez and the consolation of a Monongahela rye in Monsieur Ude's Café.

His consolation was short-lived.

Barely had he savored the first sip when a planter reminded Claiborne that last summer's tobacco was still sitting in store unsold in plantations all over the Natchez region, and the planters, already in debt to the merchants, were getting in hock over their heads.

Natchez tobacco, like New Orleans tobacco, was not in great demand. Inferior to the strains yielded by the rich soils of Virginia and the Carolinas, it was difficult to sell at the best of times, as the planter knew only too well, but which he claimed was: "All the more reason the government should step in and take it off our hands. Why, with all that Virginia tobacco to use as leverage, it'd be nothing for them to sell it. When the dons were running things, they didn't have this advantage. Worse, they were stuck with the New Orleans crop as well. You can say what you like about the dons, but let me tell you, Governor, they came through for us planters. Not like those Republicans in Washington today." The planter, in need of consolation himself, gulped down his whiskey and ordered another.

"I trust Mr. Jefferson is doing the best he can for the planters, allowing that he is one himself."

"Sure. As long as they live in Virginia."

Resolved not to lose his temper, Claiborne swallowed his pride with his rye, gesturing to Monsieur Ude for a refill.

"One must try to see these matters philosophically," offered Monsieur Ude, who could afford to be philosophical since his income depended neither on River traffic nor the sale of tobacco. "It isn't possible for the President to make everybody happy."

"Happy?" the planter shouted. "I'm talking about selling my tobacco for cash. Natchez is coming apart at the seams and you're talking philosophy and happiness. Even a Republican would have better sense than that."

"Natchez is getting exactly what it deserves!" interjected a grimlooking man seated at a table near the portico. "What is this town but an eyesore, a boil upon the face of the earth? The people of this Territory are a set of malicious, deceiving, horse-thieving sharpies. Characters convicted of the blackest crimes, who escaped from the chains and prisons of Spain, find refuge here. The perverseness of this place is beyond redemption." The stranger's voice was soft and melodious, strangely at odds with his words.

"Your sidewalks sink with the weight of pimps, whores, gamblers, adventurers, prospectors, flatboatman, and other abominations. The drunkenness of your slaves and Indians on Sundays is a defilement of the most debased kind. You wallow in barrooms, bordellos, and gambling dens, stinking with females, spitpoisons, Flatheads, mulattos, and their foul offspring. And you don't blush at carrying this illegitimate issue to be recorded in the public registries as your *natural children*! Natchez is a vile, sordid, Godless place!"

Monsieur Ude was the first to recover. "You are confusing the riffraff of Silver Street with us, my friend. A serious mistake, but one that may, perhaps, be forgiven a stranger."

"Forgiven, you say? It is *you* who should beg the Lord to be forgiven your detestable sins. Now! Before your conniving Gallic brains are flushed in your bowels by an excess of liquor."

Monsieur Ude didn't take too well to this advice, especially considering that he drank only a little wine with meals. *"Ça alors!"*

"Blood and tobacco!" The planter laughed, aiming a brown stream of tobacco juice at a brass spittoon. "You're wasting your breath, stranger. Preachers don't fare too well around here. Nobody's interested in religion. The dons tried it and had to give it up. They even imported Irish priests to do the job, seeing as their own couldn't talk English. There's still a few around, every single one a drunk by now. Isn't that right, Ude? You wouldn't want to end up like that now, would you, preacher? The way I see it, you best pick up your satchel, jump on your Opelousa, and head for more receptive territory."

The preacher rose. "Natchez is doomed!" On reaching the door, he turned to point an accusing finger at Governor Claiborne. "And *you* are responsible."

The planter kept on laughing while Monsieur Ude mumbled some soothing words in the Governor's direction. But Claiborne had had enough for one day. He stalked out of the café, disgusted with Upper Natchez, Lower Natchez, outlaws, flatboatmen, preachers, planters, French café proprietors, New Orleans, France, Spain, Washington, and the governorship of the Mississippi Territory.

When, on entering the Gouvernatorial mansion, he was presented with a dispatch from Secretary of State Madison, telling him of Monroe's appointment, the young Governor merely shrugged, unable to appreciate the good news at the moment.

At the Chancellor's quarters in Paris, the news of Monroe's appointment was greeted with even less enthusiasm . . .

M onroe?" Mrs. Livingston repeated, smiling. "You must be mistaken, Robert." Her husband's hearing being what it was, he often misinterpreted what people said.

"Are you suggesting I suddenly lost my capacity to read?"

"*James* Monroe?" Mrs. Livingston insisted, not sure they were speaking of the same man. "Governor of Virginia?"

"Read for yourself." Livingston handed his wife Madison's dispatch.

Mrs. Livingston had no need to take in the several pages of Madison's precise script to realize it was not her husband who was mistaken. His dejected attitude quite convinced her that it was she. "How peculiar of Mr. Jefferson to settle on a negotiator who proved himself a failure at negotiating. Mr. Monroe is not a clever man, Robert, you know that."

"He's shrewd enough to further his ambitions."

"Shrewd he may be, clever he is not." She had been Monroe's dinner partner once. "I told you, at the Knox's, remember? I found conversation with him painful."

"You find conversation with Bonaparte painful too, Mary."

"You know very well that what I object to in the First Consul is his lack of social grace. Mr. Monroe is a gentleman, who wouldn't dream of embarrassing a lady. The First Consul, on the other hand, wouldn't dream of censoring his speech because there are ladies present. In fact, it wouldn't occur to him to measure his words no matter *who* is present. Fluency is hardly what is lacking in General Bonaparte. More ideas come to him in a moment than come to most men in a lifetime, and to Mr. Monroe not at all."

She stopped abruptly arrested by her own statement. Not knowing she was going to utter it, there now existed no doubt in her mind as to its accuracy. She had meant to comment on Monroe's inability to formulate a sentence quickly and with ease, but some instinct — a sense of fairness — had prevented her condemning him on such flimsy grounds.

Many a gentleman's speech lagged behind his mind. This was not uncommon in men (Women didn't seem to have this handicap. Perhaps the female tongue was located in a spot more congenial to the brain?). An acquaintance of theirs in New York stammered frightfully, though this in no way obstructed his comprehension, and it was precisely there that she had felt James Monroe to be deficient.

"How can Jefferson humiliate me in this way?" Livingston burst out. "Not a day goes by without my trying to settle this matter! I have presented my arguments again and again to the powers that be, and again and again I have been rebuffed. If Bonaparte was at all interested in my country's proposals, he would have reacted long ago. He's a man of quick decisions and nobody in France has the power to prevent him from making any decision he likes. But it doesn't fit his scheme to share any part of Louisiana with the United States, even for a price . . . " Livingston reached for a bottle of *marc* on the table and Mrs. Livingston rushed to get him a glass.

"Thousands of Frenchmen have already died in Saint Domingue and still Bonaparte keeps sending reinforcements. In his report to the *Corps Législatif* earlier this month he demanded no less than five-hundred-thousand men to 'defend and avenge the Republic'. *Defend and avenge the Republic?* What is he talking about? *Five hundred thousand men!* Does he think such massive movement of troops will go unnoticed? Are we fools who fail to grasp the significance behind the great fleet of ships preparing to sail from Holland?"

"A fleet still stuck in the ice, Robert," Mrs. Livingston ventured to interrupt.

Livingston didn't hear. "Jefferson warned me not to fight by strategy against those exercised in it from the cradle, unless I cared to be outwitted. I suppose he thinks a rigid Republican like Monroe will endear himself to the autocratic First Consul and outwit Talleyrand. By appointing him, Jefferson is just playing into French hands, giving Bonaparte the perfect excuse to postpone a settlement. The minute Talleyrand finds out, he'll stop negotiations until Monroe's arrival, mark my words! If only I could speak to the First Consul directly. If he hears me quoting Talleyrand often enough, he'll get irritated and will contradict his minister." Livingston's voice trailed off, already mentally engaged in a *tête-à-tête* with Bonaparte.

Mrs. Livingston heaved a small sigh, pondering the vagaries of politics. The Livingstons of New York had helped elect Jefferson president, and President Jefferson had elected to appoint the head of the Livingston clan to a coveted post in Paris, though why it should be coveted became more mystifying by the hour.

There was no money in it certainly. The Republicans were even stingier than the Federalists, of whose stinginess Jefferson complained when *he* was holder of the coveted post, lamenting his salary didn't allow for his affairs to be conducted in a way fitting the office (hmph!). But as President he didn't hesitate to curtail that same salary if, in doing so, he could appear the economizing democrat to the American people.

A Jefferson who had returned from Paris cloaked in red silk suits with ruffles and paraded through Philadelphia in the red-heeled shoes of the French nobility (though he cheered the Revolution — riding two horses in two opposing directions at once, as was his wont), presently shuffled through the President's House in worn-out slippers and the kind of clothing which made Senator Plumer from New Hampshire mistake him for a servant. Mrs. Livingston wasn't impressed. Politicians never took a stand where a *stance* would do. For as long as she could remember, the Livingstons had been dedicated Federalists. Then, suddenly, to defeat Hamilton (or his father-in-law Philip Schuyler, rather) they had switched to being dedicated anti-Federalists and, consequently, Republican-Democrats. The about-face had neither surprised nor upset Mrs. Livingston. None of her in-laws had pretended to act in the name of democracy. No Livingston had changed tailor to impress the American people with his republicanism. And that was just what so irked her about the President. It always must appear as though every one of his actions was inspired by a higher motive. "I never liked him, you know. He is not at all sincere, in my opinion."

Still wrapped in his *tête-à-tête* with the First Consul, Livingston assumed the reference was to Bonaparte. Conditioned by more than three

decades of conjugal life in which his own concerns automatically supplanted whatever concerns were in the mind of his wife, his assumption
was natural. "I thought sincerity was one of the few virtues you were
willing to grant Bonaparte, Mary."

"Much is made of Colonel Burr's supposed propensity for schem-
ing," continued she, pursuing her private course, "but if the Colonel
were halfways good at it, *he* would be president today and Mr. Jefferson
vice-president, not the reverse—they *did* receive an equal amount of
votes—and I, for one, am sorry it isn't so."

Bonaparte hastily vacated the Livingston mental terrain (Livingston,
backed by his sizable clan, had done his utmost to make Burr the loser
in the presidential election). "Don't be foolish, Mary. A man as ambitious as the Colonel is dangerous and has to be checked."

"If he had become president he would have been checked, wouldn't
he? How much higher could he have climbed? A president needn't as-
pire further. Are you claiming Mr. Jefferson was less ambitious? I
would be disappointed to think you were taken in by all that talk about
retirement to the simple life of Monticello. A double lie that. A plantation with hundreds of slaves is the simple life? I daresay it was the simple life in the President's House Mr. Jefferson had in mind. Colonel
Burr, at least, doesn't make a secret of his ambition. In all the years I've
known the Colonel, I never once heard him express a desire for the
simple life—anywhere."

Livingston couldn't help smiling at this allusion to Burr's love of the
lavish, which was plunging him ever deeper under a continually growing mountain of debts. It wasn't that Mary was wrong in her character
evaluations; merely that the convoluted byways of politics escaped her.
Burr as president would have eliminated the Livingstons as the main
political force in New York, which they had become, once again, after
Hamilton's father-in-law had been ousted from the Senate. To achieve
that end the Livingstons had had no choice but to manipulate Burr into
Schuyler's senatorial seat. To have helped Burr into the President's
House, however, would have amounted to no less than self-destruction.
"I have no illusions about Jefferson, Mary. It is *you* who are taken in—

by your emotions. You like Colonel Burr and you are determined to keep on liking him. Very well. I shouldn't expect any lady, my wife included, to resist the Colonel's undeniable charm. I myself quite enjoy his company, but I shall be wary of him nevertheless, even at the card table."

"Robert!" Mrs. Livingston rose to her half-boots in disbelief. Was her husband implying the Colonel cheated at cards? "You can't possibly mean it!"

"Have a drop of this," Livingston suggested, picking up the bottle of marc and repairing to the cabinet for a glass. "It will settle your nerves."

Mrs. Livingston found it a dubious proposal. "It's barely afternoon, Robert." (Her alcoholic intake was regulated by the clock.) Aware he was enjoying her indignation regarding his remark about Colonel Burr, and not one to deny him the pleasure (and remembering that port had tasted no different in the morning), she accepted the glass, trying not to cough as she swallowed some of the liquor.

"You're a good girl, Mary."

She smiled, knowing this was his way of pronouncing her the best wife a man could wish for. He was bearing up remarkably well under the humiliating news. "You mustn't let this ill-advised appointment get in your way," she said — an attempt at consolation she regretted instantly, as it swept Livingston into a veritable tidal wave of self-pity.

"Twenty-four years as Chancellor of New York!" he cried. "I was the first Secretary of Foreign Affairs ever elected by Congress! Was Monroe a member of the committee to draft the Declaration of Independence? Was *he* the one who ratified the U.S. Constitution and drafted a constitution for New York? Was *he* a delegate to the Continental Congress? Was it *Monroe* who swore George Washington into office? Am *I* the bumbler who was recalled as minister from this very city by President Washington for insubordination and went back to the United States in disgrace? I am to be assisted by a blockhead! — who'll need to read over his orders every day of the interminable Atlantic crossing before the meaning penetrates his skull!"

"You must forestall him." Here, at least, was one reason to rejoice in the slowness of transatlantic transport, Mrs. Livingston thought. Her husband's anger was justified. If Mr. Jefferson found it necessary to appoint an envoy extraordinary, why hadn't he chosen Colonel Burr or Senator Morris, or another gentleman of comparable eloquence? The appointment of an envoy was insult enough in itself; to fill it with James Monroe was a direct slap in the face to Robert. Her husband was extremely capable. True, sometimes he tended to be overconfident of his abilities, but then, he had never before been faced with an opponent the size of Talleyrand. To cast Robert against a man of Talleyrand's caliber was unfair of the Fates.

When two men fought on the *Boulevard du Temple*, to see who was the strongest, the contestants were invariably of equal weight. The spectators would have protested the pitting of a small man against a large one, because, no matter how dapper a fighter, the small man was bound to lose. To be triumphant, a man had to just barely rise above his opponent. If he surpassed him by a hair the crowd would pronounce him great, while it would forget the very existence of the one surpassed.

"I must forestall him and press my case now," Livingston decided. "When is the next reception, Mary?"

"At the Tuileries? Oh Robert, you think it's wise to bypass Talleyrand?"

"When is it? Refresh my memory."

"Don't remind me, please. I suffer heartburn just thinking about racing through another one of those official dinners."

"You shouldn't try to partake of every dish."

"A futile attempt if ever there was one. I find it barbaric the way guests have to wolf down the exquisitely prepared food in order to keep up with the First Consul."

"Would you rather dine with the Second Consul and be tied to the table for six hours?"

"The Second Consul invited us only once."

"That's because you broke one of the cardinal rules, Mary. One isn't expected to speak during one of Monsieur Cambacérés' great gastronomical feasts."

"I only asked for the salt." Mrs. Livingston smiled, relieved at her husband's speedy return to normal. "I'm so happy to see you determined not to give up, Robert. A hair, you know, is all it takes. One hair can make the difference between success and failure, between remembrance and oblivion, Robert, remember that."

"I made a mistake offering you *marc* so early in the day, Mary. It muddles your thinking."

"Well I'm pleased to know that it cleared up yours."

"Oh, Madame Bonaparte!" cried Fortunée, biting into a chocolate wafer, "you simply must have it read to you. Madame Cottin has outdone herself this time. I counted no less than fourteen funerals."

Josephine's kind, coffee-black eyes filled with horror. "I couldn't bear it. So many deaths! It isn't natural. I like stories where the sun shines and people are happy."

"But the deserving always do end up being happy in the end, Mother," said Hortense, who rather liked the strife in Marie Cottin's novels.

Josephine was doubtful. "One has to suffer through such an unbearable number of pages before one arrives at the end. And then, I fail to see how anyone can be truly happy with so many people buried."

"I agree," said Thérèse Cabarrus. "Fourteen funerals is seven too many. Madame Cottin exaggerates. If I had a reader, like you, Madame Bonaparte, I should be quite prepared to feel morbid, but I refuse to struggle to the cemetery — in the most inclement weather, if I know Madame Cottin — fourteen times on my own."

The ladies all enjoyed this remark. Even the footman smiled. Around Mme Bonaparte he needn't pretend not to hear. Her disposition was such that she delighted in the happiness of all living creatures, regardless of kind; and all kinds of living creatures, in turn, delighted in the happiness of Mme Bonaparte. Stiffly correct in his consular livery, the footman took advantage of the general merriment to ask: "Would Madame like to have the coffee served now?"

"That would be nice. Yes, Polidor, thank you," Josephine chanted in her slightly-lisping, indolent Creole way of speaking. "But wait, Polidor, don't remove the wine. I think the ladies will like to finish it." The ladies were old acquaintances and she knew their taste. The spirited, pleasure-loving Fortunée was, like herself, from Martinique. And Thérèse, smart, witty, stunningly beautiful — certainly one of the most beautiful women of the century, thought Josephine, nearly as pleased with the circumstance as was her friend — had everything, except . . . except . . . No, she wouldn't spoil their little get-together by thinking about *that*. This was just like old times.

They could have fancied themselves at Croissy. Of course, no room at Croissy, however lovely, could have equaled the splendor of this drawing room (her favorite), with its yellow and brown satin walls and satin-covered mahogany chairs. One of the few rooms in the Tuileries to retain the heat, the ladies could afford to cast aside their ponderous coverings and be reflected in the draped looking-glasses in all their abundant mature charms: Thérèse, regal in blue-corded silk; Fortunée, irresistible in her *point d'Angleterre* gown. Hortense, who was less pretty, could bask in her youth, which would sustain her for several years to come. (And she *did* have beautiful hair.)

The only thing missing, Josephine reflected sadly, was spring, when the gardens would be bursting with color and the air enchanted with the sounds of birds. Winter was the only season she could reconcile herself to the windows being placed so high. If everyone remained seated, the bleak-ness outside would go unnoticed, because inside the delicate fragrance of roses and spring blossoms, brought from the hothouses of Malmaison, wafted from tables and hairdos into the farthest corners of the room. Ah, what could be more delightful than to sit amidst the silken drapes and exquisite garniture of this charming room, savoring a delicious *déjeuner* on silver-gilt plates, surrounded by one's dear old friends and devoted daughter, imagining it was spring?

She was being silly to fret, to let those little darts of guilt penetrate her consciousness. Hadn't Bourrienne assured her the First Consul was meeting with Bacler d'Albe, his mapmaker? — always a guarantee her husband would be absorbed all morning. Was she determined to add to her wrinkles for the sake of some foolish fears? Félicité approved. Didn't she? With the languor that characterized all her movements, Josephine bent down to caress the tiny mutt, nestled in fluffy-furred contentment at her mistress's lace-drenched feet.

"No, I haven't, Madame Cabarrus," Hortense was saying. "I think General Bonaparte has consulted her lately. And, of course, my mother sees Mademoiselle Lenormand regularly."

"Is General Bonaparte thinking of starting another war with England, Madame Bonaparte?"

"Madame Cabarrus, please!" Josephine looked shocked. "I sincerely hope not. Where will we get our muslin? There is no muslin superior to Indian muslin; I don't have to tell you. Lyon produces some marvelous silks and velvets, but muslin, *ah non, pas du tout*, not at all like Indian muslin."

"Very true," agreed Fortunée.

"What has Mademoiselle Lenormand to say about it?" Thérèse persisted. "Does she see France at war in the near future?"

"My dear Thérèse, I have no idea." (What woman would put this sort of question to a seeress, Josephine wondered. Only Thérèse could possibly conceive of it.) "Speaking of Mademoiselle Lenormand, you really should go see her," she urged warmly. "A lady in your position ought to know what the future holds. Mademoiselle Lenormand is amazingly accurate, isn't she, Fortunée?"

Thérèse shook her head. "I cannot abide the company she keeps. The frogs, the cats, the toads, the cocks, they all tend to make me worry more about the present than about the future."

"You must make your distaste known," Josephine smiled—a smile of some mystery, borrowed from the Mona Lisa to hide her bad teeth. "Mademoiselle Lenormand is very versatile. She has thirteen different ways of replying to your questions—Yes, Polidor, by all means, go. We can manage, thank you—the examination of corpses, the evocation of shadows, the apparition of spectres, water reflected in a mirror, ashes cast to the north wind, fingernails, egg-whites, fire, a rooster fed on special grain and put between the letters . . . "

Her voice wavered on hearing Félicité beginning to growl, an unmistakable sign that her husband was afoot.

" . . . of the alphabet . . . "

Mortification spread over Mme Bonaparte's olive-skinned face as she watched the opening door. Before the First Consul was fully inside, his spouse had miraculously unearthed a batiste hanky from her pocketless muslin gown and held it in front of her mouth, prepared to burst into tears.

Dressed in a green cavalry uniform that had seen better days, Bonaparte's vivid dark eyes took in the visitors while Félicité yapped at his boots. "Well, well, well," he smiled (a smile Josephine knew would give way to a torrent of abuse in a matter of seconds). "If it isn't the beautiful Madame Tallien . . . *Pardon*, I forgot that you are between husbands. A pity!" He bowed his head in greeting—"Madame Cabarrus"—then turned to Fortunée: "I see that you are wearing clothes, Madame Hamelin. My congratulations!"

"Bonaparte, please," Josephine begged. "They are my friends! You can't expect me not to receive them."

"I do indeed expect it, since you gave me your word."

"But you can't! You can't!"

After the customary leaps at the First Consul's footwear, Félicité settled down to a subdued growling under Josephine's chair, alert to any sudden moves or an increase in vocal tones on the part of the intruder, ready to spring to the company's defense. The intruder's not reverting to form confused her thoroughly. She let out a few, unfocused yaps, not knowing how to behave. Her mistress was equally confused, but, being human, instinctively fell to exploiting the situation. "You haven't stopped seeing *your* old friends!" she cried bravely, casting a fearful eye on a Ming vase within her husband's reach. "How can you demand it of me?"

"*My* friends don't go walking naked on the Champs Elysées in broad daylight."

"She did it only once, Bonaparte," Josephine excused Fortunée. "And on a dare. You know how these things are."

"And don't call me Bonaparte in public; how many times do I have to tell you?"

"In public?" Josephine stared at him in gentle reproach. He always started on that when he was annoyed. Everyone present knew that she had never called him anything else. Was it *her* fault he had been given a Christian name too bizarre for her tongue to pronounce?

"Do you hear your daughter calling my brother Bonaparte? Do you call your husband Bonaparte?" he asked Hortense.

Hortense smiled. "No." The very idea struck her as comical. Yet she couldn't imagine her mother calling her stepfather by any other name.

"But, Bonaparte, your brother's name is Louis!" Josephine could no longer hold back her tears. "If you had been named Louis, I would gladly have called you Louis. As it is, what am I to do?"

"You can call me *General* Bonaparte."

Josephine looked through her tears at Thérèse for a clue as to whether this was a proposition made in earnest or a pleasantry. But Mme Cabarrus was too engrossed in her own concerns to notice. She sat primly on her striped-satin chair, playing with a corner of the tablecloth and sipping coffee and wine in absentminded succession. Exclusion from the Consulate would be a terrible blow to her, Josephine knew, abjectly miserable at the thought. "Ahh, Bonaparte," she wept, "have you forgotten? If it weren't for Madame Cabarrus we might never have met. Have you forgotten it was she who introduced you to me?"

"Yes, and afterwards you couldn't remember."

" ... When I think you said of her that 'one is glad to kiss her arms or anything else one can' ... ! You, who don't know how to flatter." Her husband neither complimented nor insulted women; he merely made spontaneous remarks which were interpreted as one or the other.

"It is all because you are now living in the Tuileries," Fortunée said flatly. "Because your husband is First Consul."

"This surprises you, Madame Hamelin?" Bonaparte asked.

Thérèse suddenly seemed to have found her voice. "General Bonaparte, won't you reconsider? Please?"

"My dear Madame Tallien . . . I don't deny that you are charming, but think what you're asking. You've had two or three husbands and about eight children by everybody. Now consider—what would you do in my place? I, who am trying to restore some decorum. My wife is a good woman who can't refuse anybody anything. If you are truly her friend, you will allow her to be respectable." If this was an allusion to Josephine's countless lovers of the past, he was quick to dispel it. "To see an unhappy face disturbs her well-being; and faced with the loss of her well-being, her reasoning falters. Every day she is approached by people carrying petitions addressed to me, asking for positions, favors, my interposition in this or that, financial assistance, and so on. To every one of these petitioners my wife promises her intervention and satisfactory results. They leave, happy as she likes to see them, not suspecting that she will never read their letters, which will end up in the hands of Fouché, the very last place they'd like to see them."

Aware of the truth in her stepfather's words, Hortense nevertheless felt compelled to defend Josephine. "My mother can't help being what she is any more than you can help being what you are." Daughter of a frivolous mother, Hortense had grown into a serious young woman, fiercely loyal to her stepfather (as was her brother Eugène) and deeply attached to Josephine, both of whom she had the insight to appreciate on their own terms. She didn't particularly mind the presence of her mother's old friends, yet she understood that these living reminders of a tumultuous past (the trio had shared no end of lovers) would not stand the First Consul's wife in good stead. But, knowing her mother as she did, how could she not plead her case? Josephine's distress might not be profound, still it was genuine all the same. "Your decision makes my mother very unhappy."

"For the moment. You and I know, Hortense, that your mother's system has the remarkable capacity to reject grief overnight. Tomorrow she will have forgotten, whereas I, ladies" —he was looking primarily at Thérèse—"am bound to think of you occasionally." He clicked his heels together in salute. "Ladies!"

In the moments following the First Consul's departure, the yellow drawing room was steeped in stunned silence. Then Thérèse burst out in sobs and Josephine fell into her arms, weeping desperately. Hortense sighed, and Fortunée profited from the others' inattention to appropriate to herself the remaining bottle of Chambertin.

The dinner was held on the second floor in the Gallery of Diana. Small dinners were usually served in one of Mme Bonaparte's two drawing rooms downstairs, but this was a grand affair, attended by the upper crust of the diplomatic corps, generals, and other worthies, accompanied by spouses, daughters, mothers, and as many female relatives as could be squeezed inside under the cover of a specific invitation.

Bonaparte had no interest in food other than to satisfy his hunger. On establishing himself in the Tuileries, he quickly made it clear that he had no intention of wasting three to four hours at table as was the custom. That he was occupying a royal residence little impressed him. "Who hasn't lived in this palace?" he shrugged to Bourrienne, "brigands, members of the National Convention . . . "

Meals were served *à l'ambigu*, meaning the several courses were deposited on the table simultaneously, those to be kept hot placed on plate warmers holding spirits of wine or boiling water, a practice the First Consul adopted as another expedient to get the business of eating disposed of in a hurry. The cooks racked their brains to create culinary extravaganzas representing fortresses and other battlefield vistas to capture their employer's attention.

They had outdone themselves this afternoon with an Egyptian pyramid constructed of layers of *mille-feuille* pastry dough, filled with *crème patissière*, apricots and apples, and guarded by tiny chocolate Mameluke soldiers.

His Egyptian campaign still fresh in his mind, no doubt, Bonaparte swiftly attacked the pyramid and ate one of the Mamelukes causing the Second Consul to groan audibly at the other end of the room and the hostess to signal to the footmen, in full Consular livery for the occasion, to set about handing the many dishes to the guests.

Livingston had reason to be pleased, chance having deposited the First Consul diagonally across from him, directly opposite Mrs. Livingston, which was less fortunate. Bonaparte, who descended on a seat at random, oblivious to his wife's discreet efforts to guide him to a designated spot, and with the *invités* following in some confusion, had landed slightly left of the table's center (attracted by the pyramid?), flanked by an unlikely pair of dinner partners. To his left was the antiquated Mademoiselle Montansier, of Timoléon memory, who cackled delightedly at the host starting the meal with the dessert and who talked incessantly, and to his right was a Polish countess with a glass eye that somehow managed to reflect the passion shining in her seeing eye, both of which were focused adoringly on Talleyrand. Next to this Countess Tyskiewitz was Madame Bonaparte and her daughter.

Dressed in white silk stockings and white satin breeches, in a green uniform with red collar and facings, Bonaparte looked resplendent devouring *pâtés, oefs à la Russe*, truffled Moyenne pasties, mutton, roast beef, sole in aspic — all of it at breakneck speed, with most of the guests in hot pursuit. What appeared like mountains of food disappeared from silver-gilt plates into mouths, chased by Clos Vougeot, Chambertin, Château Lafitte, or another of the standard wines the First Consul favored.

Livingston stole a glance at Mrs. Livingston, who looked the picture of genteel serenity, toying with her *pâté*, but whose sensibilities he could fairly guess were in a state of upheaval, being so close a witness to the Bonapartian approach to food. The fact that she was saddled at her right with yet another Bonaparte — the syphilitic Louis, who wore shirts worn by skin-disease victims in the hope of curing his many ailments — didn't help.

Countess Tyskiewitz was less successful in presenting a serene facade, though her distress was not due to the proximity of any Bonapartes, but rather to the enormous distance separating her from Talleyrand, seated with Fouché at the extreme end of the long table. That the reception was indeed an official one could be ascertained by the presence of Mme Talleyrand, which Bonaparte wouldn't tolerate at any other time.

Except for Mlle Montansier, whose desire to speak was greater than her appetite, the meal proceeded in relative silence, the main sounds being that of forks and knives clashing furiously against silver plates—a state of affairs which Livingston, with his faulty hearing, couldn't regret. The only person whose conversation interested him was that of the First Consul, and the First Consul was not in the habit of whispering.

Livingston happily concentrated on the mutton while Countess Tyskiewitz divided her attention equally between a fried bobolink and Talleyrand, and Mlle Montansier explained the finer points of opera. The First Consul had charged the retired actress with reintroducing Italian opera to the Parisians, and Mlle Montansier was unable to contain her enthusiasm for the project.

"You and Madame Livingston must come and see us at the Théâtre Favart, Monsieur Livingston," her thin voice piped through an upper register that penetrated all ears. "Italian opera is a most wondrous form of art."

"Would you keep quiet and eat!" Bonaparte ordered. "You get skinnier by the hour. One of these days you'll wake up and won't see yourself in the looking glass."

Mlle Montansier giggled like a girl. "Ah, General! You say the most amusing things when you're in a good mood. General Bonaparte and I were nearly engaged once," she beamed at Livingston, who stopped chewing to stare at his host in shock, but the First Consul, usually quick to take offense, winked, explaining between two bites of quail: "Mademoiselle was sixty-five and had a little nest egg. I was twenty-six, a poor soldier. Barras thought it a perfect match."

Mademoiselle agreed. "The poor boy owned only one coat; remember, Madame Bonaparte? He looked so pale and thin I took pity on him." She lowered her voice and leaned across the table toward Mrs. Livingston. "With his mother a widow and all those brothers and sisters to support, you understand, Madame . . . The General is so loyal, always taking care of everyone in the family. Isn't that the truth, Madame

Bonaparte?"

Josephine seemed neither annoyed nor embarrassed by the old lady's familiarity. "Always."

"Tell me, Monsieur Livingston, what is the cost of a loaf of bread in the United States?"

Livingston was speechless. In all of his fifty-seven years he had never purchased a loaf of bread. At the Clermont manor bread was baked once a week, he seemed to recall.

"You seem to forget, Mademoiselle, that the American States are bigger than France and Poland combined," Countess Tyskiewitz pointed out.

Mlle Montansier wasn't going to be chastised by a Polish countess. "Are you saying, Madame, that people living in countries bigger than France and Poland need not eat?"

"I have been admiring your gown, Madame," Mme Bonaparte sang to the Countess. "The embroidery is simply exquisite."

"In the United States the price of bread is not regulated by the government, Mademoiselle," said Mrs. Livingston.

"My dear! Did you hear that?" Mademoiselle cried at the First Consul. "How can the poor people in your country afford to buy bread, Madame Livingston, if their government allows the bakers to charge what they please? Bakers must be kept under constant surveillance, as I'm sure you are aware. If the cost of a four-pound loaf has gone down to twelve *sous* in France, it is surely not thanks to the bakers but to General Bonaparte. What sort of man can your president be that he fails to concern himself with the price of bread?"

"It is very possible you met Mr. Jefferson when he was minister here in . . . " Livingston searched his memory. "1784 or 85 I think it was he arrived."

"Oh but I *did* meet Monsieur Jefferson!" she shouted triumphantly, "Didn't I?" She looked inquiringly at Livingston. "A tall, red-haired gentleman? Extremely gracious and elegantly dressed, yes? I must say, Monsieur, I find it very difficult to believe that a cultured gentleman like Monsieur Jefferson would let himself be dictated to by the uneducated bakers. He quite enjoyed our presentations in the Rue de la Loi, you know." Her voice took on a confidential note. "I was with the National Theatre then. A very fine company, if I say so myself."

"I hear," said Bonaparte, "that the Americans have adopted the deplorable English custom of banishing the ladies from the dinner table once the meal is over. If I were you, Madame Livingston, I should be greatly offended at being turned out by the men for two or three hours while they are guzzling their wine."

"Did you know, Bonaparte, that Monsieur Livingston and Madame Livingston's brother are inventing a ship propelled by steam?" Josephine chanted, blessing chance which had allowed her to overhear this information earlier (and Livingston's deafness which prompted him to speak unduly loud) and make use of it now to distract her husband from the present subject.

"A steamboat!" Bonaparte shouted, abandoning his coffee cup at the thought. "I have been approached about the possibility. A most interesting proposition. Remarkable! Remarkable. Ha! I have always maintained that it will be the Americans wiping the English from the seas. How far along are you, Monsieur, in the practical application of your invention?" Livingston hastened to point out that the invention wasn't his. "Many a man has been fascinated by the prospect of a steamboat, General. There is Mr. Fitch, for one; and Mr. Rumsey; Nicholas Roosevelt; Mr. Stevens, my brother-in-law; and now Mr. Fulton. And I, of course, am deeply interested . . .

'Of course you are interested. You must! One must."

" . . . but it will be many years, I fear, before we can hope to see the idea translated into practice. There are difficulties . . .

"You will overcome them, my dear Monsieur."

"We shall be propelled by steam over the waters of the world!" crowed Mlle Montansier. 'How very exciting and extraordinary. Pray heaven that I live long enough to see it happen."

"Heaven can do nothing if you don't eat," said the First Consul, piling a major section of the pyramid's base on a china dessert plate and planting it before the skinny Mademoiselle. "A little less talking may help too."

"I'd say," the ill-humored Louis Bonaparte suddenly chimed in. "I am getting a headache from all your pointless chatter."

"You look lovely in blue, Mademoiselle," Josephine offered. "The color compliments your complexion."

"Do you happen to know a gentleman by the name of James Monroe, Monsieur Livingston?" asked Hortense. "He is the Governor of Virginia."

Livingston turned to his wife, whose expression confirmed that his ears weren't at fault, then back to Hortense. "Why, yes . . . " He had yet to inform the Consulate of Monroe's appointment, convinced the news would bring negotiations—already lagging miserably—to a complete halt. "Are you familiar with Mr. Monroe, Madame?"

"Oh yes," Hortense smiled. "Very much so. I was at Madame Campan's with Monsieur Monroe's daughter. Eliza . . . Mademoiselle Monroe, actually it is Madame Hay presently—she was married, did you know?—she and I are faithful correspondents. She wrote me her father will soon be coming to Paris on government business and she will accompany her parents. I am overjoyed at the prospect of seeing her again, you can imagine! After one, two, let's see . . . " She started counting on her fingers. "Nine years."

Livingston nodded. He had caught enough of her excited babble to feel alarmed at this unsuspected connection of the Monroes. But exactly how close a connection was it? "I expect that Madame, your mother, and the First Consul are equally overjoyed."

"Oh yes, well, I suppose my mother is, but General Bonaparte cannot recall his having met Monsieur Monroe."

"I am not surprised," said Mrs. Livingston, thinking out loud. "The expectation of meeting one's former schoolmates is unlike any other," she added quickly.

"Does Monsieur Jefferson still play the violin?" cried Mlle Montansier.

Neither of the Livingstons had any idea.

"How many years have you been married, Madame Livingston?"

Bonaparte wanted to know.

"Thirty-three, General," Mrs. Livingston obliged.

"A third of a century! Splendid. Excellent. Have you any children?"

"Yes, General, two," smiled Livingston, aware of the First Consul's infatuation with families.

"Ha! Did you hear that, Josephine? *That* is the kind of lady you shall invite to gossip with you in the morning."

"I would be delighted, Madame Livingston, if you should do me the honor," smiled Josephine, Mona Lisa-like, not at all put off by her husband's brusque request. "Several ladies of my acquaintance would be equally delighted, I am sure. Madame de Genlis speaks very highly of you."

"Poor Madame de Genlis," mused Bonaparte. "When she speaks of virtue she seems to be making a discovery."

"Are you musical, Madame Livingston?" inquired Mlle Montansier.

"The honor would be entirely mine, Madame Bonaparte," glowed Mrs. Livingston, possessed of a fleeting desire to absolve the First Consul of any and all sins. "Not very, Mademoiselle."

"Madame Bonaparte plays the harp," Mademoiselle went on.

"Only one tune," said the surly Louis. "Always the same tune."

"Do you play the harp, Madame Livingston?"

"I'm afraid not, Mademoiselle."

"You can consider it a blessing, my dear fellow," Bonaparte assured Livingston, as he rose from his chair and everyone around him scrambled to do likewise.

"The General is not musical either . . . " Mademoiselle shook her puny head. "A pity."

The guests followed the First Consul into the next room where people not invited to dine were to be presented. Mrs. Livingston would have been content to send for Tranche and head home at this point and, in so doing, perhaps retain her softened impression of the host a while longer, something she knew would be difficult, watching the presentations.

Already the First Consul stalked before the line of ladies and gentlemen waiting to be introduced, hands in back, looking as if he were reviewing a division of artillery soldiers and delivering comments to match—"Splendid teeth!" he shouted at one girl. "Big feet!" at another. "Who has piled up your hair like that?" he inquired of the wife of a diplomat—leaving guests unfamiliar with military inspections stammering and stunned.

Mme Bonaparte, grace and gentleness personified, tiptoed in her husband's wake, administering to the wounded; dipping into her inexhaustible supply of charming asides and compliments, dispensed in her soft, lilting voice.

When Ambassador Whitword joined the Livingstons, Mrs. Livingston excused herself. Bonaparte being so near and civil (for him) at table, had increased Robert's belief in the possibility of a brief *entretien*, on which he had pinned his last hope for success. She thought it best to leave her husband to his pursuits and crossed the room—brilliant with the light of dozens of candles reflected in the crystal chandeliers—to the spot where she had noticed the Countess de Genlis, a lady whose writings and courage Mrs. Livingston much admired.

Mme de Genlis seemed to be in the midst of settling a lover's quarrel. The girl was very young and plump, with the red cheeks of someone fresh from the provinces. She was half-naked in a flimsy Greek tunic that didn't suit her and was crying desperately. The boy, whom the Countess introduced as "the poet Millevoye", looked bored and sickly, and wore huge spectacles. Beside him, looking very annoyed, stood Marie Henri Beyle, an ill-mannered young man from Grenoble who admired Bonaparte and talked of writing under the pen name of Stendhal.

It appeared that the girl, whose name was Ninon, was Beyle's niece. Ninon had made the long trek from Grenoble to Paris by herself with the sole object of meeting the First Consul. Not knowing what to do with her, Beyle had palmed her off on Mme de Genlis, who had dressed her in this gauzy attire, only to have Bonaparte advise Ninon to "go home and put on something warm," demolishing whatever expectations she might have had of replacing the beautiful Mademoiselle Georges, current Bonaparte favorite.

In an effort to cheer up the crying girl, Josephine had dispatched Millevoye to read some of his verses to her. "*Alors là, vraiment,*" said Mme de Genlis, "Madame Bonaparte's choice was unfortunate." She brought her elegant head nearer to Mrs. Livingston's to whisper: "Madame Bonaparte means well, but she rarely if ever reads anything and she imagines all poets to be consumptive or too sensitive to eat, their spirits lost in a world of flowers and birds. Millevoye over obliges Madame Bonaparte by looking as though he were suffering from several dragging illnesses at once. Physically, we can all see how well he lives up to expectations. Spiritually, alas . . . " The Countess sighed.

Poor Millevoye's spirit soared only through desolate landscapes, full of dying poets and dead leaves, and other subjects in varying stages of decomposition. Anyone darting through flowerbeds was his natural enemy. Life was a dark-tinted entity to Millevoye — forever wilting, languishing, disintegrating into death. Good health appalled him. One myopic glimpse of the full, rosy cheeks of Ninon and he had recoiled in horror, sending the girl into a new frenzy of tears.

" . . . The boy has no eye for flowers," Mme de Genlis explained, "nor an ear for birds. He is, how shall I put it? From the elegiacal school, you see, Madame Livingston. Not the sort of thing to cheer up a girl from Grenoble. It is well Ninon didn't hear his verse." The Countess reproached herself her own role in the drama. "But what was I to do, Madame? The girl wanted to make an impression on the First Consul, and the First Consul seems unimpressed by understatement . . . " She hesitated, reluctant to speak ill of someone instrumental in getting her back on her feet. The Count de Genlis had been decapitated in 1793 and she herself had returned to France from exile only the previous year when Bonaparte allocated her a pension of six thousand francs. "Oh, stop it!" Mme de Genlis suddenly lost her patience. "What have you got to cry about at your age?"

Beyle paid no attention to his weeping niece, selecting the moment (and these civilized surroundings) to lecture the tubercular Millevoye on the City sewers. " . . . You Parisians, who think yourselves so advanced — you are barbarians! Your streets stink; you can't take a step in them without being covered with black mud, which gives a disgusting appearance to the populace, forced to travel on foot. This comes from the brilliant idea of turning your streets into a sewer. It's *under* the streets that sewers should be laid . . . " All of this while swallowing half a platter of canapés and gulping down wine. Mme Bonaparte would never take *him* for a poet, Mrs. Livingston decided, wondering how the refined Mme de Genlis managed to be friends with Beyle.

"But, Henri, you know very well that I am not a Parisian," protested Millevoye. "I am not responsible in the matter."

"I just finished reading your *Mademoiselle de Clermont*, Madame," Mrs. Livingston started, about to express her admiration, when the First Consul's voice boomed across the room, arresting further conversation.

"You are then determined on war!"

Everyone turned to look at English Ambassador Whitword to whom the words were addressed. Lord Whitword kept his wits. "We are too well acquainted with the advantages of peace to think of war."

"If England is so appreciative of peace, why is she exciting troubles in Saint Domingue? Why does she keep a naval armament in the neighboring seas? Why does she have ships of war in the Gulf of Mexico? England has taken from France Canada, Cape Breton, Newfoundland, Nova Scotia, and the richest portions of Asia!" Bonaparte interrupted his tirade on noticing Constant, his valet, whose presence reminded him that Mlle Georges was waiting in his private apartments.

Without further ado, the First Consul energetically stalked out of the room, Constant in tow, dashing Livingston's hopes for a *tête-à-tête*. After a few moments of astonished quiet, the guests resumed their conversations.

If only he had known of it, the Chancellor would have drawn a certain balm from the clamor and fury in Congress . . .

February 1803

The debate in the Senate had been raging for several days. Pennsylvania Avenue, rarely overtaxed by traffic, now was entirely empty. Anybody who could afford the time had repaired to the one finished wing of the Capitol to watch the fight. It was the only theatre in town and better fare than was to be had on the New York or Philadelphia stage, without any billboards advertising the outcome, which was uncertain.

Creaking and groaning on its axles, the Royal George trundled in daily from Georgetown, disgorging excited locals of all ages (in their starched Sunday best), who had come to trudge through the yellow mud beside congressmen and senators lodging in Georgetown, who were the coach's regular passengers. The ladies forgot their loo tables and social chitchats and tried to outdress one another before racing ahead to claim the best seats. All four foreign attachés were in attendance, to report on the proceedings to their respective governments: Louis Pichon to France, the Marqués (and Marquésa) de la Casa Yrujo to Spain, Edward Thornton to England, and Peder Pederson to Denmark. The Federalist and Republican press were highly visible (and highly partisan), quoting from the debate in their newspapers anything which made the opposition look the loser, slinging no end of unflattering copy at it in the process.

Meriwether Lewis had come to have a look at the combatants in their morocco-leather lined scarlet seats on the Senate floor and experience some of the fuss in the flesh. The gallery was graceful enough when viewed from below, he thought, but something of its charm was lost when you found yourself stuck behind one of its Ionic columns, next to a grandpa with a boy crawling over his knees.

"Let's not await the arrival of the French! Since a solemn treaty has been violated, let's not hesitate to occupy places that ought to belong to us . . ."

Lewis didn't need to torture his neck to recognize the speaker as

Senator James Ross of Pennsylvania. A rabid Federalist, Ross had been talking of his resolutions for over a week and, finally, they were being debated.

"... The people of the West are ready to fight. It would be excessive simplicity to suppose New Orleans will be yielded to us spontaneously, or even by treaty with Bonaparte. We can no longer await the uncertain results of diplomatic procedures. New Orleans ought to belong to the United States. Never was there a more favorable time to annex to the Union a place without which half of our states couldn't exist. It's easy to seize on it, as France is on the verge of going to war with England. It is time to teach the world that America is as dominant in this part of the globe as other nations are in Europe; that we fear none of them; that our youth is over and we are prepared to make use of our strength!"

Senator Breckinridge of Kentucky disagreed. "A minister is sent to the offending nation with an olive branch for the purpose of an amiable discussion and the settlement of differences, and before he is gone we invade the territory of that nation with an army of fifty thousand men!"

"Why submit to a tardy, uncertain negotiation?" Ross wondered. "The Westerners cannot go to market. They have no resources but the products of their farms. You allow the Spaniards to lock them up. You tell them their crops must rot in their hands, yet they must pay taxes. Is this justice? Why not seize what is essential to us as a nation? The Westerners are tired of negotiation. They are impatient to fight. Is this spirit to be repressed by negotiation? When in possession of New Orleans, we will negotiate with more advantage," he concluded, paraphrasing Hamilton in the New York *Evening Post*.

"Why negotiate when war will serve?" cried White of Delaware.

James Jackson of Georgia jumped to support Breckinridge. "Didn't France capture our vessels and imprison our seamen during the administration of Washington, so much eulogized by the gentleman from Pennsylvania? Did President Washington resort to war? No, sir! And after him, did President Adams appeal to arms? No, sir! He sent a new set of ministers who were received by the French and who made a treaty which was ratified."

"I have heard," smiled Ross, "that the French may be willing to sell the Isle of New Orleans if certain influential persons at the Consulate were to be given two-million dollars . . . "

"Order! Order!" shouted Wright of Maryland. "How dare a senator betray in public information received in confidence?"

Vice President Burr, who presided over the debate, picked up his gavel "Gentlemen, gentlemen . . . "

"You should've been here yesterday," Grandpa told Lewis, under the cover of cheers and boos rising from the gallery. "They nearly came to blows. That one there . . . " He pointed a bony index finger at someone beyond Lewis's vision.

"Ross!" the boy shouted.

" . . . and the one in the black britches. 'Course they cleared us out in a hurry so's not to show us the fact. Me and Bud have been watchin' every day, ain't we, boy? Bud thinks the Federalists are bound to come out ahead."

"You're a Federalist, are you, Bud?" smiled Lewis.

"Bud's a Republican, like me," the old man quickly corrected. "He just thinks the Federalists are better talkers."

"Order! Order!"

"And fighters, it looks like," said Lewis, at the sound of a new round of cheers and boos in response to a fresh commotion on the floor.

"Gentlemen, please!" Colonel Burr was pounding his gavel, though from the expression on his face it was plain that he wasn't unduly disturbed.

"That man never upsets himself," declared Grandpa, following Lewis's gaze. "Say 'thank you, ma'am'," he ordered the boy, who accepted an apple from the bonneted lady beside them.

"No, sir! Do not repeat it or I shall be forced to demand satisfaction!"

"Who's that talkin', boy?"

"Thank you, ma'am. I don't know that one, Gramps."

"That's Senator Rutledge," Lewis obliged.

"A Federalist, I take it, making so much noise? Who's the fellow he's shouting at?"

"Order!"

"That's Ellery, from . . . It sounds like he's being challenged to a duel. I wonder what happened . . . "

"Gentlemen! Gentlemen!"

"If it's a fight, never mind, we ain't gone see it," claimed the old man. "They'll clear us out in a hurry so's not to show us the fact."

He was right. The debate was to be continued behind closed doors. Colonel Burr was forced to clear the gallery.

Gouverneur Morris, Federalist Senator from New York, was attended to by his two French valets, who were torturing his hair into papillottes. Clad in a silk embroidered robe, Morris leaned back in a cushioned Chippendale chair, his wooden leg resting on a matching footstool. He was reading a letter from Robert R. Livingston, a longtime friend, while the valets fussed. Looking up, he spotted Vice President Burr through the window and sent one of the Frenchmen to fetch him.

"You find me in *déshabillé*, Colonel," Morris limped up to greet Burr, pointing to his greying hair which branched out like some exotic tree in a multitude of ringlet curls tied with paper bows. "Appearances must be kept up, even in the wilderness. I hope you will ignore the exterior man for the interior one who delights at this unexpected chance to congratulate you, Colonel, on your performance in the Senate. You are presiding over the debate with skill and impartiality." A note of regret seemed to creep in the Senator's last words. "Sit down, Colonel, please. Have you dined?" And when Burr nodded. "Gaston, *offre à boire au colonel.*"

Gaston rattled off the names of several cordials: "Bergamot, ratafie, aqua mirabilis, eau de vie, royal usquebaugh, *mon colonel?*"

"*Un cognac s'il-vous-plait*, Gaston," Burr interrupted the litany.

"*C'est ça. Pour moi aussi*," Morris added, waving both servants out of the room when the drinks were poured. "I wasn't aware you spoke French, Colonel."

"I know how to ask for a cognac. If I had spent nine years in France, as you have, Senator, I might have asked for champagne."

"Confirming my belief that you would have made a splendid emissary to France."

Burr smiled graciously. "Thank you, Senator." The point, however, was no longer moot. Monroe's nomination had been confirmed by the Senate. "I am confident Mr. Monroe will spare no effort to succeed in his mission."

"As he succeeded in his first mission in that country? Being recalled by President Washington for disobeying orders! Jefferson has taken special care that a stone that the builders rejected should become the first of the corner. The President believes in payment of debts by diminution of revenue, in defense of territory by reduction of armies, and in vindication of right by the appointment of envoys. And what an envoy! Are our interests to be defended by an ambassador who cannot formulate a cohesive sentence before giving it a quarter of an hour's thought first?"

"Not everyone shares your talent for mastering foreign languages, Senator."

Morris's genteel eyebrows went up in mock surprise. "Who said anything about *foreign* languages?" Encouraged by Burr's smile, he went on: "Let's face it, Monroe is dense, his uncompromising republicanism unrelieved by any social grace or sense of humor. Talleyrand will laugh at Monroe. No, he won't condescend to laugh. He will ignore him."

"Which reminds me . . . Did you hear Rutledge challenged Ellery to a duel, apparently over this very business?" What reminded Burr was that Morris himself once crossed swords with Talleyrand in Paris over a lady.

"Ellery backed off. In the great Republican tradition he is all talk and no action."

"He is also terribly near-sighted."

"Or so he claims. Imagine Chancellor Livingston's reaction when he hears he is to be assisted by Monroe . . . " Morris waved in distress at the papers lying on the mahogany table near his chair. "What can I possibly write the Chancellor to console him for this ignominy . . . " His voice wavered. He watched Burr drink his cognac, shaking his papillotted head. "When I think it could have been you, my boy, sitting at this moment in that big box they call the President's House . . .

Burr's smile broadened at being addressed this tenderly. Senator Morris was fifty, which made him all of four years Burr's senior.

What is the matter with you, Colonel? Do you believe all things will come to he who is complacent? Then, let me tell you that you are mistaken. You've been lucky so far, but don't fancy your luck will hold out forever. I don't understand you, Colonel, really I don't. Eminently qualified for this mission as you are, the administration passed you up in favor of an incompetent, and the fact merely seems to amuse you. I suppose you were equally amused on reading Cheetham's attacks on you in the *American Citizen?*"

"Cheetham is a hired hand."

"You know it and *I* know it, but the public doesn't know it. You simply can't keep on going through life looking as if you're enjoying yourself. In politics, especially, this leaves the wrong impression. Already you are at a disadvantage by having been born with a handsome face. People don't like to read satisfaction on a face like yours, Colonel. Yet you are not at a disadvantage where your mind is concerned. I have watched your adroitness in court in New York, your technical precision, your compelling persuasion of juries. I admired you as a member of the Assembly and as Attorney General. In the Senate, too, you make a striking impression, presiding with ease and dignity, always understanding the subject before you, stating the question clearly and confining the speakers to the point, but even here you persist in enjoying yourself." Morris paused to regain his breath and lubricate his vocal chords with a swallow of cognac. "As you know, tomorrow will be my turn to speak in the debate."

"I am looking forward to hearing you, Senator." Burr meant what he said. Morris was one of the most erudite speakers in the Federalist Party. In both parties.

"As you know also, it will be my farewell address as well. You heard

the arguments of my peers. This issue cannot be resolved by negotiation. Chancellor Livingston himself admits to that. It is our duty to support the Westerners and take back by force what is ours by right."

"Assuming I agree, Senator, what would you have me do? I have no
power."

"Be discreet, my boy. Enjoy yourself only when the Republicans
have the floor. Your objectivity in presiding over this debate has been
rightly praised by both parties, but the praise will end with the debate.
Neutrality is a virtue of the moment, admired only so long as is convenient. There is no longer a place for you in the Republican Party. You
have conceded the throne to that Virginian democrat and he will never
abdicate in your favor. It is high time you realize the precariousness of
your situation and start containing your joy. Remember — the gavel is
yours. Handle it with a mind serious upon your future political fortune.
With any sort of luck we shall be at war long before Monroe reaches Le
Havre. *That* is the only solution to the problem. War will vindicate the
West and return my party to the top all in one brilliant stroke. So stop
smiling, Colonel, and you may live to be a part of it."

While the debate in the Senate raged on, Jefferson, Madison, and
Monroe conferred in the President's study.

"I was hoping that by expanding my law practice, I might put a dent
in some of my debts." Monroe's voice matched the stony quality of his
face. "I haven't yet recovered financially from my last mission, and this
new one can only get me in deeper." He leaned away from the large
study table, switching his muscularly-compact weight to the back legs
of his chair, allowing Jefferson to reach into a drawer filled with miniature garden tools.

The President's greyish-red head bobbed up and down in accord as
he retrieved a piece of string from the drawer. "Public service wasn't
meant to make a man rich." (His own expenses invariably exceeded his
income) "But who else is there to plead the cause of the West?"

"Whom the Westerners themselves would accept as their spokesman?" lisped Madison in support.

"There you have it in a nutshell!" Jefferson's gangly frame waded between the profusion of small and large tables to one of the windows. He picked up the wandering branch of a winter-weary begonia and secured it to its main stem. "Nine-thousand may not be a princely sum for duty abroad, but it's the best we can do. The Government will cover any traveling expenses, of course, as well as postage, couriers, and so on."

"And Mrs. Madison and I have agreed to take up your offer and buy the silver and Sèvres plates," Madison promised. "The pieces we saw were quite handsome."

"That will help," sighed Monroe, grateful for any extra cash. His raw-boned body shifted awkwardly on the faded chair while he tried to formulate his gratitude. "I am deeply touched by your confidence in me."

"I can think of no one who deserves it more," the President replied warmly. He reclaimed his seat at the table, setting to leaning on one hip, as was his wont. "And every reasoning mind in the country agrees. From the moment news of your appointment reached the West, tempers there have cooled down considerably. Of the essence now is speed. We must take advantage of this temporary calm and negotiate a settlement before the mood changes. You will take yourself to New York as fast as the winter roads permit and set sail immediately. The moment in France is critical; only the trouble in Saint Domingue delays French possession of Louisiana. Bonaparte is in distress for money for current needs . . . " He stopped speaking when the mockingbird, safely enclosed in his suspended cage, seized on the moment to drown his master's modest voice under a furious warble. Jefferson took off his grey corduroy coat and draped it over the cage before turning back to Monroe.

"You will be authorized to purchase the city and isle of New Orleans and., if possible, East and West Florida as well. For this, you can spend up to fifty thousand *livres tournois*, or about nine thousand two hundred fifty dollars. The least you should settle for is a permanent reshipment depot on the lower Mississippi near New Orleans. All of this will be explained in great detail in your instructions—Mr. Madison is hard at work giving them shape and form—which will be sent after you to New York. Study them carefully during your passage and inform Livingston on your arrival. You and Livingston will proceed jointly and succeed where he alone failed."

Monroe nodded gravely. His opinion of his own abilities surpassing his opinion of Livingston's, he saw no reason to doubt the success of the President's dictate. "To what do you attribute Livingston's failure?" he wondered. "Is it lack of application?"

"I don't think our minister lacks application," smiled Madison, who was not without a certain sympathy for Livingston (no representative could be expected to delight at the appointment of an assisting party) and, in his official correspondence, was trying to soothe the minister's bruised ego as best he could.

Jefferson's sympathy was minimal. "Application misapplied, I wouldn't wonder. Livingston is an alumnus of the New York Federalist kennel, full of old tricks he can't unlearn, concerned first of all with fattening and preserving his own hide. His objectives are likely to take on so many shapes that no instructions could be squared to fit them. I'm not sure Johnny Randolph wasn't right when he said of Livingston 'brilliant but utterly corrupt, he shines and stinks like rotten mackerel by moonlight.'"

Monroe laughed—"Leave it to Randolph"—but Madison frowned at the opposing wall, singling out the territory of Canada among the several maps for his disapproving gaze. "Damaging judgments come naturally to John Randolph, but if Livingston's corruption had half the sheen Randolph imagines, he ought to come off looking better than he has, next to Talleyrand."

Jefferson shook his head. "You don't try to beat a Talleyrand at his own game, Jemmy. I have seen enough of that fox in my days abroad to know there is nothing in Livingston's bag of tricks to startle him. Honesty is as good a weapon as any I can think of to disarm Talleyrand. And we couldn't dispatch a more skillful deployer of that weapon than our old friend here." He winked at Monroe whose grey features blossomed pink under the praise. "The country depends on you, James."

Monroe nodded. He understood that. But what of the cries for war by the opposition? "What of the warmongers on the Hill? What if they get their way?"

"We must pray they won't."

"I doubt they will," said Madison. "They may have the orators, but we have the numbers."

Monroe wasn't sure. "I hear the Senate's fighting something fierce."

"Good!" The President smiled. "So long as the Senate is fighting, the country remains at peace."

After stabling their horses at 14th Street, the President and Lewis plowed home on foot in the crisp February evening. A thaw had set in the day before and progress was slow. The dark, brooding facade of the President's House looked inhospitable, a trifle sinister even, with a fluttering speck of candlelight in the porter's lodge the only discernible sign of life.

The lodge was empty — the porter, as usual, off visiting elsewhere. Jefferson and his secretary sat down in the poorly lit space to exchange their boots for less muddy footwear. "I don't mind telling you, I'm glad that's over," Jefferson confided. "The excess of toasts we had to endure tonight taxes the brain." They had just returned from McLaughlin's Tavern in Georgetown where the Republicans had given Monroe a sendoff dinner.

"Drinking the toasts, sir, or listening to them?" Lewis wanted to know.

"Both."

"And here I was hoping we'd have a nightcap before turning in."

"*Your* idea of a nightcap is drinking one final glass at a time. Somebody ought to sit you down sometime, Meriwether, and explain the meaning of the word to you."

"You could explain it to me while we have one," quipped Lewis, confident that nothing tonight would disturb the President's good mood. "Tomorrow your special envoy will be on his way to New York. In the Senate things are not going according to plan for the Federalists. Most importantly, a replacement for myself has been found in the person of Lewis Harvie. What more can a president ask for?"

"A nightcap?"

"You read my mind."

"Let's go to the study where it's warm." Already Jefferson was pacing through the hall, lit by a few strategically placed candles and streaks of natural light suddenly beaming through glass panes by the appearance of the moon.

Lewis paced after him. "Speaking of Lieutenant Clark, sir, I think he should be made a captain." He smiled when the President turned to offer him a puzzled stare. "It wouldn't look right if we weren't of equal rank. To the crew, I mean."

Jefferson returned the smile. "I am only the President, Meriwether. I don't have the power to transform lieutenants into captains." He stopped walking when the porter came sauntering from the northeast corner, a hand aloft to indicate he had a message.

"Major Lee, come to see you." The porter pointed behind him in the direction of the common dining room. "He's been eatin' dinner."

"Light-Horse Lee?"

"Yessuh."

"Dear Jesus!"

When Jefferson pushed open the door to the dining room, Major General Light-Horse Harry Lee jumped to his feet and saluted. "Mr. Jefferson, sir." Standing very erect and looking solemnly at the President in the doorway, he came straight to the point. "Mr. John Walker of Albemarle County demands satisfaction, sir! Your choice of weapons and place!"

Jefferson sighed. It was as he had feared. "Sit down, Major, please. Would you care for a nightcap? Would you care for a brandy?" he corrected himself.

While it was plain the Major drew a certain pleasure from being the bearer of the challenge – Light-Horse was no admirer of Jefferson – he, like the President, was a Virginian, and the gracious dispensation and acceptance of hospitality was an indigenous Virginian force before which personal dislikes wavered temporarily.

"Don't mind if I do." Light-Horse sat down, shaking his head. "A sorry business."

Lewis, who had witnessed the scene from the hall, discreetly shut the door and leaned against it to utter a string of curses at James Thomson Callender, the muckraker responsible for this development.

"M-m-hmmmm . . . " The porter, too, had witnessed the scene. Nodding to Lewis and mumbling to himself, he dragged his portly person off to inform his fellows.

Since the Sally Hemings story was collapsing under the strain of repeated use – even the most startling of revelations could only be revealed once, Lewis decided – Callender had been scouring the Albemarle countryside, desperate for fresh information. Betsey Walker had decided to rescue Callender, startling her husband rather than the country with her revelation that the President had tried to seduce her on numerous occasions some thirty-five years earlier.

The American public somehow stood skeptical before a woman who, after decades of silence, suddenly confessed to having been the innocent victim of Jefferson's repeated attacks on her virtue. A Jefferson who "possessed that ardor of constitution" which prompted him to pursue the virtuous Betsey for a full ten years, undaunted by the fact that John Walker was his friend and that his intended prey wasn't possessed of the necessary constitutional ardor to respond to his advances, causing Tom Paine to quip: "We have heard of a ten year siege of Troy, but who ever heard of a ten year siege to seduce?"

Lewis was inclined to agree.

And now that, thanks to the good offices of Callender, John Walker had achieved the dubious status of being the nation's number one cuckold, he wanted to reclaim his former unsullied self through a duel with President Jefferson.

Lewis's eyes rolled up at the peeling plaster on the ceiling as he climbed the stairs to his cavernous room. "What next?" Halfway up, he decided to sit and wait it out. A minute later the President was shaking his arm. Lewis was about to voice his surprise at the shortness of the interview, when the clock in the public dining room began to strike an interminable number of times. "What happens now?"

"I'll have to jump on my horse tomorrow and try to talk Walker out of it." Jefferson sagged on the stair next to his secretary. "Light-Horse will try to set up a meeting at Montpelier."

"You're going to *Virginia?*" Lewis was wide-awake now. "But that's three days' riding! I'll be in Philadelphia by the time you get back. Why don't you take Walker at his bluff? You're a good shot! Tell him to come here. Your choice of weapons and place, remember? I heard Light-Horse."

"I'm turning sixty next month, Meriwether. Are you urging me to shoot another elderly gentleman before the whole of Washington? I can just see what the Federalists would do with *that*. Why, the mere idea of Walker and I fighting a duel is too preposterous to contemplate. The mere idea . . . " Jefferson gestured at the bottom of the stairs as if he were trying to conjure up a tableau of the event there. "And over Betsey Walker!"

"Yes," Lewis nodded. "I must admit I agree with you there. What on earth did you see in Betsey Walker? *That's* the part strikes me as preposterous. Did you?"

"Did I what?"

"Seduce the elderly Betsey?"

The words were out before he knew it. Lewis held his breath, ready to be told off in no uncertain terms. Jefferson did not take kindly to any prying into his personal affairs. His private life was a jealously guarded secret. Nothing could induce him to comment on it. Even at the height of the Sally Hemings hysteria, when the ballads and commentary in the papers had descended to a level only to be described as vile, the President could not be baited into a reaction, to the distress of those who wished him well and sincerely commiserated with his plight. It was almost unnatural, Lewis thought. It was . . .

"She wasn't always elderly." Jefferson's voice sounded impatient but it wasn't the impatience with a prying question Lewis had expected. It was the impatience of a sixty-year-old man with a twenty-eight-year-old one, at the younger man's presuming the older one never to have been twenty-eight. "What happened happened exactly once, while John was away at Fort Stanwix. And seduction is hardly the word for it — it wasn't a great tour de force to convince Betsey — though I wouldn't embarrass her by saying so. As a gentleman I can do no less."

"Yes," Lewis swallowed, determined to be no less a gentleman himself, though not for Betsey's sake.

"But I am not inclined to fight any duels — over Betsey Walker or anyone else."

"Yes.

"Yes, yes? Why are you so agreeable? Are you asleep?"

"No!"

"Imagine if someone should come by right at this moment." Jefferson smiled. "We must present an interesting sight. President Jefferson and Captain Lewis having a chat on the stairs in the dead of night." He got up and stretched. "Let's go to the dining room."

"Who will come by? It must be going on one."

"I was under the impression that you wanted a nightcap."

"In that case . . . " Lewis scrambled to his feet and followed the President across the hall.

Nothing came of the duel, as the President had predicted. Walker was persuaded to be satisfied with a written admission of guilt on Jefferson's part, which, while stressing his own guilty role, exonerated Betsey of all complicity.

Callender has since been silenced for good. A few months ago — on July 17th to be precise — he was discovered drowned in the James, in a section of the River where the water reaches only to a man's knees, giving rise to the theory that James Thomson Callender's passage to the other side could not have been accomplished without assistance. The fact that his remains were rushed to the grave that same day did nothing to put the speculation to rest.

Of course, so long as the physical assault of newspaper editors by rival newspaper editors, lawyers, and other opposing factions continues to remain unpunishable by law, it would be excessive simplicity (to borrow a phrase from Senator Ross) to suppose the practice will die of its own volition.

But to go back to February: As the President was forced to saddle his horse and battle the winter roads to Virginia, the Surveillant *was approaching her first port of call . . .*

February 1803

The *Surveillant* was anchored a small distance from the harbor, her passengers and crew unable to go ashore. Captain Girardais had given strict orders no one was to leave ship. The people on deck were silent. Wherever their vision stretched, it was met with devastation. The plantations of Duplas, Vaudreuil, and others had burned to ruins; scorched skeletons etched eerily against the evening skies by the campfires of the slaves, present masters of Saint Domingue. The surviving remnants of the French army — soldiers wasted by want and disease — could be seen acknowledging their new masters as far as the City gates.

How had this calamity happened? Who had allowed it to happen? What had become of the regiments? Where were the commanders? Where was Leclerc?

Flames leapt up from the little island called La Tortue, painting the surrounding waters an unnatural red in the quickly descending night. Human forms were running wildly through the burning glare, arms beating like windmills — the pursuers and the pursued howling with like hysteria. The planter who owned La Tortue was dragged from his flaming house, only to be slaughtered like an ox by a mob of maddened slaves.

As the bloody spectacle unrolled before the terrified witnesses aboard the *Surveillant*, the flare swept through the greenery concealing the ship and drew whimsical designs on their horror-frozen faces. All came to realize that Saint Domingue, once the pride and glory of their homeland, was lost forever.

There would be no regiment here to escort the *Surveillant* on the final leg of her long voyage to Louisiana. The brig would have to make a solitary entrance, hoping that no English spies cruising the Gulf would guess the nature of her business, and that General Victor's fleet had met with favorable winds and was not far behind.

When, at the first sign of daylight, the *Surveillant* left Cape François,

the advance party was a far more sober lot than that which had so exu-
berantly set sail from the Bay of Biscay more than six weeks earlier.

MARCH

T he sea had been calm for two days. A heavy fog had settled on the 400-ton *Richmond,* causing her to move slowly, wearily, one knot to the hour at best. Eliza Monroe climbed onto the rudder trunk to stare through one of the high, sloping stern windows of the small, ill-lit cabin. Her eyes, accustomed to seeing the broad sweep of ocean and sky, met with an impenetrable wall of grey mist.

Her hair and clothing felt damp. The air in the stern cabin was moldy and smelled of vomit and urine. Before the bunks the curtains drooped with humidity. An excess of moisture everywhere, but no water for bathing. Being a man, her father could plunge (and probably freeze) in one of the bathing tubs on deck. For women there existed no such facilities. Her parents claimed the *Richmond* was a merchant vessel and not equipped to carry passengers. Eliza wasn't fooled. She remembered all too well the crossing of nine years ago not to know that comfort had no place in transatlantic travel.

When you weren't being flung out of your bunk by a nasty sea, a variety of objects landing on and beside you on the slimy floor in the process, you were being subjected to the violence of boredom. Eliza turned from the window to sit down on the trunk, looking at a small brass clock with Roman numerals. Barely two days at sea, a meanly rocking ship had lifted the clock right out of its hollowed wooden niche on the wall to send it flying onto Eliza's right shoulder. Her father had plied its base to a knotted hole in the wood with one of her mother's knitting needles. Unable to cause any further physical damage, the clock now had turned to mental abuse, ticking persistently with the pretense of advancing time. It read five minutes after one presently. In an hour, Eliza knew, she would look again, and it would be ten minutes after one. The ship creaked with the regularity of a rocking chair. Eliza sighed deeply, thinking of her husband and her parents' roomy house in Richmond she had left behind. To realize that they were only two weeks into the voyage, that the ship hadn't yet covered half the distance to Le Havre, was maddening. She suddenly understood why Theodosia Burr wished for an accident when she traveled.

"Travel is no fun, Mother."

"It isn't meant to be, dear." Mrs. Monroe's fingers automatically continued knitting a baby bonnet as she looked up at her daughter from the sofa.

"I wish it would storm."

"Eliza! What a horrible thing to say. Do you want your father to be deathly ill again? Travel is by definition unpleasant. For all of us but even more so for your father. Poor James . . . He's had a rough time of it. For you to wish for a storm just to relieve your boredom is an unbelievable show of selfishness." The pale, classically sculptured face of Elizabeth Monroe was flushed with indignation. "You would do well to remember, Eliza, that you're here at your own insistence."

"I know, Mother. I'm sorry. I didn't mean it the way it sounded. I just wish George could have come along. I . . . " She stopped as the door to the cabin opened, sending in a waft of foul air coming up from the hatchways.

Monroe hastened to step inside and close it. His complexion pasty, his bluish eyes hollow and watery, he smiled as he took off his coat and proceeded to pour himself a glass of port. "Not a blasted thing to be seen on deck. A pig escaped from a pen and nobody can find it in the fog."

Eliza jumped from the rudder trunk. "I want to go look."

"Be careful up there, Eliza." Monroe punctuated the warning with his glass of port. "Stay near the house on the poop deck. And put on a scarf. It's awfully chilly. You want me to go fetch Ben or Felicity to go with you?"

Her father's admonitions aroused Eliza's impatience. "I don't need any slaves to escort me to the poop deck." In her haste to snatch her jacket from the hook of her bunk, she nearly upset the chamber pot. "Oops." She smiled mischievously before shutting the door. "I'll try not to fall overboard, Father."

The deep lines in Monroe's forehead pursed as he drank his wine. "I don't know if we were wise in taking her along, Elizabeth. A woman's place is beside her husband."

"Eliza's only seventeen, James. She has an entire lifetime to station herself next to George. Do you want to abandon your only daughter to the company of tobacco-chewing Virginians at seventeen?"

"George is a good man. If I didn't think he were I wouldn't have agreed to the match."

"George's qualities are not the issue, James. A man's ambition is reflected in his wife, and a wife can be no better than the society that forms her. It is George, who will be the beneficiary of Eliza's stay in Paris. Anyway, no one forced his hand."

"Eliza may have, though now she seems to have second thoughts."

"Her mood flies from one extreme to the other. One minute she can't contain herself at the prospect of seeing Hortense and her other friends, and the next she sits brooding in front of the window like a monk." Gathering the Venetian-striped broadcloth skirt of her dress to avoid contact with the floor, Mrs. Monroe walked toward the table. "I feel like having a little port myself."

"You think you should, in your condition?"

"Don't be silly, James."

An expression of wonder and admiration lit up Monroe's severe face as he looked at his wife. Not only was Elizabeth a great beauty blessed with an extremely agile mind, but she possessed a constitution rivaling that of the hardiest sailor aboard. Pregnant, though not yet visibly so, she endured the cramped quarters, the stench, the ceaseless hassle and noise of a groaning and tossing ship like a hardened salt. Was there a man on this earth luckier than he?

"I'll drink to the success of your mission."

"Let's hope your confidence in me is justified."

"Can you doubt it?"

"Maybe I overestimate my talents?"

"Of course you do, James. That's your strength. A man ought to overestimate his talents. How else is he going to convince those who underestimate them?"

Monroe smiled. "For all we know the affair may already have been settled. I can't imagine Livingston not doing all he can to make my presence in Paris superfluous."

Mrs. Monroe shrugged. "Livingston so far has succeeded only in failing. I can't see any reason to worry about Livingston. For one thing, he has no access to Madame Bonaparte as you do. We can bless our lucky stars that Eliza went to school with Hortense."

"The First Consul's reputation isn't that of a man influenced by his wife."

"Would you rather the connection be Livingston's?"

"No!"

"Of course we would have been smarter to cultivate a friendship with Bonaparte, but who could have dreamed that Madame de Beauharnais would marry that obscure little Corsican. I knew he was her lover, you know. I remember one morning, I was waiting in her house downstairs, when he came storming in the salon, dressed only in one of Madame de Beauharnais's white silk peignoirs and a pair of black army boots, her little dog yapping and chasing after him. When he saw me he grinned and asked if I hadn't any belladonna on me by any chance."

"Belladonna? Isn't that a deadly poison? What would you be doing carrying belladonna? What would Bonaparte be wanting with poison?"

"Do away with Félicité."

"Bonaparte wanted to poison our maid?" Monroe was stunned.

"Not Felicity, James. Félicité, Madame de Beauharnais's little dog."

"A mutt no bigger than a cat. Why didn't he kick it, if he had on army boots?"

"James . . . " Mrs. Monroe's voice hovered between impatience and amusement. "You talk as if he actually meant to kill the dog."

"Well, didn't he?"

"Of course not. It was a joke."

"Then explain why the dog came to a violent end in Italy? Wasn't that the same dog?"

"Maybe dogs aren't meant to go on military campaigns."

"Eliza said the poor mutt's head was bitten off. Hortense told her so in one of her letters."

"By the cook's big mastiff, James. Not by Bonaparte."

"Then why didn't Bonaparte punish the cook? Why did he discourage the cook from tying down the mastiff? What good was it to buy his wife a new dog when that big mastiff was still running loose in the camp?"

Elizabeth Monroe smiled. "You'd better not let on about that to Madame Bonaparte. I don't think it will help your cause."

"I have grave doubts about Madame Bonaparte helping my cause under any circumstances. The best that can be said for her is that she means well."

Mrs. Monroe's smile deepened. "You're probably right."

As the Richmond *proceeded on its course toward Le Havre, the* Surveillant, *at last, reached the shores of Louisiana . . .*

March 1803

T he dawn was not an hour old, leaving the sun swaddled in a modest morning haze. The moon still glowed overhead. The Mississippi was very wide now, 1200 to 1500 fathoms, Mme Laussat guessed. And probably as deep. The water was the color of dark amber, and Governor de Salcedo's launch slid through it without a sound.

Marie Anne Laussat smiled. A few days ago, when they finally had set foot on *terra firma*, she had made a solemn vow never again to wander from it.

Sixty-nine days, suspended between water and skies, including several days of bobbing amongst floating trees and ominously lurking alligators, waiting for the winds which were to take the *Surveillant* ashore: that had been the worst of it. To see the little church and frame dwellings of La Balise so near yet unreachable had set everyone's nerves on edge.

A pilot station situated in what seemed like a swampy locale, La Balise barely qualified as *terra firma*. No matter. It stood fast. Didn't displace objects and people, a condition Mme Laussat had come to view as a luxury. And then, there was muddy (but saltless) water for bathing, a luxury in itself.

New Orleans was still some eighty-seven miles away, their host, Juan Ronquillo, informed the Laussats. It would take another five to six days of traveling by water and overland to reach their ultimate destination. Ronquillo was chief pilot of La Balise, single-handedly regulating all traffic in the Mississippi Delta, a part of the river which required experienced navigators to successfully negotiate the countless invisible inlets, sandbars, floating obstructions and debris — when the wind collaborated. When the wind was adverse, river traffic simply stopped.

"I wish you would stop scratching, Pierre. It makes me want to imitate you."

The mattresses at Ronquillo's house were stuffed with Spanish moss, which made for a wonderfully light and springy bed, ideal for the climate. Unfortunately the moss was home to a legion of microscopic red sand fleas, which promptly descended on any humans who came near it, in particular, it would seem, on male humans of French blood.

In the bottom of the night, Mme Laussat had been roused from sleep by a figure seemingly preyed upon by St. Vitus dance. Candle light revealed the figure to be a husband of bloated features and scarlet skin, punctuated with welts left by mosquito bites.

"You shouldn't scratch," Ronquillo had advised the next morning, "or you might be mistaken for an Indian. You're lucky to be here before the mosquito season. Wait till you get to Fort St. Philippe." He smiled, flashing an uneven row of bright teeth in an unblemished, honey-complexioned face.

Marie Anne Laussat was reasonably sure that her husband's dislike for all things Spanish had taken root with Juan Ronquillo's smile. Up to then, Pierre had been merely chauvinistic, an inoffensive affliction he shared with thirty million other Frenchmen, herself included. But when they had arrived at Fort St. Philippe the following day, Pierre had gone beyond chauvinism.

"Marry a short man," her father had warned two weeks before she was to wed Laussat, "and sooner or later he will act his size."

Marie Anne had smiled indulgently at the time. Her father was full of sayings appreciated only by himself—he had pronounced his future son-in-law ambitious and a good match, after all—but at St. Philippe she began to wonder. Ronquillo's pleasantries perhaps were not in the best of taste, but he had shown himself a most gracious host, not deserving of the label "swine" Pierre had attached to him.

"Monsieur Ronquillo has been very patient with the girls," she reminded her husband, "showing them the Commander's quarters, the guard house and the powder magazine. Whatever his faults . . . " Mme Laussat was thinking primarily of the chief pilot's fondness for rum. "A man who likes children must have a tender heart."

"The Spaniards all like children. Haven't you noticed? It comes naturally to them. They are children themselves. Who else but a child could speak the execrable French they do with the confidence and exuberance they display? And, just like a child, expect to be complimented after each sentence? They like dressing up and making noise, entirely in the manner of children. Not even Bonaparte owns the number of medals Captain de Salcedo sports on his uniform. Never in peacetime have my ears been assaulted by so much booming and shooting as they have since our arrival in Louisiana. You don't think this endless noise is meant for *our* pleasure, do you?"

"You said you expected them to fire a few salvos to celebrate our arrival."

"What, I wonder, have the Spanish got to celebrate? The loss of this enormous colony to us? A few *pro forma* salvos, I'm not sayi—" Laussat stopped short as Captain de Salcedo came into view.

"This afternoon we will stop at the Duplessis plantation," he beamed good-naturedly at his guests. His thumb was frantically massaging a spot under the belt of his white, bemedaled uniform, a gesture that endeared him to Laussat.

The army of gnats, mosquitoes, and mites swarming over the swamps of St. Philippe at least selected its victims at random—feasting on Spanish and French with equal voracity. So much so, in fact, the small garrison stationed at the fort had to be changed periodically.

It was at Fort St. Philippe that Captain Manuél de Salcedo, eldest son of Governor de Salcedo, had appeared on his father's splendid launch to escort the Prefect and other French officials to New Orleans. With him were Don Beniño García Calderon—Second Lieutenant of the Louisiana Grenadiers, and following on a slightly smaller vessel, Intendant Juan Ventura Morales.

The Laussats and some of the French officials had boarded the Governor's boat, while the rest took refuge in that of the Intendant.

The trip to New Orleans was proceeding smoothly and at a leisurely pace. When possible, sleep was had on the nearest plantation. Meals were likewise taken there, or at a farm along the way. Irrespective of the origin of their ancestors, wealthy planters, and poor farmers had in common a generosity which prompted them to share whatever they had with whomever entered their home. Such was the custom, a local development owing nothing to the Old World (which partook of it with a mixture of suspicion and delight).

"Duplessis is of French descent." The Captain knew this would please Laussat. He felt no urge to venture beyond the call of duty in pleasing the French Prefect, a man ignorant of boats, the military, and the Castilian tongue, and who lacked the charm to compensate for this ignorance. A man too insignificant to make a soldier and too grandilo-quent to make a diplomat. The kind of man who might blame his wife if Duplessis were Spanish.

"Good morning, Madame."

"Good morning, Captain."

Beyond the thick sandbars the palmettos and cypresses stood mo-tionless against an endless sky: No leaves swayed; no vines moved. The gigantic canebrakes had ceased to rustle. Wild animals paused in the underbrush, parrots and smaller birds no longer shrieked and twittered. The Intendant's boat was nowhere to be seen. The sailor busy in a cor-ner of the deck stared inquiringly at the Captain, as if expecting to hear a command that would reanimate the scene. The silence seemed to frighten him. Again Marie Anne smiled. To her this was the wonder of it, the mystery of this exotic country.

But already the world had gone back into motion. The moon van-ished. Insects were buzzing above the water. Wild turkeys flurried nois-ily out of the reeds and into the trees. The sun was casting off its de-mure veil, preparing to look everyone straight in the face. In a matter of minutes the children would be awake. "I'd better go and look in on the girls."

"Pedro is watching them," de Salcedo reassured her. "The cook," he specified, realizing that roughly one-fourth of the sixteen sailors aboard answered to the name Pedro.

Laussat shook his head. How typical of the Spanish to bring along a cook when neither the Governor's nor the Intendant's boat carried pro-visions or was furnished with the necessary equipment to prepare a meal. "How far is the Duplessis plantation from New Orleans, Captain?"

"About eleven leagues."

"What does that mean in terms of traveling time?"

"I hope to be in the city tomorrow afternoon. If all goes well, we should be at the Gentilly plantation by nightfall." He smiled. "Gentilly, too, is French. We will rest there and leave before dawn to arrive in time for breakfast at Sancier's."

"Another Frenchman?"

"There are seven brothers Sancier, Monsieur Laussat. Every single one of them a Frenchman.

I f Spain mourned the loss of Louisiana, it was not visible in the behavior of her officials at New Orleans. The reception accorded the French delegation on arrival in the city was enthusiastic and, thought Laussat, typically Spanish. Cannons roared, shots rang out. The French tricolor was raised to flap in unison with the Spanish flag. There were introductions, speeches, applause and embraces. Not since he was a toddler had Laussat been kissed so fervently and so often.

Any man who could lay claim to a uniform had stepped into one and had attached to it any available silk- and hardware. The crowd at the Place d'Armes was awash in brilliantly colored sashes and the glitter of sabres and swords. The few males, who had never borne the King's arms, strutted about in tall boots with big flaps, their faces encased in high collars and triple cravats. Contrasted with this masculine display of feathers, the ladies emerged effortlessly elegant in gowns of superior imported silk, the more stunning for the fabric being devoid of the customary excess of gold and silver. Those less well off were no less captivating in dresses of calico and muslin, moving with that casual grace which seemed innate to the Creole woman, regardless of class.

The next day, which was Sunday, a High Mass was celebrated in the church near the Cabildo — the City Hall, after which the entire Cabildo membership flocked to the house reserved for Laussat at the east gate — a lovely residence belonging to the aging Marquis de Marigny — to present themselves and bid the family welcome. The clergy and local merchants followed suit. So did deputies of commerce, officers in the service of the Governor, and a procession of local residents. Governor de Salcedo himself put in an appearance.

On Monday another Mass was celebrated and, on its completion, the Governor invited the Laussats for a ride in his beautiful carriage, taking them as far as the bayou St. Jean. In the afternoon an elaborate dinner was laid out at the Gouvernatorial mansion at the corner of Toulouse and the levee, featuring indigenous specialties.

The soft-shelled turtle was a Mississippi dweller Laussat had come to appreciate in the past week. Local culinary wizards transformed this mean-tempered reptile into a delicacy called gumbo, which was served with corn. There was eel, redfish, mountains of oysters, pickled okra, teal duck, goslings, partridges, wild rice, pomegranates, spiced peaches, sweet oranges, Havana bananas, figs, hot chocolate, café-au-lait, and an endless pouring of wine, taffia, and brandy to accommodate the toasts.

Raising their glasses in honor of the new arrivals were the major commanders, the Vicar General, Intendant Morales, the rich merchants Faurie, Burthe, Vinache, Neurisse, and Daugerot – and the representatives of the Church. And a Spaniard whose name and title in themselves constituted a toast: Don Maria-Nicolas Vidal-Chavez-Etcheverry de Madrigal y Valdez, who was *Teniente Governador Civil y Auditor de Guerra de los Príncipes de la Luisiana y de la Florida Occidental, Juéz*, etc.

It was Lent, accounting for the absence of beef, veal, and lamb at the table. Raised a Roman Catholic, Laussat, like the majority of his compatriots, was no longer too clear on the details of his religion, which he practiced without much conviction. (Bonaparte was trying to rescue the creed from the disrepute into which it had fallen after the Revolution, not because of any personal devotion but because he deemed it a beneficial, unifying influence on France.)

The Spaniard looked with horror on this cavalier approach to the True Faith. In the colonies his horror had dissipated somewhat due to constant exposure to the Creole mentality, which was impossible to harness into a discipline of any kind. Undaunted by local lethargy, Spanish colonial officialdom persevered in its adherence to religious ritual, abstaining from eating red meat on Wednesdays and Fridays during Lent. Only today was Monday. Was there perhaps a law Laussat had forgotten which allowed one to eat game but forbade the consumption of domestic meats on Mondays?

"The grass freezes in winter," Governor de Salcedo replied.

"Yes?"

"The colonists don't grow grass for hay. It is spring now, the time of year when cattle fatten. Do not commit the error, my dear Prefect, of buying meat now. It tastes abominable."

"Surely, Governor, the colonists are familiar with the practice of collecting hay?"

Governor de Salcedo smiled. His son had described the French Prefect as self-important, naive and not very likeable. But the Governor disagreed — a man who had taken an instant dislike to Morales, as had Laussat, automatically came in for a certain share of his affection. That he didn't bother to conceal his dislike was rather undiplomatic of the Frenchman, but it could only enhance the Governor's own delight on discovering this unexpected ally.

"They are, Prefect, they are . . . " The Governor carefully snipped the tip from a cigar and lit it on a nearby candle flame before settling down in his silk-upholstered Louis XV side chair. "Right at this moment, when the flesh of grazing cattle is unpalatable, they are quite sensible to the idea of collecting hay." He nodded, blowing a puff of blue smoke over Laussat's head.

"Yes, Governor." Laussat grew impatient. "But it is in late *summer* that hay is gathered."

"Quite so. I remember it well."

"Why then, wasn't it gathered?"

"The Louisianian is not an ant or a squirrel, Prefect."

"Are you saying that he has less sense than these creatures?"

"Our people here deal only in the present. The future they trust to the Lord, as do we all." De Salcedo lowered his head to bring his voice nearer Laussat's hearing and switched to a more important conversational topic: "I am endeavoring to have Morales transferred to Puerto Rico. He undermines my authority here. I don't doubt he criticizes me in his dispatches to Madrid. Why else would the Court appoint Casa Calvo as interim governor? They are trying to unseat me . . . "

The prospect of having to concede authority to the Marqués de la Casa Calvo hovered before the old Governor's mind's eye like a frightening spectre. The fact that Casa Calvo wasn't expected until May did nothing to disperse the dreadful vision, made more dreadful still by his consumption of an indefinite quantity of spirits, obligatory accompaniment to each of the many toasts.

Why couldn't Casa Calvo remain in Havana? Or go to Puerto Rico? Wasn't there some honorable position in Puerto Rico to satisfy his ambition? For the Governor at his advanced age to have to receive that intriguer Morales at his own table was already more humiliation than he could bear. How was he to endure the presence of a second usurper? . . .

Before the astonished eyes of Laussat, Governor de Salcedo silently slipped to the cypress floor. A merchant and a Capuchin monk propped the inanimate form back into a semblance of its former position on the Louis XV chair, the merchant whispering that the old fellow's days were numbered, the monk urging the fainted man to confess his sins and forgive his enemies.

The Governor half-opened his eyes. "I have no enemies," he protested weakly. "I have shot them all." His own words startled him back into acute consciousness. Using his damask napkin to wipe off the sugared water Laussat had sprinkled on his face, he hastened to correct himself. "Almost all."

"One does not contemplate the shooting of one's enemies during Lent," the Capuchin admonished. Then, realizing that his statement seemed a dispensation to do so at any other time, he added piously: "Lent is a time for doing penance, for *forgiving* one's enemies."

Governor de Salcedo nodded sadly. His aim wasn't what it used to be, anyway. Accepting the cigar Laussat had retrieved from the floor, his watery eyes were focused on the Capuchin's round face. "May one contemplate the removal of one's enemies to Puerto Rico during Lent, Father?"

The Monk had never been asked the question and was forced to consider it for a moment. Puerto Rico was just another colony. Where was the harm? He was a guest of Governor de Salcedo, after all, and the Governor set an excellent table, even during Lent. "I know of no ruling against it, my son."

"I wasn't aware he had fainted," Mme Laussat told her husband. "Nobody at table mentioned anything about it. Poor Governor. I can't help feeling sorry for him."

"Don't waste your pity. The man is literally collapsing from decrepitude, yet he insists on maintaining a post he can no longer adequately fill. There is a time for entering and a time for exiting, Marie Anne. A clumsy entrance is less offensive than a graceless exit."

"Yes, well . . . " These were sentiments easily tripping off the tongue of a man of thirty-five. An additional thirty-five years might severely compromise that ease. "The Spanish will all have to make their exit shortly, won't they? So why not let the old man be? What difference can it make?"

The Laussats were waiting at the gate of the Governor's Hotel for their carriage, presently en route to deliver home another guest. The Marigny house was only three hundred steps away, but Laussat had been advised not to venture forth on foot at night, as a host of criminal elements roamed the streets.

"Let's get back inside, Pierre. What time is it?"

Laussat retrieved his gold pocket watch. "A few minutes after three."

Inside the gambling had started in earnest. An *ambigu* had been served on a large walnut sideboard, but few of the card-players rose to savor any of its many dishes.

"Would you care for something from the buffet?" Laussat realized he was hungry. Dinner, while copious, was many hours in the past.

Mme Laussat shook her head. "I prefer to sit here where the driver will notice me on entering."

"Do you mind if I go and have a bite?"

"Of course not."

Eight tables had been set up for the games, illuminated by dozens of wax candles and several oil lamps. A giant cypress punkah waved steadily back and forth above the player's heads, swatting mosquitoes and other uninvited nocturnal visitors and displacing great quantities of smoky air. The mulatto boy pulling the cord to regulate the punkah's movement was yawning.

Gaming was even more of an addiction in Louisiana than it was in France, Marie Anne thought. A veritable obsession that swept through every layer of society like some malignant contagious disease, affecting rich and poor alike. Planters gambled away their crops, sea captains the cargo entrusted to their care, *émigrés* from Saint Domingue the properties they had fled and which might no longer exist. The lower classes were said to play for lesser spoils with even greater fury.

Faced with a deck of cards, perfectly reasonable and intelligent men lost their wits, possessed of a fever that made them impervious to everything else. The few ladies present at the dinner had left, and with good reason. Mme Laussat had been told that a ball to entertain the ladies usually followed a dinner, but there had been no ball tonight. Perhaps because it was Lent.

Entrenched at the second table, Governor de Salcedo grinned broadly, cigar in hand, indicating that what he was in the process of revealing must be a winning hand. Marie Anne smiled up at the hangings over the transom in exasperation and amusement. That a person of his years and poor health would be better off in bed at three in the morning obviously didn't occur to the Governor. Her smile absentmindedly took in the Governor's son, who approached with a glass of champagne in his hand.

"Voilà, Madame." Captain de Salcedo handed Mme Laussat the champagne as if she had asked him a moment earlier to please fetch her a glass, prompting her to accept it as if she had. "Thank you, Captain. Your father seems in good spirits."

"Of course. He is winning, Madame."

Marie Anne sighed. "Of course."

"You don't approve of gaming?" He seemed disappointed.

"You might as well ask if I approve of the weather, Captain."

"I see you are philosophical. An excellent attitude for Louisiana. The people will be very happy with you!" The Captain thought over his words for a moment, then approved them with a nod. "Yes! Good night, Madame."

"Good night, Captain," Mme Laussat smiled, wondering at his hasty retreat. Her eyes above the glass followed the handsome figure of the officer as it described a *demi-tour* — back to the card tables. Of course! She should have guessed. An excellent attitude for Louisiana indeed … Blinders would be more appropriate. Nothing here was what it seemed. Experience of life elsewhere didn't apply and peripheral vision only added to the confusion.

Nationalities were blurred. The Spanish had lost their sharp edges and the French their past. One of the Sancier brothers had taken great pains to convince Pierre (in a patois barely recognizable as French) that his forebears had been amongst the first settlers at Mobile. Yet he couldn't say what part of France they had come from and was surprised to hear that Europe and France were not one and the same. Social lines were equally blurred. At the Duplessis plantation, Duplessis had introduced as his own ten mulatto children, who were indistinguishable from the slave children with whom they cavorted on the grounds. The women of color wore a *tignon* but, aside from this headgear, their dress showed nothing to set them apart from the rest.

When Pierre had voiced his surprise at this during breakfast at the Ursuline Convent (where the Laussats had gone to pay their respects), the Mother Superior admitted: "It is true that there seems little distinction among the classes so far as dress goes — you are not the first newcomer to remark on it, Monsieur — but you must keep in mind that most of these ladies will gladly submit to a diet of nothing but Indian gruel for six days in order to flaunt about in silk robes on the seventh. We would see the Saint Louis Cathedral empty on Sundays, if they were not able to show themselves in their ribboned frippery. It is the only thing that will rouse them from their indolence. No one here has any concern for the hereafter. However much we may deplore the situation, we must accept it as the will of God because there is nothing to be done to alter it. A little more *café-au-lait*, Madame?"

"In view of the Spanish presence, I would have expected a more pious attitude in general," observed Laussat. To say nothing of the good Sisters themselves, whose arrival on these shores far predated that of the Spanish monks, and whose religious authority had not been touched by the anticlerical rage of the Revolution back home. But like a child taken from his mother who, forced to rely on memory, reconstructed an imperfect picture of her later on, the Ursulines, after seventy-six years away from the Mother House in France, were conjuring up faulty images of that spiritual order and the duties it prescribed. How else to explain the religious laxity rampant among the colonists? "As a person of the cloth, how do you account for this absence of devotional spirit, Reverend Mother?"

"It is very difficult to persuade a people who are not interested in the means of securing their salvation, Prefect," the Mother Superior smiled patiently. The black cross over her white starched bib dangled in mid-air as she bent to replenish the cups of her guests and cut some fresh slices of the corn-and-rice bread the Sisters had baked that morning. "Personally, I am convinced it is the climate at fault. Have you noticed the wealth of vegetation everywhere? The orange blossoms and the magnificent Spanish dagger blooming over the rampart? Everything here grows of itself. No encouragement is required. A climate which induces its soil to sprout forth all manner of ostentatious growth isn't likely to induce a sense of humility or a fear of mortality in its human outgrowth."

"You are very tolerant toward the colonists, Reverend Mother."

"And so, my dear Prefect, should *you* be if you expect to remain among them. What is your opinion, Madame?" —

"I want to go home. I am dropping with fatigue," mumbled Madame Laussat, rubbing the sleep from her eyes. "Ah, Monsieur Morales! I beg your pardon. What did you say?"

"My carriage is at your disposal, Madame." The cool brown eyes of Intendant Morales were speckled with gold reminiscent of a tiger's pelt.

"I must admit I am tempted to accept your kind offer, but our driver is due back at any moment. Thank you."

"As you wish, Madame. Good night."

Ah, there was Pierre returning at last. "Did you ever see a portrait of the Duke of Alva?" she asked.

"There's one in the Cabildo. Why?"

"I am reminded of that portrait whenever I look at the Intendant."

"I wouldn't tell him, if I were you. The Duke of Alva used to bury people before they were dead."

"Is it in honor of these exploits that they keep his likeness in the Cabildo? Tell me, Pierre, why did Morales close the port to the Americans? Was it to spite the Governor, as people say?"

"I didn't know you were concerned for the Americans."

Marie Anne shrugged. The Americans meant nothing to her. "Madame Vinache was telling me the closure is beginning to hurt New Orleans. Can't you do something about that?"

"Don't burden your mind with these matters. Where can our driver be, I wonder?"

"Probably gambling away the carriage."

There was a sudden upset at the tables. One of the officers jumped up, shouting: "The Americans have escaped!"

The Spanish authorities recently had captured the Mason gang, put the bandits under lock and key, and then decided to return the lot to Natchez, where its arrival was awaited with bated breath. Mason *père & fils*, James Mays and his club-footed sister, and Little Wiley Harpe of "the terrible Harpes", had been escorted to their destination the previous Saturday and, it now appeared, had escaped that very day during a violent storm on the Mississippi.

Governor de Salcedo made his cautious way toward the door, unable to contain his joy. This unexpected development came as a direct result of measures taken by the Intendant who would be personally blamed for it. "The officials at Natchez will be fuming," he promised Laussat in a voice quivering with pleasure. "They were already getting out their rope." The Governor's watery eyes were overflowing as he shuffled outside. "Imagine," he wept to the French Prefect. "News like this and winning at *bouillotte* too."

Like Mme Laussat (and the lady who related the foregoing to me), I seem to have developed a soft spot for Governor de Salcedo. Of course, we none of us ever had to take orders from the Governor, though Duke Biggs, who has, admits de Salcedo "is no worse than some I knows is nearly as mad."

He was here again this morning – Biggs that is, for he now has taken it upon his impecunious self to court that bastion of virtuous (and propertied) widowhood, Mrs. Hagedoorn, a proposition which strikes me, as it must strike anyone acquainted with both individuals, as utterly lacking in promise. Yet the virtuous Mrs. H. has revealed to Duke that her Christian name is Perpetua, information certainly not released to any man since the day Mr. Hagedoorn perished in the late war.

I find it all very curious indeed, but then, my understanding of the intricate steps of courtship and the nuptial pas de deux is limited to observation from my seat in these bachelor's quarters, and what I am able to make out leaves me to pronounce most couples unsuited to dance, at least with the partner at hand. A notable exception is the Livingstons, whom years of practice have drawn together into one graceful silhouette. And never was this more apparent than during the difficult times in Paris in the spring of 1803 . . .

APRIL

April 10, 1803

T he Easter Mass at 11 A.M. in the Cathedral of Notre Dame was spectacular, Mrs. Livingston thought. Mounted police and soldiers outside, mountains of flowers and candles inside. Four regiments of cavalry preceded the succession of coaches, driven by grooms in full livery, bearing the three consuls, the ministers, and ambassadors; Bonaparte and his generals in gala uniform, the diplomats in their most elegant dark silks, the ladies in opulent Lyon velvets and embroidered satins. The official procession was welcomed by the Archbishop, Monsignor de Belloy. Bonaparte, Cambacérès, and Lebrun settled on a dais in the choir, while Madame Bonaparte ascended to a seat in one of the oblong, elevated pulpits.

The assemblage glittered and coughed beneath the thirteen tableaux depicting the Stations of the Cross and the marble-based statues of serene-faced saints and martyrs. The glazed eyes of the agonizing Jesus in the ninth station were fixed in supplication on the flowered garland in Madame Bonaparte's hair. A carved, painted figure Mrs. Livingston identified from a bronze plaque as Saint Rochus had a perplexed expression on his full face, as if he were pondering the origin of the open sores in his flesh and the presence of two dogs at his feet. Unfamiliar with the myths and sanctified beings crowding the Roman Catholic landscape, Mrs. Livingston pondered along with him. Exotic smells wafted through the vaulted halls. Weighed down by the gold thread in his holy-day chasuble, the old Monsignor turned slowly, his voice quivering with years and emotion as he sang to the congregation. A burst of organ and male voices vibrated from the choir loft in response.

Mrs. Livingston wasn't a Roman Catholic and had no intention of ever being one. Only, at moments like these, when one's senses were being pleasantly assaulted from every direction, it was difficult not to fall prey to a vague longing for things indefinable.

This was the second Easter Mass in Paris since the Revolution. Mrs. Livingston was not an admirer of the First Consul but there was no denying the man had a clever side to him; always knowing just how far he could go, how much he could get away with. His instincts were uncanny. The previous year he had elected himself first consul for life and, while there had been some grumbling, the deed was done. One step at a time seemed to be his motto, with regard to the satisfaction of his personal ambitions as well as where it concerned the granting of the wishes of the people.

Having known want himself, he was well placed to anticipate the people's needs. No matter how enthusiastically the French might have cheered the Revolution and the new calendar which followed in its wake a decade earlier, the fact remained that the revolutionary calendar, with its lovely monthly names of *Brumaire, Germinal, Fructidor*, etc. counted ten days to the week. Those working for a living had to do so nine rather than six days. The laborer looked forward to a shave and a clean shirt on the seventh day, not the tenth. If Bonaparte re-instituted the Mass on Easter Sunday, and on all the Sundays in between, could the abolishment of the *Décadi* be far behind?

A vision in white lace and gauze, Madame Bonaparte looked ravishing in the ambo. Mrs. Livingston recognized other ladies. Seated two rows ahead, the Countess de Genlis was adorned in a hat of the same festive green as her coat. Majestically upright in green and gold, she bore no resemblance to the untidy individual Mrs. Livingston had visited the previous morning.

One would think she was accustomed by now to the informal morning dress of the Parisian. Actually, she had been disappointed rather than shocked on being confronted with Mme de Genlis's disorderly person, unable to reconcile the great lady of her acquaintance with the female clad in a robe which would have required more than one serious washing to yield back its original burgundy color and velour suppleness. A Countess de Genlis enthroned amongst piles of paper, volumes of verse, watercolor sketches, toothbrushes, an ink-stand, pots of partly eaten jam, eggshells, a roll, an empty coffee cup, paper flowers, a candle stick, a tress of false hair and a piece of leftover brie.

This was especially regrettable since a gentleman had come to call.

Of course, this impossible young man by the name of Beyle, alias Stendhal, who couldn't refrain from calling things by their given name, à la Bonaparte, hardly qualified as a gentleman. Yet the Countess seemed no more disturbed by Beyle's unvarnished accounts than Beyle seemed concerned with the unpolished appearance of his hostess. Wearing a frayed coat of an uncivil brown and trousers splattered with dark matter, Beyle's attire was on a par with his speech.

Mrs. Livingston politely accepted the cup of hot chocolate Mme de Genlis offered, wondering if she had arrived too early. Hers was a very special visit. Not one she would care for other people to know about. But Beyle showed no inclination to depart, slurping his chocolate with slow, childlike sips, and telling stories in between. And, for whatever reasons of her own, Mme de Genlis gurgled with pleasure at whatever he said.

"How was it at Mademoiselle Duchenois'?" she prompted him. "Did you spend an interesting evening, Monsieur Beyle?"

Beyle shrugged, picking up the piece of leftover Brie. "These gatherings of actors and writers are always the same. I found five cads there, sitting in a circle with an old lady dwarf who prided herself on playing the piano, and soon proved her pride misplaced. La Duchenois stooped under the weight of her gowns and the cyrus around her neck. Millevoye peered through his spectacles for a full five minutes and still managed to mistake somebody's lap for a chair."

"Ah, Monsieur Beyle . . . " The Countess twisted the tress of false hair in delight. "What else? Oh, do tell us more!"

To Mrs. Livingston's relief, Beyle claimed he was late for an appointment. Maybe it was something beyond the grasp of the inartistic temperament, she thought, eager to overlook the bizarre behavior of her hostess. Artists were eccentric, and there was evidence aplenty of the lady's artistry. But what of Beyle? What writing was there in existence bearing the name Stendhal? Of course he was still very young. Not that she was likely ever to reach for the fruits flowing from this man's mind. Hearing him speak was painful enough.

"Mademoiselle Lenormand is here, Madame."

When the servant girl announced the arrival of the famous seeress, Beyle hurriedly stalked out. Mrs. Livingston became aware of an eerie feeling in her stomach. If Robert should find out about this he would be furious. Worse, he would laugh. Yet it was with him in mind that she had asked for this encounter. Mlle Lenormand's predictions were simply too accurate too often to be dismissed as coincidence. If her powers weren't wondrous, why would important people like Bonaparte, the painter David, Mme de Staël, Talma, and countless others consult her? There was nothing to be lost in hearing someone labeled the sibyl of St. Germain. Regardless of whether the prediction proved favorable or not, peace of mind was sure to follow. For herself in any event. If Robert couldn't accept the verdict, so be it. There came a time when the patience of even the most devoted wife ran out. Robert's frustration and despondence had been indulged beyond endurance. It was entirely possible, Mrs. Livingston thought, that if this New Orleans matter was brought to her attention one more time, she might scream.

Mlle Lenormand wasn't the imposing figure her fame would indicate. Young and sharp-featured, she promptly deposited two caged toads on Mrs. Livingston's knees. One was horned — a frightful sight to behold; the sort of creation one imagined one could meet up with in the outpourings of Beyle. Was this really necessary?

"Your lover, dear lady, will return to you forthwith," Mademoiselle Lenormand said pointedly.

Mrs. Livingston momentarily forgot about the proximity of the amphibians to stare in astonishment at Mme de Genlis, then at the seeress. Was this promise intended for her? At no time in her life had she known a man other than Robert. "I have no lover," she gasped finally.

"Of course." Mademoiselle's voice was soothing. "I understand, Madame.

Mrs. Livingston wasn't pleased. Sibyl of St. Germain or no, assumption did not an oracle make. "Mademoiselle . . . "

Sensing the irritation of her guest, Mme de Genlis quickly interjected: "Madame Livingston knows the whereabouts of her lovers, Mademoiselle. She isn't here today to inquire about love. The object of her concern is her husband, Monsieur Livingston."

"A business matter?" Mademoiselle whisked away the cage from Mrs. Livingston's lap and placed it on the eggshells. She poured over Mrs. Livingston's left palm for several long minutes. "Your husband is alive," she concluded. "What is the question? The question?" she repeated, pressing the tips of her fingers against her temples and closing her eyes.

"Well . . . " Mrs. Livingston didn't quite know how to formulate it. "I would like to know if my husband will be successful in settling a matter in which he has been unsuccessful so far?"

Mrs. Livingston suddenly wished she were elsewhere. This wasn't what she had anticipated. The young, impatient draper's daughter had nothing about her of the fortuneteller. If it weren't for the unorthodoxy of the caged toads, one might mistake her for a governess. This didn't inspire confidence. Standing in the middle of the cluttered room with her hand pressed to her forehead and her eyes closed, she looked like a young bourgeoise suffering from migraine.

"Yes." Mademoiselle opened her eyes, smiling. "Your husband, dear lady, will be successful."

"Really?" Mrs. Livingston couldn't help herself. "When?"

"Any day now, Madame." She retrieved the cage and turned to Mme de Genlis. "I must say goodbye."

"Surely, you will have a cup of hot chocolate, Mademoiselle?"

Mademoiselle had no time to indulge in the drinking of hot chocolate. It wasn't her custom to leave the Rue de Tournon to see clients at home. The Countess thanked her profusely for the great favor.

"I suppose I had better get dressed?" she asked then, as if dependent on Mrs. Livingston's consent. "Madame Bernadotte is expecting me to *déjeuner.*"

Mrs. Livingston rose. "I won't detain you another moment." She expressed her gratitude for the arranged interview and headed for the door. "I wish you a pleasant lunch, Madame."

"Pleasant? You must have in mind a different Madame Bernadotte. I am speaking of the chubby little Désirée Clary, who has made it her vocation in life to weep through every meal."

"Tears are the fashion," Mrs. Livingston replied automatically, distracted by Mlle Lenormand's prediction.

"You are thinking of Madame Bonaparte or Madame Talleyrand? Yes . . . " The Countess gave an understanding nod. "But the tears of these ladies follow a classical pattern. Madame Talleyrand, for one, refuses to weep unless there is a gentleman near enough to be moved into offering his assistance. Such a use of tears commands respect, you will agree, Madame, especially by one so devoid of the capacity for thought as Madame Talleyrand. Madame Bonaparte's flow seems more spontaneous, true, but hers is a more generous nature overall. It would be doing Madame Bonaparte a grave injustice to assume her weeping to be without design. Behind Désirée Bernadotte's tears there exists no such intelligence. She cries because the soup is cold, or because it is too hot; because the General is out, or because he is in; because the sun shines on the strawberries, or because it is too early in the season for strawberries . . . In short, she weeps only for pleasure, which is the more painful to her guests since she expects to be consoled by them. If tears are the fashion, Madame, it is not a fashion becoming to all."

Looking at the happy green *tenue* of Mme de Genlis in the Cathedral, Mrs. Livingston hoped the weeping Désirée served a good lunch at least. "An odd person, this Mademoiselle Lenormand," she mumbled to the perplexed Saint Rochus.

Yet, somehow, a feeling of optimism pervaded one after seeing her. And the feeling seemed to have communicated itself to Robert— without his knowing the cause, for she had not yet found the courage to confess to her little adventure.

Unable to see her husband, who was segregated in the right aisle with the other gentlemen, Mrs. Livingston's thoughts were focused on him. "Whoever you are, dear Saint Rochus," she prayed, "please put in a good word for Robert on this beautiful Easter Sunday."

April 10

I n spite of the elaborate Easter Service and other measures pointing up Bonaparte's desire to do away with the Décadi, the Consulate (and the country) still followed the revolutionary calendar and, after the Mass, the First Consul called an emergency meeting. Hastening to the Palace of St. Cloud were Admiral Denis Decrès, Minister of the Navy; François de Barbé-Marbois, Minister of Finance; and Charles Maurice de Talleyrand-Périgord, Minister of Foreign Affairs.

Talleyrand was less than thrilled. The time was spring — even the revolutionary calendar admitted to it being *Germinal* — but the weather was proving both misnomers. In the princely-decorated room where the First Consul awaited his ministers a fire flared high within its marble confines; egged on by a freezing wind blowing from the north, it struggled valiantly against the profusion of unreceptive marble and stone. On a hot summer day this exquisite room, in this palace built for kings, must be a haven, Talleyrand thought, as he reached for the Louis XV chair nearest the hearth and Marbois and Decrès seated themselves on identical chairs at a nearby table.

Energetically pacing up and down the stone floor and brandishing a paper in the air, Bonaparte wasted no time. "Our good friend George III is up to his old tricks again!" Still pacing, he read from the paper in his hands.

"His Majesty thinks it necessary to acquaint the two houses of Parliament that, as very considerable preparations are being made in the ports of France and Holland, he has judged it expedient, though these preparations are avowedly directed to colonial service, to adopt additional measures of precaution for the security of the dominions; and he relies with perfect confidence on their public spirit and liberality to enable His Majesty to adopt such measures as circumstances might appear to require for supporting the honour of his crown and the essential interest of his people . . . "

Bonaparte dropped the paper on the gold-inlaid surface of the table before Marbois and Decrès. "Needless to say, Citizen Ministers, which majesty is speaking here. Only an Englishman could circumlocute a call to arms in this way."

Decrès nodded. "Obviously, they know about the cession."

"*Justement!*" The First Consul pointed an index finger at his minister of the Navy and held it there. "That's it exactly. Louisiana is nothing compared to the conquests the English have made all over the globe, yet the jealousy they feel at the restoration of this colony to France is so obsessive, they will risk everything to take it from us. This is how they will begin the war, make no mistake about it, gentlemen. Very well. If George III wants war, he shall have it. But he shall not have the Mississippi that he covets. The conquest of Louisiana would be easy for the English, if only they took the trouble to descend there. It is their love of subterfuge and circumvolution alone that is delaying that descent. I haven't a moment to lose in putting it out of their reach. I think of selling the colony to the United States."

Decrès and Marbois gasped. Talleyrand yawned. Not used to acknowledging the world before eleven, he had been forced to rise early that morning to attend Easter Mass and now be a witness to a scenario for which he could have furnished the dialogue. The First Consul had informed him of his decision to sell Louisiana to the United States a few days ago. Talleyrand had been surprised but could see nothing harmful to France in the ceding of a colonial possession that had been a vast financial drain in the past. He wasn't an expansionist. It was true that the British couldn't be trusted, but it was equally true that the British Ambassador had approached him with a bribe to help prevent the outbreak of hostilities between England and France.

He had accepted the bribe, of course, though none was necessary to convince him of the desirability of keeping the peace, especially at a time when France could ill afford another war. But Bonaparte's prime genius was military and his own, if any, was diplomatic, two talents that didn't travel gracefully arm in arm.

Once he was decided, there was no swaying the First Consul. The decision might seem as if ripened under the collective wisdom of ministerial council and, on occasion, this was the case, though, once formed, it emerged a purely Bonapartian creation. For the British to entertain hopes that either he or Lucien Bonaparte (the brightest of the First Consul's brothers was a party to the bribe) might persuade Bonaparte into following a course not his own, proved their fundamental misreading of his character.

Napoleon Bonaparte had decided to make war on Britain and to finance that war with the proceeds of the sale of Louisiana to the United States. Whether or not his ministers agreed would in no way affect his decision.

Marbois would approve the sale. A native of Lorraine—a Frenchman with the mind of a German—Marbois was fascinated with sum totals, numbers and percentages, wandering within the maze of France's entangled finances with energies stirred to rapture. Order and balance were his muses. The excessive pouring over numerical symbols had made him far-sighted and wary. He walked with measured steps in the middle of the road, carefully watching traffic on either side while holding on to his purse. It was whispered that Marbois and Talleyrand were alike in their love of money. The very thought struck Talleyrand as absurd. His own love of money was selfish—indifferent to that belonging to others. The idea of millions of *livres tournois* rolling in the Republic's coffers in the event Louisiana should be sold hardly set his blood afire, unlike Marbois, whose mathematical turn of mind would have him twisting in ecstasy at the prospect.

The passionate Decrès, on the other hand, would protest the sale. A soldier in every honorable sense of the word—brave, loyal, dutiful—the forty-one-year-old Minister of the Navy was territorially oriented. That he believed in the American cause and had fought in their war under the Count de Grasse didn't detract from this orientation, any more than Marbois would be influenced by the affection for the United States he had developed during his years as First Secretary to the French Ministry there, and by his having married an American. This unfortunate female, twenty years Marbois's junior, had suffered a nervous collapse and was presently living locked away in a house near her husband's chateau at Noyers.

Talleyrand couldn't help wondering why the young woman's reputedly wealthy merchant father had made no effort to reclaim his only daughter, if only temporarily. Talleyrand had been an exile long enough to know the balm inherent simply in being at home, among one's own kind. Mme Marbois's unstable mental health was of fairly recent date. Maybe it was not irreversible? Marbois was a staunchly moral man; not one likely to accept a bribe or deflect the nation's revenue into his own pockets. Mme Marbois would never lack for proper care and attention. But was this really all that could be done for the poor creature? Or was it the lot of the staunchly moral to be devoid of intuition, imagination, insight? One of those ironies of life from which the immoral like himself could derive comfort? The reward for allowing one's illegitimate children to call one "papa" and help them along in this world? The thought so amused Talleyrand, it roused his consciousness to the scene before him. Was he being addressed?

"If we may be allowed to intrude upon your pleasant reveries, Citizen Minister, perhaps you would answer the question?" Bonaparte seemed to be saying.

"Certainly," Talleyrand replied amiably. "What is the question?"

"The First Consul has heard the Admiral's and my own views on the United States," Marbois said. "He would now like to hear yours."

Talleyrand shifted his position in the chair so that the fire would favor his left leg instead of his right. "I was ostracized by Philadelphian society for escorting a handsome lady of mixed blood through the streets of their city. President Washington refused to receive me. The present American President, Monsieur Jefferson, thought it wiser not to invite me to Monticello"

"All of this is irrelevant!" Decrès cried. He turned his flushed face to Bonaparte. "The colony of Louisiana has just been ceded to us. It depends on you, General, to preserve it. We are still at peace with England. It wouldn't be wise to abandon our most important future colony for the mere possibility of war." He tugged impatiently at the collar of his admiral's uniform, the constriction of which hampered his flow of words. "This premature decision will cause nothing but regrets. Louisiana will be an inestimable resource of trade. Just look at Paris! All the luxury you see there is the result of colonial industry. There can be no navy without colonies, no colonies without a powerful navy."

"Yes, yes . . . There's no need to tear apart your coat, Denis. I haven't yet sold the colony." Unable any longer to watch his old comrade's vain struggle with his apparel, Bonaparte decided to lend a helping hand. "Stand still. There! I can't very well sell it, can I, when it isn't yet in my possession? If, however, I leave our enemies the least time, I shall only transmit an empty title to the Americans. They ask for only one town, but I already consider the entire colony as lost."

"General Bonaparte, please!" His neck liberated, Decrès's words were able to keep pace with his passion. "The political system of Europe is preserved only by a skillfully combined resistance of many against one. If we are to submit to the tyranny of England, our trade and navigation will collapse. You cannot, by your resignation, acknowledge England as the sovereign of the seas. To renounce Louisiana is to admit that no one can possess colonies except at her pleasure. It doesn't become you to fear the kings of England."

"If I feared the kings of England, Admiral, would I challenge them? Ha! At last." Bonaparte turned toward the opening door and the young servant girl who was making a rather clumsy entrance carrying a tray laden with dishes, butter rolls, garnished sandwiches, silverware, condiments, and steaming pots of coffee and chocolate. "Two hours to prepare a simple meal! Are you all asleep in the kitchen?"

"No, General, only Pelagie," the girl replied earnestly, flustered by her disclosure being met with smiles. She let down her burden on the table near Marbois, covering George III's message to Parliament. "Shall I wake her?"

"Let's not get reckless." Bonaparte picked up the nearest roll. "The less Pelagies snooping about the corridors, the better—Why do you suppose we came here?—Ha! These are good." He wiped the butter from his mouth with the back of his band and sat down at the table, motioning for the girl to leave — "Thank you" — and for Decrès, who stood brooding by one of the silk-draped windows — "Come, Denis" — to join them.

"Louisiana can indemnify us for all our losses," Decrès countered ardently, ignoring the invitation. "There isn't a single port, a single city in the world so destined for importance as New Orleans. The closeness of the American States already makes it one of the most commercial on the globe. The Mississippi doesn't reach there until it has received twenty other rivers, most of which are bigger than the finest rivers in Europe. Forts exist. Fertile land is being exploited. The climate is like that of Hindustan and the distance only a fourth as great. Navigation to the Indies, by doubling the Cape of Good Hope, has changed the course of trade in Europe, ruining Venice and Genoa. What will happen if, at the Isthmus of Panama, a simple canal should be dug to connect the one ocean with the other? The revolution which navigation will then experience will be more formidable still. Louisiana would be on this new route and the inestimable value of this colony will then be realized.

Bonaparte put down his knife. "Maybe you will also tell me that the Americans are destined to become too powerful for Europe in a few centuries? Personally, I don't hold with such remote fears. I'm confident that we can shortly expect rivalries among the states. The confederations called perpetual only last till one of the contracting parties finds it in its interest to break them. Even so, Louisiana will be more useful to the policy and — yes, Denis — to the commerce of France, in the hands of this growing power than if I should try to keep it."

"I agree with the First Consul," said Marbois, reaching for the silver coffeepot with one hand while passing the plate of open sandwiches to Talleyrand with the other. "We shouldn't hesitate to give up that which we are bound to lose. War with England is inevitable. How shall we defend the colony with our inferior naval forces against that power? The American States have a dispute with the Spanish government and threaten New Orleans. Louisiana is barely inhabited. There aren't fifty soldiers in the entire Province. Can we rebuild fortifications that are in ruin and construct a chain of forts along a frontier four-hundred leagues long?" He paused to wash down a bite of ham and bread with coffee, then turned his bespectacled face to Bonaparte.

"If England lets you undertake this work, Citizen First Consul, it's because she will enjoy seeing you deplete your resources in efforts from which she alone will derive the benefit. Louisiana is open to the north by the Great Lakes. If the English show themselves at the mouth of the Mississippi, New Orleans will fall into their lap. The takeover would be easier still for the Americans. They can reach the Mississippi by several navigable rivers. To be masters of the colony, it would be enough for them to enter it . . . "

Decrès stared angrily at the drapes. Everybody was eating as though the subject under discussion were a bauble to be pawned to pay the tailor. In the First Consul's case this wasn't unduly disturbing — even with enemy cannon staring him in the face, General Bonaparte experienced no loss of appetite — and Marbois, well, Marbois was a functionary — a man with the soul of a grocer — who had in common with Bonaparte only that he, too, came from a country annexed by France. But Talleyrand was French to the marrow. Nothing in the Foreign Minister's arsenal of schematic weaponry directed toward power and riches was positioned at the expense of the country. This was the redeeming factor. France came above all else to Talleyrand and, because of it, he stood absolved of all else. Why then, didn't he speak up?

" . . . The colony has existed for a century, but the latest counts of its population and resources attest to its weakness. If it becomes French . . . "

Decrès could it endure it no longer. "How can you keep silent, sir!" he burst out to Talleyrand, "when the whole of France is at stake?"

Talleyrand's hooded eyes opened slightly in surprise. "I can see no dismemberment of the mother country in the ceding of a colonial possession, Admiral. A possession, moreover, which has proven to be anything but profitable in the past."

"Don't get so worked up, Denis. There are no enemy sails in sight here." Bonaparte pointed to the chair he had just vacated. "Sit down. Drink your coffee before it gets cold. You shouldn't be fooled by Citizen

Talleyrand's inattention. His eyes may be closed but his ears are wide open." The First Consul grinned at his foreign minister, who was repositioning himself near the fire. He lifted a few logs from the iron-wrought stand and threw them on the flames—"There!"—before returning his attention to Marbois:

"Go on, Citizen Minister."

"As I was saying, if Louisiana becomes French and acquires importance, there will be in its very prosperity a germ of independence developing before long. The more the colony prospers, the less chance we stand of keeping it. The exclusive rights that the parent countries exercise over these remote settlements get more tenuous every day. The people feel humbled at being dependent on some small country in Europe, and will liberate themselves as soon as they become aware of their own strength."

"The efforts of the French to establish colonies on the American continent have proven everywhere abortive, whereas the English seem everywhere successful," Bonaparte mused. "Why is that?"

"Because the English are patient and industrious and don't fear the silence of newly settled countries. The Frenchman requires society. He needs to talk to his neighbors. He starts on the experiment willingly enough, but at the first setback drops the spade for the chase."

"Then how do you explain our success in the West Indies?" asked Decrès, finally propelled by hunger to investigate the remaining edibles on the tray.

"The slaves do all the work in the West Indies," said Marbois.

"Are you pretending they don't elsewhere?"

"I can't decide whether to maintain or abolish slavery," the First Consul admitted. "Who works the land in Louisiana?"

"Slavery has given the colony half its population," Marbois told him. "An inexcusable blunder was made in suddenly granting the slaves of Saint Domingue a freedom for which they were not prepared. Of all the scourges that afflict the human race, slavery is the worst. But, without dwelling for the moment on how it could be abolished, let's just say that the colonies where it is practiced are more a burden than an asset to

France. The colonial laws are in collision with those at home. For what good purpose should you subject yourself to embarrassment in Louisiana, Citizen Consul? The holding of yet another colony with slaves will bring us more expense than profit."

Decrès begged to differ. "If we must abandon Saint Domingue, General, Louisiana will take its place. Consider the injury to France if the colony becomes a competitor in producing those things of which we now enjoy the monopoly. Spain has been unable to prevent experiments with the vine, the olive and the mulberry tree, and all have succeeded only too well. If Louisiana becomes free, Provence and our vineyards will face a fearful competition with a country new and of boundless extent. If, on the other hand, it is subjected to our laws, any sort of culture competitive with our own would be prohibited."

"Do you hope to establish the exclusive system in a country next to the United States? My dear Admiral . . . " Marbois smiled, shaking his greying head. "The reign of prohibitory law is over. The sugar cane and coffee tree are cultivated everywhere and at small expense. There are lands in the tropics far more extensive than our West Indies islands and fit for the same culture. Monopoly is impossible when production is so widespread. The Louisianians won't let it strangle their trade. Do you propose to fight resistance by force? Don't expect from the colonists any attachment to your person, Citizen First Consul. They admire your fame and exploits, certainly, but the love of nations is reserved for those rulers they see as the authors of their happiness. The Louisianians have lost all recollection of France. Constantly varying laws, quarrels in which they are strangers, parent countries which barter them like merchandise, all have killed affection for masters two-thousand leagues away . . . "

When Talleyrand opened his eyes again it was night. Floating momentarily between a state of wakefulness and dream, he was suddenly seized by a terrorizing vision of his future fate. Nothing in the room had changed except time, which had passed and would continue to pass without his knowledge, his body trapped in some space beyond it, his consciousness condemned to witnessing the same tableau in perpetuity.

Season would follow season; kings would die; great events would shake the world, while he would be strapped to a chair in a drawing room of the Palace of St. Cloud, a helpless spectator to a play he had seen before, featuring players who doggedly stuck to a text he knew by heart.

The silk handkerchief trembled in his hand as he mopped the cold sweat from his brow, an activity proving that at least he wasn't dead, as he had believed for one incredible moment. Vague recollections slipped into his mind. There had been a dinner, he remembered now. Brandy glasses and flasks containing various beverages sitting on the gold-and-leather tabletop assured him that time was running its normal (if paralyzingly slow) course. Candles and oil were burning down in familiar fashion. He noticed an urn with still warm coffee on the lacquered stand next to his chair, a fresh cup and saucer beside it.

He was wide-awake now. A glance at his pocket watch told him he had napped a mere ten minutes. How much longer was he to be a hostage to this predictable performance? The coffee was good.

"It would be best, Citizen Ministers, if you would all spend the night here," Bonaparte was saying. "Everyone is tired. We shall continue the discussion in the morning."

Talleyrand nodded. Here, at last, was a variation in the script (Tomorrow they could return to the text). "I am curious," he found himself asking Marbois, "have you any news from Madame Marbois's father?"

Marbois lowered his silver-framed spectacles to stare at Talleyrand with naked, startled eyes. "My father-in-law died in ninety-three. I didn't realize you knew Mr. Moore, Monsieur.

Talleyrand smiled. He had never met Mr. Moore. "I am sorry to hear it."

April 11

Dressed in the previous day's military attire, minus the hat, the First Consul stormed into the room, waving the dispatches he had just received from the French Ambassador in London. "The English," he shouted by way of greeting, "now want Lampedousa, which doesn't belong to me, and at the same time want to keep Malta for ten years . . . " He stopped momentarily to assure himself of the presence of his ministers, who sat shivering in their city clothes in the palatial morning chill.

"This island, fortified to the limits of military genius, would be another Gibraltar to them. Giving it up would be robbing the southern provinces of trade with the east. And, if that weren't enough, gentlemen, they want me to immediately evacuate Holland! Irresolution and deliberation are no longer in season! I renounce Louisiana!

"I know the price of what I abandon, since my first diplomatic act with Spain was the recovery of it. I renounce it with the greatest regret, but to try to keep it would be folly.

"I direct you, Citizen Marbois, to negotiate this affair with the envoys of the United States. Don't wait for the arrival of Monroe. Talk today with Livingston. I will need a considerable amount of money for this war and I don't care to start it by levying new taxes. I want fifty million and for less than that I won't treat. Is that clear?"

Decrès seemed crushed, but resigned to the inevitable.

Talleyrand, too, kept silent, happy to see the meeting ended. Only Marbois, after having pleaded in favor of the sale the night before, suddenly expressed concern for the people of Louisiana.

"Do we have the right, Citizen Consul, to abandon what the Germans call the souls? Can the souls of the colonists be subjected to a contract of sale?"

Bonaparte didn't hesitate: "Go and send your maxims to London. I'm sure they will be greatly appreciated there. In the meantime, contact the American Minister. Present him my offer without any subterfuge.

Observe secrecy and recommend it to the Americans. No one outside this room knows of my intentions. You will keep in touch with Citizen Talleyrand. Inform him of your progress." He turned to his foreign minister: "If I followed *your* advice, France would confine her borders to the left bank of the Rhine and make war just to maintain them and prevent dismemberment of the country."

Talleyrand smiled his enigmatic smile. "I see no danger of that happening, Citizen First Consul." When Bonaparte gave him a long look, he added: "Dismemberment of France, that is."

April 11

L ivingston couldn't recall how often he had sat in this charming room of the Hotel Gallifet in the Rue du Bac, waiting to see Talleyrand. About as often as he had come up against the Foreign Minister's uncooperativeness would be a safe guess. This couldn't be the case today. His presence at the Foreign Ministry was "highly desirable" the message read. Highly desirable?

As recently as *Germinal 1*, or exactly eighteen days ago, Talleyrand had stated in no uncertain terms that Monroe should be waited for and heard "in order that every matter susceptible of contradiction, be completely and definitely discussed."

News of Monroe's landing at Le Havre on Friday had reached Livingston yesterday, on his and Mary's return home from the Easter Mass. Talleyrand had been informed. The trip from Le Havre to Paris could be made in two to three days. So why, with Monroe virtually beating at the city gates, was his own presence at the Rue du Bac highly desirable all of a sudden? Talleyrand was up to something. This much was clear.

"Ah, Monsieur Livingston . . . " Tapered fingers extended, Talleyrand limped from a nearby room. "I see with pleasure that you received my message. Enter, sir. Be seated, please." As usual, the Foreign Minister was civility personified.

"The pleasure, sir, is entirely mine." Livingston sat down in one of the copper velvet chairs, waiting for the familiar retinue of manservants to finish their silent ritual with decanters and glasses. Talleyrand was fond of *chinoiseries*. Wherever the eye turned, it was met with translucent porcelain figures, bronzes, ivory statues, and other carved exotica. Livingston nodded toward an amber-colored liquid on being presented with a lacquered tray of flasks. At last, the liveried retinue departed.

"Your government, Mr. Livingston, ought to be well persuaded that the First Consul bears the same affection for the American people that has animated France at all times."

"I don't doubt it, sir." The amber liquid tasted like a mixture of cognac and a certain liqueur the name of which escaped Livingston at the moment. "And I won't delay in conveying these sentiments to my government. However, if you permit me, Mr. Talleyrand, the persuasion of my government would be made a lot easier if the First Consul gave some evidence of his affection. There is still the unresolved matter of New Orleans."

"Perhaps your government would be interested in purchasing the entire colony of Louisiana, Mr. Livingston?"

"What?" Livingston's first reaction was to smile. What new trick was this? Or had he misunderstood? "The entire colony of Louisiana, you say, sir?"

"The entire colony without reservation, yes, Monsieur Livingston. The First Consul has decided to give up Louisiana and he intends for the United States to have it."

After endless months of stalling and hedging in the matter of ceding a single town, Bonaparte suddenly "intended" for the United States to buy the entire colony? How was he, a mere minister, expected to make such a momentous decision? He had received no instructions for this completely unexpected eventuality, as Talleyrand and the First Consul must know. The price would be far in excess of that authorized by Congress for New Orleans. Something wasn't right.

Livingston stared at the flask of amber liqueur without seeing it. Talleyrand loved to spring surprises on people. A dinner Mrs. Livingston and he had attended in these very rooms came to mind. Talleyrand was justly famous for his *petits soupers*. No one in Paris could rival the Epicurean rewards of his table. There was the Second Consul, of course, but Cambacérès was a fanatic who served his guests sixty dishes and denied them the pleasure of speech. At Talleyrand's the conversation was as choice as the cuisine.

As the majordomo announced the dish to be served next, silence fell into the room. The majordomo was a performer aware of his own importance, who would describe the dishes with great dramatic flourish, as if he were declaiming Racine. The delicacy in question was an enormous salmon, an incredible catch, and Talleyrand's majordomo carried it like a treasure on extended arms for the select gathering to admire. "There isn't another salmon like it!" the host exclaimed, and went on to detail the unique properties of that giant among fish, that miraculous catch. He was still at it when the majordomo tripped and fell face to the floor, sending the culinary wonder sprawling all over the diamond-shaped tiles. The guests howled in despair at the catastrophe.

Only Talleyrand retained his Talleyrandian composure. "Bring on the other one!" he ordered.

This sort of prearranged incident was called "mystifying" — and was very much in vogue. There was a man by the name of Musson who was the professional mystifier *par excellence*. Livingston doubted, though, that the Foreign Minister had made use of Musson's expertise to set up the salmon episode. In the labyrinth that was Talleyrand's mind, the elements needed to achieve mystification were likely to spring up naturally. Was this another such dubious diversion?

"The First Consul expects negotiations to start today."

"But Mr. Monroe is expected to arrive tomorrow."

"It is unlikely, sir, that Mr. Monroe will be better prepared than you for a decision which goes infinitely beyond anything you have asked from us. The First Consul well realizes this. He, therefore, would like you to meet with Monsieur de Barbé-Marbois this very evening and begin the discussions." Noticing the look of surprise on Livingston's face, Talleyrand smiled. "It is he the First Consul has elected to negotiate this matter with you and with your colleague when he arrives. You are acquainted with Monsieur Marbois, I believe?"

"Yes and so is Mr. Monroe." Talleyrand seemed unaffected by his being passed over in favor of Marbois. No doubt because, whatever the outcome, there was no likelihood of a bribe in any dealings with the Americans.

"As you know, Mr. Livingston, London is well aware of your country's measures to obtain New Orleans. But it can't guess at those we are taking now and in which the First Consul wants to observe the greatest secrecy. I highly recommend that you do likewise. Your country has everything to gain from this advice."

Livingston nodded. He was too stunned to speak.

April 11-12

he First Consul estimates the price at eighty-million francs," said Marbois, adjusting the silver-framed spectacles through which he watched Livingston's reaction.

"Eighty-million," Livingston repeated matter-of-factly.

Let's see . . . That came to about fifteen million dollars. "Eighty-million francs!?"

"Do you consider the price too high, Mr. Livingston?" Marbois smiled, a smile suggesting only a fool would answer the question in the affirmative.

"I couldn't say." Livingston was quite candid. He could afford to be. There was no need to analyze the utterances of Marbois for any hidden meanings as there was with Talleyrand. The fact that Marbois hadn't hesitated to slap another thirty million francs to Bonaparte's asking price wouldn't have changed Livingston's opinion, had he known of it. Rather, he would have interpreted the addition as merely the exercise of a businessman's acumen—one who instinctively understood that his client's property was of far greater value than supposed. "How can I say, when the extent of the colony isn't known?"

"You will receive Louisiana to the extent that it had in the hands of Spain, when Spain ceded it to France," Marbois assured him. "The First Consul was specific on this point."

Livingston couldn't help smiling. "I don't doubt the First Consul's good intentions, Mr. Marbois, but this hardly tells us anything specific with regard to that extent, does it?"

It was a little like buying a cat in a sack. The sack had been tossed from nation to nation over the centuries in exchange for other goods, the country holding onto it satisfied to glimpse the creature's size and feel its weight, not a one troubling to trace its outline and establish its true worth.

"This is a circumstance that can't be helped and which, for all we know, may well turn out to your country's advantage. The First Consul has charged me to make you the offer without any subterfuge. He is determined on the United States having the colony."

"Yes . . . " So much was obvious by now. Not only was Livingston convinced of Bonaparte's determination to sell Louisiana, but he was also equally convinced of his impatience to have the business done with — now, this minute, tonight. It was after midnight, for heaven's sake! All of a sudden everybody had to conform to the Bonapartian rage for speed, meeting in the dead of night, etc.

The old saying "Rome wasn't built in a day" could never have managed its solid footing in the language if Bonaparte had been around to direct the Roman architects. His selection of the straightforwardly pedestrian Marbois over the pirouetting Talleyrand proved his intent to march from point A to point B in record tempo.

And he had better pull on his boots and march along, Livingston thought, unless he wanted to be left by the wayside.

Or worse, be surpassed by that other pedestrian marching in from Le Havre — Monroe.

If only he could prevent this plodding rival from entering the race — elicit some sort of official writ denying him participation. The march was already in progress, after all. The First Consul had seen fit to give the starting signal before Monroe could submit his presence. If you weren't at the starting line, you couldn't very well run in the race, could you? Which was no more than fair. Why should Monroe share in a possible victory resulting from an effort in which he had invested no energy whatsoever?

But how to convey this viewpoint to Marbois? How to extract the desired disqualification papers from an individual used to writing only in numbers, whose drawing hand was dispiritingly clumsy?

Suddenly, unexpectedly, Livingston's being was flooded with longing for Talleyrand. Now there was a man uniquely poised to instantly grasp the essence of the matter, whose expert hand was up to the required task.

It was one o'clock in the morning. He would plead fatigue with Marbois, Livingston decided., and be at the Rue du Bac when Talleyrand opened his eyes. There wasn't a moment to lose. Monroe would be marching on Paris this very day.

I don't think any fair-minded individual will argue the Chancellor's contention that whoever is not at the starting line shouldn't be allowed to enter the race, certainly not anybody who had watched him run himself ragged across this very terrain. But Monroe's good opinion of himself, already inflated by the President's attention and further bloated by the elaborate official reception at Le Havre, was floating above such common considerations — a state of affairs encouraged by the ambitious Elizabeth Monroe (and observed by Colonel Benthalou, who related it to me)

In case you are wondering, Colonel Benthalou was, like many an American at the time, in Paris trying to collect on a claim against the Directory, a task proving nearly as arduous and futile as the Chancellor's. And as long — - prompting the Colonel to have his spouse leave Baltimore and join him in Paris. Mrs. Benthalou made the crossing alongside the Monroes on the Richmond, *and Benthalou, eager to be reunited with his wife, had gone to Le Havre to fetch her . . .*

April 12

"T hese French highways are as bad as any road in Virginia," sighed Monroe.

"I wouldn't go *that* far," said Mrs. Monroe.

With the procedure of greetings and the blasts of cannon still ringing in their ears, the Monroes had set out from Le Havre for Paris on Saturday. Trundling through the innards of France's countryside for three days, they had seen a few carriages, a broken-down cabriolet, an ancient diligence, and a coach or two, indicating that vehicles were no more abundant today than they had been during the years following the Revolution.

In Le Havre this had not been so evident, as all means of transportation converged on the bustling channel harbor. The local authorities had reserved a coach and driver for Monroe, and a military wagon with infantry soldiers had been waiting at the dock to take the cabin furnishings and other goods off the *Richmond* and proceed forthwith to Paris with them.

"We certainly can't complain about the reception, Elizabeth."

Elizabeth Monroe shrugged. She had expected no less. The French had always favored her. The favoritism was a result of her looks (they had dubbed her *la belle Américaine*). but then, beauty was the only means by which to gain favor with the Parisian — the foreigner's prime access to his generosity.

After a night of sleep attended to by that species of angels who invariably hover over feather mattresses on the sea voyager's first night on dry land, the Monroes — scrubbed, rested and fed — piled into the reserved coach with the cocoa-colored Felicity (Ben, the other slave accompanying them, had been sent ahead with the soldiers and furniture).

"Mother is partial to anything French, Father. You know that." Eliza, crammed in between the *embonpoint* of Felicity and a heap of luggage in the back, lurched forward to make herself heard above the croaking axles and rattling windows. Felicity's turbaned head bobbed up and down, either in agreement or with sleep.

"I'm not partial to this infernal coach, I'm sure," Mrs. Monroe replied. "I wish your father had inspected the springs before we left."

"Oh, I can't believe we're nearly there!" Eliza shouted. "I'm so excited! Paris! Imagine? I was still a child when we left six years ago. Too bad George can't be with us. Oh, isn't it wonderful, Mother . . . ?"

The coach went veering upwards and came clunking down, upsetting passengers and luggage all in one moment. They had arrived at the last roadblock. Jerked back into reality, Felicity tried to assemble the baggage into its former position while Monroe retrieved a pillow from the mud-caked, carpeted floor and brushed it with his hands before replacing it behind the regal back of his handsome spouse. Outside, the driver paid the toll for the final stage of the trip.

"And I have you to thank for it, Father!" Eliza cried, as the rusty conveyance clattered back into motion.

"And Mr. Jefferson," Monroe smiled.

"Don't be silly, James. Who else could he have appointed?"

"I agree with Mother! Who else is there who enjoys the full confidence of the President of the United States of America, except my father?"

"Well, there's Mr. Madison for one," Monroe said. "Of course, his being the Secretary of State, Mr. Madison could scarcely leave the country on a diplomatic mission."

"And it would ill become the country if he did," Mrs. Monroe concluded. "Let's face it, Mr. Madison is a devotee of the desk, a collector of quills, who would neither be audible nor visible in debate. Don't misunderstand me, James. I'm as grateful as you are for Mr. Madison's help in financing the private costs of our trip. What I question is your readiness to step aside for him. I'm proud of you, James. Eliza and George are proud of you. We are all proud of you."

"And I'm proud of you, Elizabeth. And of you, Eliza, and of George . . . "

Mrs. Monroe held aloft a kid-gloved hand in a plea for silence. "Tell me, James, did you ever wonder why a race as difficult to please as the Parisian nicknamed me *la belle Américaine?*"

Monroe's stern face softened at the recollection. "Because, obviously, the Parisians considered you the most attractive American female in town."

"Not attractive, James. I will not be called attractive. Not by you. Not by Paris. Which is the point I am trying to make. In life, one receives the tribute one exacts. Remember that, Eliza, when you are introduced to Parisian society. If you are satisfied with being *la jolie Américaine*, than that's all you will be. Modesty is a virtue becoming only servants."

Felicity blew a puff of air at the nearest rattling window, prompting Eliza to say: "That's not what I was taught in school."

"What is taught in school has no bearing on life, Eliza. I am serious, James. You are as good as any Madison or Jefferson."

"Jefferson? That's a tall order."

"*President* Jefferson, Mother?"

"Yes, Eliza. *President* Jefferson. Do you think your father a lesser man than Mr. Jefferson?"

"No, of course not."

"There! You see, James?" Elizabeth Monroe's almond-shaped eyes widened meaningfully as she glanced at her husband. "And neither should you."

Monroe smiled at the back of the driver through the dirty panel of glass. "I just wish you'd pick somebody a little less tall for your comparisons. Robert Livingston, say."

"Robert Livingston? James, don't be absurd."

Eliza waved her hands at Felicity in mock contempt. "Mr. Livingston is *quantité négligeable.*"

"Why, Eliza . . . " Mrs. Monroe turned to face her daughter, the expression on her classically chiseled face a mixture of surprise and delight. "You *do* remember the language, after all. Did you hear that, James? Eliza, I'm so proud of you."

"I'm proud of you, Mother. And of you too, Father."

Monroe was touched. "And I am proud of you both."

While the Monroes were thusly being transported over the French provincial roads, Chancellor Livingston hastened through the streets of Paris in order to keep ahead of them . . .

April 12

The Foreign Minister does not receive anyone before eleven, Monsieur."

Livingston blinked absentmindedly at the valet. He had expected as much. "I'll wait if you don't mind."

What better place to rest his tired mind and bones than amidst the deep reds of this lovely room where daylight entered haltingly, respectfully, as did the visitor.

What he ought to ask Talleyrand was for him to write some form of letter or note. It could start by expressing Bonaparte's friendship for the United States, his desire to give a striking indication of this friendship by ceding to it the whole of Louisiana, and so on. After that, they could work to mature the treaty before the official reception of Monroe, who could appear later as a contrasting party . . .

"Firmin. Are you here, Firmin?"

Livingston sprang to his feet. "Good morning, Madame."

The way Mme Talleyrand peered about the furniture, Livingston assumed she was hunting for the unzealous, undersized canine usually reclining near Talleyrand's bureau. She looked a woman capable of naming a dog Firmin.

"Monsieur?" Her blonde hair undone as if it had just left the pillow, the svelte body wrapped in an indifferent grey robe, Mme Talleyrand fixed her myopically beautiful, violet-blue gaze on Livingston's face, obviously trying to attach a name to it. Devoid of cosmetic embellishments, her skin was as fair as that of a child.

Livingston hastened to refresh her memory. 'Robert Livingston. At your service, Madame."

"Monsieur Livingston, of course . . . " She flashed a row of small even teeth in a smile designed to disguise the hesitation in her voice. "And how is Madame Livingston?" The violet-blue eyes brimmed with the desperate hope that indeed there *was* a Madame Livingston.

"Very well, thank you." He felt an urge to be pleasant. "I am delighted at this unexpected opportunity of seeing you again, Madame."

Was it her fault she wasn't a genius? She wasn't so stupid that she didn't realize she wasn't. Not every woman emerged a Mme de Staël, and a good thing it was too. It was the pedantic Germaine de Staël whom Talleyrand had in mind when he claimed that "one must have loved a genius in order to appreciate the happiness of a fool." Such quips by the Foreign Minister at the expense of his wife could only encourage his foppish friends to ridicule the poor fool at every turn. Not surprising that Mme Talleyrand had grown hesitant at the sight of an unexpected presence.

"My husband promised to lend me Firmin," she explained. "Hippolyte broke his leg and my other valet complains of the extra work." She flashed another smile in Livingston's direction. "He's probably hiding. Firmin doesn't like to serve in my apartments. You haven't seen him by any chance? Your name and accent sound foreign, Monsieur. Are you English?"

"I am American, Madame."

"Are you, now? My first husband was English. I was born in India, you know. Oh, but I met Madame Livingston. I remember now."

"Mrs. Livingston and I had the pleasure of dining with you recently."

"No, no . . . " She waved a small white hand. "I mean long before that. Weren't you minister during the Directory?"

She was confusing him with Monroe. Livingston's urge to be pleasant evaporated. "No, Madame," he said stiffly. She richly deserved the reputation of beautiful dolt she enjoyed. "I haven't seen Firmin."

His brief encounter with Talleyrand didn't end on a much happier note. The Foreign Minister deliberately misunderstood while insisting that he understood perfectly.

"It is you, Mr. Livingston, who refuses to understand. that the matter is out of my hands entirely," he said in his most irritatingly-patient voice. "There is nothing I can do. You must address yourself to Monsieur Marbois. It is the First Consul's wish."

"And one must never go against the First Consul's wish, must one?"

No sooner did Livingston hear his own words than the anger that had inspired them vanished. This sort of language wouldn't help him any. He was about to smooth the gaffe over with some diplomatic varnish, when he noticed Talleyrand's smile.

"It is wiser not to, Mr. Livingston."

Livingston thought he would go home and take a short nap (he had been late returning from Marbois's the previous night and, once in bed, couldn't get to sleep), but found himself wandering the streets of Paris instead. He knew that Skipwith, the American Consul, had rented a house for Monroe, probably near one of the main thoroughfares: the Rue du Bac, Rue de Lille, or the Rue de l'Université. The Parisian was, of necessity, an inveterate walker. Even the better classes often saw themselves forced to rely on their own feet for transportation. The imposed exercise was just as well, thought Livingston, seeing the enormous amounts of food they consumed. Of course, any self-respecting Parisian loved strolling along the boulevards — the Rue Royale and the Rue St. Antoine — or lingering on the Pont des Arts to watch the passing barges, floating mills, and wash-houses on the Seine. When the sun put in an appearance, the well-dressed *papas* and *mamans* likewise emerged with their marriageable daughters for the traditional promenade.

The young couple and elderly matron walking ahead of Livingston suddenly dashed for the safety of the buildings to the right. Instinctively, Livingston followed suit. A year and a half of plowing through the passages and byways of the French Capital had taught him that any such sudden moves by pedestrians signaled the approach of a cabriolet.

"*Assassins!*" The chaperoning matron angrily shook her umbrella as the two-wheeled vehicle came tearing around the corner, splashing mud in all directions. As he inspected his trousers and. topcoat, Livingston noticed a wagon loaded with furniture in a side street, its team of horses eye-deep in a canvas bag of feed attached to their neck. An infantry soldier stood guard while two of his colleagues were hoisting a sofa up the steps to a house. On the wagon was a chair and footstool covered with the same flowered fabric as the sofa, a writing desk, a leather trunk, a table, a chest of drawers, and a variety of items such as might be desirable in a private cabin on an extended sea voyage.

The house was a typical bourgeois city dwelling, not very different from the one where he himself lived, with steps leading from the street directly into the parlor. The door to the room behind the parlor was closed, but it was likely to be identical in size and shape. Beyond it, or to the left and right, would be a clutter of interdependent bedrooms and, stuck somewhere in between, a dark little cubbyhole called a water closet. The domain ruled by the Mme Tranches of this world — the kitchen — would be situated outside or as far from civilized scrutiny as possible.

Livingston was about to ask the identity of the owner of the furniture, when his ears perked at the unmistakable sounds of a Virginian drawl. He climbed the flight of steps to see a middle-aged white man of Negroid features directing the placement of the sofa.

"Ici?" The soldiers held the heavy contraption above the black-and-white flagged floor left of the fireplace.

"Lessee . . . " The man seemed undecided, or else he was enjoying himself.

Of course. A slave. He should have guessed. Those Virginian democrats couldn't bear to travel without their slaves.

"Is this the residence of Mr. Monroe?" The question was a mere formality, confirmed by the servant.

"Has Mr. Monroe arrived yet?"

Again a confirmation, followed by the intelligence that Mr. Monroe was out, "gwine' to see Mistah Livin'stin."

"Thank you."

Livingston rushed down the steps and into the street.

April 12

In spite of his misgivings, the agonizing of the past months, a rush of excitement spread through Livingston as he retraced his steps. Monroe was an American, a compatriot. Paris harbored a small flock of Americans, most of whom had come with the hope of recouping losses sustained during the Directory. There was the Consul Skipwith and other representatives, secretaries, etc., but these people knew less than he about the current state of affairs in the United States. Monroe would bring all the latest news.

Mounting the steps to his own parlor, Livingston felt something akin to expectation. His greeting of Monroe was more cordial than he would have thought possible.

"You haven't changed a bit." A well-intentioned lie. Monroe's gentle blue eyes had receded further into their sockets, and his face, already lined at 25 when he entered Congress, now looked old at 45. It was a refined face, Livingston noted with surprise, made severe by its creases and furrows. He barely knew the Virginia Governor and vainly searched his memory for their last meeting. "I regret I was out when you called."

"Mrs. Livingston has been most kind in keeping me company," Monroe replied graciously.

"Mr. Monroe complained of a deranged stomach," Mrs. Livingston said, explaining the serving of tea. Robert didn't care for tea. "I'll fetch you a glass of Madeira. Maybe Mr. Monroe would like to join you in a glass?"

"Not today. Thank you, Mrs. Livingston."

"I trust you and Mrs. Monroe are both well?" Livingston sat down. "Did you have a good crossing?"

"Personally, I found the passage grueling, but Mrs. Monroe has suffered no ill effects from it I'm happy to say." Monroe smiled. "This is all the more remarkable, considering her condition."

"Oh, dear!" With the typical female flair for decoding a euphemism covering a variety of afflictions, Mrs. Livingston had immediately identified the condition mentioned as pregnancy. "I would have imagined your children to be grown, like ours." "They are, Mrs. Livingston. She is," he corrected himself. "Eliza is seventeen. We have only a daughter."

Not blessed with his wife's decoding talent, it took Livingston a few moments to understand . . . "You're going to be a father again?" Wasn't Monroe a little old for that? Of course his wife was a good decade younger. And beautiful to boot. "Well, well, well . . . " He tapped the smiling father-to-be on the shoulder. "Congratulations, my dear fellow."

"Yes . . . " Mrs. Livingston looked as though she wasn't altogether sure congratulations were in order.

The conversation hobbled genteelly along the trail of social amenities, until it tapered to a natural end—a clearing from which all roads, Mrs. Livingston knew—would lead to Louisiana.

"Mr. Madison has shown me the correspondence pertaining to New Orleans, up to my time of sailing," Monroe started. "I'm anxious to see the rest of it."

"I have it all prepared for you." Livingston rose to fetch the letters in his study.

Mrs. Livingston carefully lit the argand lamp on the edge of the chimney mantle and the candles of a candelabrum on the table. "Don't forget about dinner tomorrow afternoon, Mr. Monroe."

When her husband returned, Mary Livingston discreetly bowed out of the parlor, taking along her unfinished glass of Madeira. Closing the door, she saw Monroe's brow knotting over the dispatches in his hands. Robert was settling down with one of the copies of the New York *Chronicle Express* brought by Monroe.

Livingston was dozing off when Monroe's voice returned him to the business at hand. "This seems to be encouraging." He pointed to a letter written by Talleyrand.

"Unless you've dealt with Talleyrand, it's impossible to have an idea of his character." Livingston picked up the *Chronicle Express* that had slipped to the floor. "Nothing he says can be relied on. Yesterday he proposed the United States buy the whole colony of Louisiana."

"The whole colony?" Monroe laughed. "Well there we'll have to disappoint the Foreign Minister. Our instructions are to obtain a town, not a country."

"Bonaparte won't deal for anything less than the whole. He wants eighty-million francs, take it or leave it."

Monroe's glee vanished. "But this is ridiculous, preposterous—I mean, if they are serious—and I will tell Talleyrand so to his face."

"Talleyrand is no longer the negotiating party. We have to address ourselves to Barbé-Marbois in the future."

"Barbé-Marbois? I know Marbois. I know him very well. Mr. Marbois is a gentleman whose high moral character rules out any indulgence in jest."

Livingston stared in amazement at the black iron stove. Did he hear correctly? Was Monroe equating morality with an absence of wit? It sounded like something Talleyrand might say—tongue firmly planted in cheek. But Monroe's jaw was far too lean to accommodate a frolicsome tongue, his own moral character probably too elevated to stoop to jest.

"Mr. Livingston . . . "

"Yes, Mr. Monroe." Livingston's reaction was instantaneous, an automatic show of attention when a voice nearby took on a certain volume and impatience, indication that the speaker mistook his deafness for lack of interest.

"I asked whether you've met with Mr. Marbois?"

"We had a conference last night during which he repeated the offer made by Talleyrand.'

"But then, the First Consul must be in earnest . . . Mr. Livingston!" Monroe jumped up from his chair. "Why didn't you tell me so immediately? You declined the offer of course?"

"I neither declined nor accepted it."

"There is no question that we must decline it. Our instructions . . . "

"We can't afford to dismiss out of hand a proposal of this magnitude. At the very least we ought to consider it."

"It is not our place to consider it, Mr. Livingston. This is a matter for the consideration of the President. And for the Congress."

"Time won't allow it. Bonaparte is in a hurry for funds to start his war on Britain."

"Bonaparte's concerns are not those of the United States!"

"They may well turn out to be to the advantage of the United States all the same."

"This argument is pointless, Mr. Livingston, since we haven't the power to negotiate for the purchase of the whole colony. If your understanding of the offer is correct. I won't rest until I've heard it with my own ears. When is your next meeting with Mr. Marbois?"

"Tonight."

"Tonight?"

"As I said, Bonaparte wants to see this business resolved in a hurry."

"Very well. I'll go with you."

"Unfortunately, Mr. Monroe, your participation in the negotiations will have to be put off until you've been officially presented to the First Consul."

"And when can I expect *that* to happen?"

"At the next official reception."

"Which is when?"

"I'm not sure. In a few weeks or so." Livingston smiled. "No need to get excited, Mr. Monroe. I have arranged for your reception tomorrow morning by Cambacérès, the Second Consul, and Lebrun, the Third. Bonaparte has decided to waive protocol in your case, which ought to convince you of his intent to have this affair settled quickly. It is in our own interest that we respond in kind."

"Not if it means exceeding our instructions." Monroe's voice was as severe as his face. "That would be insubordination."

A curious objection, Livingston thought, coming from somebody removed from this very city by President Washington for insubordination. Good old unjesting Monroe, sent by the Republic of the United

States to make treaties with the regicidal lawyers of the Directory. They must have seen him coming, this earnest American patriot, waving the banner of brotherly republican love at Carnot and Paul ("the King of the Corrupt") Barras.

"Insubordination is a word of many syllables," he began cautiously. "Times have changed. France these days is a republic only in name. Bonaparte is the man of the hour. I believe the wisest course for us would be not to commit ourselves one way or another until we both have had an opportunity to study the proposal in depth."

"I have studied my instructions, Mr. Livingston! I suggest you do likewise before embarking on a course unauthorized by the President." Years of being embroiled in New York politics had left Livingston a devious man, Monroe thought. Jefferson's distrust of him was well warranted. "Until such time when I can personally enter into the negotiations, I must warn you not to make any claims in my name.

"Then we are agreed. Excellent."

Unaware of the developments in France, Brigadier General Juan Manuél de Salcedo, Governor of Louisiana, sits down to enjoy a cigar and the good tidings brought by his old comrade, Brigadier General James Wilkinson . . .

April 13

Governor de Salcedo had not been in better spirits in months. Providence these days seemed bent on manipulating events in his favor. There was the official transferal of Louisiana from Spain to France and its accompanying grand festivities to look forward to. Instructions at last had arrived from Madrid ordering Intendant Morales to reopen the port to foreign trade (word of which had been sent to the United States President). General Wilkinson had come to offer the Governor several dozen superior American cigars and, in addition to this bounty, now was telling him that the authorities in Natchez had captured the notorious bandit Mason — forever robbing the intriguer Morales of appropriating to himself that glorious honor. A lifetime of soldierly discipline could not prevent tears of joy from welling up in the Governor's old eyes at this unexpected largesse of fate.

"How did it happen, General? How did they capture him?"

"Well, as I understand it, two strangers walked into town one fine morning with a head packed in a clump of blue clay — to keep it from spoiling, you see."

Governor de Salcedo's right hand, escorting one of the superior American cigars toward a brass receptacle, stopped in mid-air, dusting a respectable length of cigar-ash over the red brick floor of the loggia. "A *human* head?"

"Insofar as Mason could be called human, it must have been, because these fellows claimed it was his head."

"How did they come by it?" Decapitation, to the Governor, seemed too French somehow for Natchez.

"A good question, Your Honor," Wilkinson admitted. He shifted around the walnut table for the bottle of brandy the Governor — the most generous host this side of the Mississippi — had ordered in his honor. "There has been a good deal of speculation about that all over the Natchez region. The trouble with outlaws like Mason is that those who can identify them are no longer around . . . "

"Speaking of Natchez, are you planning a visit there in the near future?"

The interruption was not inspired by rudeness, Wilkinson knew. Very likely, some thought had entered the old fellow's head and he felt compelled to get ahold of it before it escaped. "I might."

"The reason I'm asking, General . . . I was wondering . . . I have written Governor Claiborne the good news about the port, of course. However, a spoken message is ever so much preferable to a written one, don't you agree? So I was thinking . . . You would do me a great kindness if, while in Natchez, you would speak . . . "

"To Governor Claiborne? Certainly. My pleasure, Governor. Any idea as to the exact time traffic will he restored? I don't suppose you can put a date on it?"

"I imagine within four to five weeks. Sometime in May, shall we say?" Governor de Salcedo nodded "yes" after consulting with himself. "That seems a reasonable expectation. But I didn't mean to distract you from your fascinating story. Go on, General, please. What happened with the Mason head?"

"Well, that was just it. Folks weren't any too sure the head in that blue clay was Mason's. Why, for all anybody knew, these two characters might have chopped the top off some poor truck farmer in order to get their hands on the reward money. Two thousand is a serious sum, and Governor Claiborne wasn't about to throw it away at some fraudulent head. I'm sure you can appreciate that, being Governor yourself?"

The Governor was in serene accord. "Absolutely."

"Finally, though, a planter — and then another — showed up to say the head sure looked a lot like Mason's. A few more people turned up to agree with them. There was a trial — don't ask me why; what they had in mind by bringing to justice a decomposing head I haven't a clue. Anyway, while all this was going on, with the two fellows getting to be mighty anxious to collect their reward, a Captain Stump from Kentucky stepped into the courtroom and identified, not only the head as Mason's, but one of the characters who had brought it in as one of Mason's gang. 'Why, that man's Wiley Harpe!' yelled Captain Stump and, so help me, he was right. The man turned out to be Little Wiley Harpe of the Terrible Harpes. The other one, too, was a member of the gang — a fellow by the name of Mays. The trial had served a purpose, after all."

"Providence is like that," agreed the Governor.

"Their necks'll be strung any day now in the proper length of hemp on Gallows Field in Old Greenville and their heads cut off and stuck on pikes on the Trace, where their rotting skulls can reassure innocent travelers and warn outlaws still active there of the fate in store for them."

"A frightful prospect," the Governor nodded. "You tell a good story, General. I shall miss you."

"Thank you, Governor. The feeling's mutual, I'm sure. But I aim to keep in touch." He would have to, Wilkinson thought. Colonel Burr and he had certain plans regarding Mexico. His long-standing affiliation with the Spanish officials would come in handy here. And, anyway, he liked the old fellow.

Governor de Salcedo smiled gracefully. Poor General Wilkinson, who believed himself as opaque as his good cigars, was as transparent as the blue curlicues of smoke those cigars generated, and — the Governor's smile deepened as the curlicues evaporated before his eyes — for all his physical bulk, as insubstantial. "You must, my friend, you must," he urged, surprised at the sincerity with which he extended this invitation to a man insincere by all accounts.

An informer to Spain against his own country, General Wilkinson now was suspected of plotting against both Spain and the United States. But, if it was true that a man shouldn't get old before he became wise, then the Governor at his ripe age ought to have accumulated enough wisdom to know that friends were not come by easily. If a young colleague like Claiborne in Natchez could curb his youthful impatience until the guilty party was identified, then, surely, a governor of his own years must be able to exercise restraint with regard to General Wilkinson.

"To begin with, I have no intention of missing the big do's coming up," Wilkinson promised with a broad smile.

"As for the future" — Governor de Salcedo passed on a smile equally pregnant with promise — "Providence will take care of it."

At about the time (I would guess) the old gentleman bids adieu to his guest, events in the French Capital are coming to a head . . .

April 13

The din in back of the house had subsided somewhat to the routine clatter of pots and plates. Whenever the Livingstons invited guests to dinner — be they only two as was the case this afternoon — Mme Tranche went into a minor trance, culminating in verbal, sometimes physical abuse of Zoé. The young, unwarlike maid was no match for the temperamental Parisian cook. An obedient follower most of the time, some inner, self-preserving device triggered a rebellious reaction in Zoé when Mme Tranche pounded her chestnut head with a blackened pot.

Except for incidents of this nature, when she considered it her duty to escort a crying Zoé back to her post and exhort an oath of future non-violent conduct from Mme Tranche, Mrs. Livingston stayed well clear of the kitchen. Experience had shown that Mme Tranche's dinners, however traumatically executed, had a way of bringing out a spirit of peace and satisfaction on their consumption.

Mrs. Livingston's only concern now was whether the cook had stayed with the agreed-upon leg of mutton as the main dish. Even though the money spent wasn't her own, Mme Tranche's sense of frugality often prompted her to ignore her employer's suggestions in favor of a better buy. The past winter, for instance, she had substituted venison for veal, because a friend of her husband had unexpectedly come into half a deer and was selling it at the price of cabbage. Mrs. Livingston wouldn't have minded if Zoé, who acted the part of major-domo and announced each dish as it was served, had had the flexibility of mind to likewise substitute venison for veal. Unfortunately, once committed by rote to a set menu, Zoé's reason couldn't be altered by mere truth.

Noticing the door to her husband's study was ajar, Mrs. Livingston rose to close it, just as the sound of a shattering dish reached the bedroom where she was dressing. In an attempt to steady her nerves, she went to the parlor in pursuit of a glass of sherry.

"The only way to face dinner with Monroe," quipped Livingston, who had preceded her there with similar intent.

Maybe Monroe could not be called a devastating wit, Mrs. Livingston thought, but he had the virtue of being a gentleman, who would not mistake the dessert for the hors d'oeuvre or remark to a lady about the soiled condition of her dress, like some people she could name. Robert's perception of Monroe was, understandably, clouded by the circumstances surrounding his visit. "Not everyone has the talent to prattle on endlessly without saying anything."

The cat, too, had deigned to put in an appearance, glaring angrily from behind the tubular, clumsy stove at the Livingstons, as was his wont, as if he held them personally responsible for the fracas in the kitchen which had forced him to seek shelter in the only other heated room in the house.

April had been balmy at the onset, inviting Paris to throw open its windows and doors at the promise of an early spring. A premature gesture, it turned out. During the past week winter had returned with all the desperate fury of a last stand, sending Parisians scurrying back to their coal cellars and woodpiles.

"Thank God for Mrs. Monroe," said Livingston.

Elizabeth Monroe, nee Kortright, was from the Livingston's home state of New York. The Livingstons knew the Kortright family well enough. They were less acquainted with Elizabeth, who was only eighteen when she married Monroe and left New York for Virginia. Mrs. Livingston seemed to recall a haughty, self-assured young bride. Most eighteen-year-old brides tended to disappear behind the ceremony of their own nuptials. Elizabeth Kortright Monroe had dominated hers. "I don't expect Mrs. Monroe to do much idle prattling either, Robert. I remember, even as a young girl she was serious and proud, very much a presence at her own wedding."

Livingston smiled. "I would hope so."

"I mean, Robert, that she made an impression."

"Next to Monroe, who wouldn't? Madame Tranche would look striking next to Monroe."

Mrs. Livingston smiled in spite of herself. "You're not being very charitable. Robert . . . " She stared over her glass of sherry at a point on the white damask tablecloth. The table had been laid out in the parlor, which also served as dining room. "I would like this to be a pleasant dinner."

"In spite of Monroe?" Livingston's flippant tone concealed a tender core. His wife wanted a pleasant dinner for a man who was his political rival and for a woman whom every woman he could think of considered a personal rival. Less because of her beauty than because of her attitude. When Monroe was Senator, his wife drove through the streets of Annapolis and Philadelphia as if she had been sired by Caesar himself. This did not endear her to most American females.

"Don't worry, Mary . . . " Livingston's voice, usually at a pitch where he himself could hear it, softened to a whisper. "If your heart is set on having a pleasant dinner, I'll do my best to help make it so."

"I only meant . . .

"Yes, I know. No talk of politics at the table." Livingston held. up his hand. "I swear."

"No need to perjure yourself, Robert." Mrs. Livingston smiled. "Let's say, not until the coffee."

Mrs. Livingston had reason to be pleased. The leg of mutton, that most dependable of standbys in Mme Tranche's culinary repertoire, had, once again, run away with the honors. The Monroes had partaken of this succulent entry with the passion common to travelers who are sitting down to consume their first home-cooked meal.

Behind the lacey curtains the windows were misted with the warmth emanating from gratified mouths and a consistently snoring stove. Candles, lit to ward off the dark afternoon, added to the genial atmosphere, which contrasted pleasantly with the enduring cold outside.

It was due to the unusual cold spell that Zoé, looking awkwardly smart in a black dress and dainty white apron, committed her sole gaffe of the day, for it was in reaction to the chilling north wind and freezing night temperatures that Mme Tranche's bucket of water in the cellar had congealed into ice, allowing her to forego the chocolate mousse in favor of that utterly delectable recent French gastronomic invention — ice cream.

Rarely to be had in summer (the icehouse was very unreliable), it was an unexpected luxury in April. Indeed, had seemed an impossibility only a night ago when Mme Tranche inspected the bucket. How Zoé could remain placidly attached to "chocolate mousse" in the face of a development that had taken Mrs. Livingston all of her willpower not to reveal beforehand, was beyond human comprehension. Especially, when it was she who had doggedly turned the handle of the ice cream mill, Mme Tranche's "condition" forbidding her to engage in such tedious labor, of course.

Mrs. Livingston's irritation with Zoé reached a level where she contemplated casting a severe, reprimanding glance at the stubborn girl, when the cries of delight at the table arrested her. Even Robert shouted like a schoolboy. Mrs. Livingston found herself smiling with the pleasure of the hostess who sees the pleasure of her guests. But the Monroes had in store a surprise of their own. Monroe went to retrieve it from the inside pocket of his topcoat at the *porte manteau*. A bottle of American peach brandy.

"The best brandy in the world!" Livingston's face was glowing.

Monroe smiled. "I am in complete agreement."

"Your offering, my dear fellow, couldn't have been more timely. We have been without for two weeks; the new shipment being long overdue." Holding the squat stem of the glass between his fingers, Livingston tenderly balanced its bottom in his palm, savoring the brandy's delicate perfume as he spoke: "I have been trying to convince the French of the superiority of this brandy ever since my arrival."

"A futile enterprise, no doubt?" asked Monroe.

"They readily accept my free samples but refuse to accept my claim."

"It is foolish to think they ever will." Mrs. Livingston didn't approve of her husband's crusade on behalf of American brandy. To promote the commercial products of the United States was the business of the Consul. Let Skipwith rub the French in a spot where they were unanimously touchy.

"Would you like to have the coffee served here or in the drawing room, Madame?" Now that dinner had been presented without any major mishaps, Zoé felt free to properly stare at the Monroes as she cleared the table. Zoé's fascination with the Livingston's guests increased in proportion to their conversation being incomprehensible to her. Her eyes dwelled on Mrs. Monroe's red velvet gown as though that garment, too, was intelligible only to foreigners.

"Zoé, dear," Mrs. Livingston tried to divert the girl's focus, "you can bring the coffee here. The drawing room is too chilly."

Zoé reminded her employer that the door to the drawing room could be left open to let in the warm air.

"Then it will shortly be comfortable, Madame."

A suggestion from Zoé? Mrs. Livingston was pleasantly startled. "By all means, Zoé. Leave the door open."

"I have never heard him give a comprehensible speech," Monroe was saying.

"Because he can't come to the point," Livingston replied.

Mrs. Livingston looked questioningly at Mrs. Monroe. Who was this person who couldn't come to the point?

"Mr. Hamilton," Elizabeth Monroe whispered.

"Oh." Mrs. Livingston was disappointed.

"Not a happy accompaniment to brandy, I agree, Mrs. Livingston."

It was no secret that everyone in the room cordially detested Alexander Hamilton, a man whose every word and action was calculated to advance his all-consuming ambition. Probably the reason why he was hated even within his own Federalist party, Mrs. Livingston thought—"That bastard brat of a Scots peddler," Mr. Adams called him—and certainly the reason why the Livingston clan had banded together with George Clinton, Mayor of New York since time immemorial, to depose Schuyler, the power behind the Hamilton throne.

Monroe was well aware of this, of course, as was Robert well aware of Hamilton's ridiculing Monroe's appointment as Envoy Extraordinary in his New York *Evening Post*. The dislike of host and guest for the person of Alexander Hamilton was common knowledge to both, but such were the superior qualities of American peach brandy that they admitted to it.

"I will not suffer my retirement to be clouded," Monroe started.

"Your retirement?" Mrs. Monroe interrupted. "What are you talking about, James?"

"I am quoting Mr. Jefferson after he stepped down as Secretary of State. Where was I?"

"I will not suffer my retirement to be clouded," repeated Livingston, who had read the letter.

"'. . . to be clouded by the slanders of a man whose history, from the moment at which history can stoop to notice him, is a tissue of machinations against the liberty of the country which has not only received him and given him bread, but heaped its honors on his head!" Monroe's head bobbed up and down for emphasis. "That, to my mind, is an accurate description of Hamilton's character."

"I prefer Mr. Adams's. It isn't so long-winded." Mrs. Monroe turned to her hostess. "Wouldn't you say?"

Mrs. Livingston shrugged. She had no love for Alexander Hamilton—a faithless husband who caused his good wife no end of grief. As a politician he was no better or worse than any other would be, given Hamilton's circumstances and intelligence. "Mr. Hamilton little interests me."

"As does politics." Livingston gave his wife an affectionate pat on the arm. "Mary claims all in politics is predictable."

"That would explain why the subject is so tiresome," said Mrs. Monroe.

"In that case, Mrs. Livingston, tell me . . . " Monroe leaned forward over the table. "Who will be the next President of the United States?"

"I can tell you that it won't be Colonel Burr." Mrs. Livingston's reply was immediate, prompted by her belief that the very powers which had been instrumental in directing Burr's rise to the vice-presidency—a post which had led to the Presidency in every instance in the past—were already orchestrating the descent of the charming Colonel, deemed by many to be as adroit an intriguer as Hamilton could hope to be.

"The question is superfluous, James, when you know that Mr. Jefferson is allowed to serve again."

"Mr. Jefferson has expressed the desire to retire from public life."

"Mr. Jefferson has expressed the desire to retire from public life ever since he entered it."

Mrs. Monroe's remark greatly amused Livingston. "No president admits to wanting to serve another term, Mr. Monroe; you know that. It has virtually become tradition by now."

"Mr. Adams did."

"Mr. Adams was not reelected, James."

"Will you be going to the drawing room soon, Madame?"

"What is the matter with you, Zoé? Why are you so set on moving us to the drawing room?"

"So I can let in the gentleman."

"The gentleman?" Mrs. Livingston didn't understand.

The front door was within plain sight. No one had rung the bell. "What gentleman?"

"The gentleman in the garden, Madame."

"In the garden?" Mrs. Livingston looked at her husband. "Are you expecting anyone, Robert?"

Livingston motioned that he didn't. "How did this gentleman come to be in the garden, Zoé?"

"When he knocked at the back door, I sent him there, Monsieur. I'm not supposed to let in callers when you are still at table."

"Madame Tranche's orders, I take it."

"No, Monsieur. Yours." Zoé looked hurt. She had taken this responsibility upon her own frail self. "Madame Tranche fell asleep from exhaustion right after the chocolate mousse."

"I'm sure I didn't say that you couldn't announce them."

Elizabeth Monroe appeared to be enjoying the situation. "Maybe we ought to inquire as to the identity of this mysterious gentleman in the garden, Mr. Livingston?"

Livingston nodded. "Now listen carefully, Zoé. Did the gentleman give you his name?"

"He gave me a visiting card." She fumbled in the pocket of her dainty apron. "*Tenez*, Monsieur."

"My god!" Livingston popped from his chair in alarm. "It's Marbois! And you send him to freeze in the garden. How long has he been there? When did he arrive?"

"Just after the *sole Véronique*, Monsieur."

"Oh, dear . . . " Mrs. Livingston couldn't decide whether to laugh or cry as her husband bounded through the drawing room and in back to rescue Marbois. The unhappy face of the maid prompted her to an encouraging nod. "You did well, Zoé. Thank you. You can go back to the kitchen now. I'll look after things here."

Monroe stared at his hostess with an expression approaching awe. "I must confess, Mrs. Livingston, your patience is exemplary."

Mrs. Livingston sighed. "I have no choice, Mr. Monroe."

"I am from Lorraine and used to the cold," said Marbois, extending a shivering hand to greet Monroe. His passing by the house had happened by sheer chance, he claimed. It wasn't his intention to disturb the company. "I beg you, please, proceed as if I weren't here."

Unable to do as he begged, the company smiled and watched the unexpected visitor sip a brandy handed him by the host.

"I am overjoyed at seeing you again after all these years," the Frenchman told Monroe. "Your arrival has been eagerly awaited, in view of certain recent developments which demand your immediate attention. But I don't want to invite the displeasure of the ladies by introducing a topic of conversation which can only bore them."

Wiping the steam from his spectacles with a large white handkerchief, Marbois smiled myopically in the direction of the gold velvet *causeuse*, where the ladies were sitting defiantly upright, recognizing the speaker's verbal gymnastics as an invitation to withdraw.

"We can go into the drawing room," Livingston suggested. "I'm sure the ladies would be glad with an opportunity to converse amongst themselves."

Marbois protested that wouldn't be fair. He was an uninvited guest. "I have imposed my presence. I fear the ladies would never forgive me." Spectacles in place this time, his smile was fixed on Mrs. Monroe.

Mrs. Livingston sighed, resigned to the inevitable, but Mrs. Monroe, smiling back at Marbois, called his bluff. "I wish more gentlemen in public life were blessed with your sensitivity, Monsieur. It is indeed a vexation when we ladies are denied the pleasure of a social gathering because the gentlemen are preoccupied by affairs of state. Your consideration demands reciprocation. After your banishment in the cold garden, Mrs. Livingston and I wouldn't dream of sending you into the unheated drawing room. And since your business is obviously urgent, we beg you to proceed as if there were no ladies present."

Monroe smiled. Whenever Elizabeth made up her mind to say something, she said a mouthful. He could see that even Livingston was impressed. Marbois, ensconced near the stove in an armchair matching the *causeuse*, took a few moments to recover.

"I assure you, Madame, nothing is so pressing that it cannot wait for a more convenient hour to be discussed."

Livingston disagreed. "And keep in suspense Mr. Monroe? who is anxiously awaiting your personal confirmation of the information I communicated to him . . . "

" . . . That the United States buy Louisiana from France for eighty million francs?" Monroe jumped in.

"Then I am happy to dispel your doubts at once, Mr. Monroe. Yes, this is the proposal of the First Consul, as I informed Mr. Livingston. As a friend to the United States, I must point out the enormous benefit your country would derive from owning this vast colony. I couldn't exert myself on behalf of a scheme I believed detrimental to the land of my wife's birth."

Monroe was quick to reassure him. "No one acquainted with you, sir, can doubt the affection you bear the United States, or your integrity." The President himself thought highly of Marbois. His *Notes on*

Virginia were the result of a query by the Frenchman. "I am confident that you are acting in good faith and assume the scheme would be beneficial for both our countries. However, I must confess surprise at the cavalier attitude with which you seem to regard the obligations of Mr. Livingston and myself. More than any other of your countrymen, you understand the American democratic process. You followed the Congress during our Revolution. Yet you casually propose that my colleague and I violate the very principles you profess to admire in order to buy a French colony. Exert yourself no longer, Mr. Marbois, because it is not within our power to accept the First Consul's proposal. Our instructions will not allow it."

Marbois stared at Livingston, who, with Monroe, had remained seated at table. "I appreciate your objections, Mr. Monroe, and can assure you that the First Consul has in mind expedience, not offense to the American democratic process. After many long weeks traveling from New York to Paris, the irritating slowness of transatlantic passage must have impressed you anew. To consult with your government in Washington and await its decision could easily take up several months. I'm afraid that the First Consul won't be dictated to by time in this matter. Has it occurred to you, sir, that your country may ultimately profit from this haste?"

Monroe considered the question. "Yes, and therein lies the danger. Thinking of the possible greater good in future, one is tempted to overstep one's authority at present."

Once again, Livingston felt the Marbois spectacles flashing his way. Unable to suppress a smile, Livingston experienced no trouble in holding back his tongue. Let someone else discover the delights of dealing with Monroe, who, perhaps inspired by the unexpected female audience, was reverting to character with singular dedication. A cautious speaker by nature, his words now took on the inflections and ponderousness of a teacher's, no doubt for the edification of said audience.

The ladies, meanwhile, sat on the *causeuse*, looking like injured mutes. The painful expression on Mary's face reminded Livingston of the time the Ambassador to Portugal had likened her eyes to sapphires.

As for Mrs. Monroe, her annoyance was almost palpable. That she chose not to exploit an already irregular situation and vent her annoyance pointed to a mind where deliberation overtook impulse.

"Yes, Mr. Marbois, I understand, but our instructions are to obtain a port of trade . . . "

In the aftermath of dinner, the warmth generated by the stove and Monroe's insistent drawl conspired to produce a feeling of drowsiness. Livingston rose to pace the floor in an effort to remain alert. Marbois, too, rose from his armchair, visibly disappointed. "I apologize for the intrusion, Mr. Livingston. Perhaps we had better postpone further discussion until tomorrow. Shall I expect you at my house as agreed?"

"Mr. Monroe and I will be there promptly at nine, Livingston promised.

Preparing to take his leave, Marbois's face hovered over Mrs. Livingston's hand, then bent over that of Mrs. Monroe. "I hope to have the pleasure of seeing you again, Madame?"

"My husband has had a trying day, Monsieur," Elizabeth Monroe replied cryptically. "I expect a good night's rest will considerably refresh his outlook by morning."

What trying day? All he had done was stick his feet under the Livingston table, Monroe thought. It was true that he had not been sleeping well. Nevertheless, refreshed or not, "I wouldn't depend on your dissuading me from my position," he warned Marbois.

"Can I depend on your attending the meeting?"

"Certainly, my dear sir. We must leave no stone unturned. That is the reason I am in Paris. Mr. Jefferson is counting on me."

Inside the President's House, meanwhile, the mood was bleak . . .

April

That doesn't mean the port is open." Jefferson dropped the dispatch from New Orleans back onto his desk. "Between reception and execution of the order God knows how many weeks will pass."

Madison tried to take the President's reaction in stride. Jefferson wasn't having an easy time of it lately, what with Meriwether Lewis in Pennsylvania there wasn't anybody around for him to bounce off his anxieties. The new secretary was willing and eager enough to please, but poor Harvie, so far, had been rowing upstream. The President didn't exactly carry his feelings on his sleeve.

Monroe had not been heard from since leaving port in New York and couldn't be expected to be heard from again until he stepped ashore in France — if, as were to be hoped, the ship had met with a routine crossing — after which there would be another interval of a few months before the writing reached Washington City.

No one had to tell Madison how living with this continual uncertainty ate into a man's mind and spoiled his thinking. All the more so when there was nothing to detract from it: no fighting Congress, no hysterical press; no expeditions to plot or John Walkers to pacify. Still, how could Jefferson fail to rejoice at the prospect of New Orleans becoming an open port once again when all the turmoil and misery of the past months could be traced directly to its closure? "Dead time between reception and execution of an order is to be expected. Meanwhile, though, word will get around and the West will settle down." Madison looked at a paper the President had pushed into his hands. "What is it?"

"Read it."

Madison switched his chair so the letter caught the light coming through the window (Not everyone could read in the dark):

> . . . Public opinion here is in a state of great excitement. The Spaniards have insulted and injured us. They have provoked our pride;

they have seen that neither interest nor national honor can determine the American Cabinet to act with energy. We have shown the world that we are well disposed to place our existence at the mercy of foreign nations. The French are in possession of New Orleans. I have seen the manifesto of the Prefect. It is like all the other manifestoes. There is not a well-informed man in this territory who does not realize that our country is ruined. Moreover, it is you, the President, alone who is to blame. It is you who, by your pusillanimity, have allowed the blood of the West to stagnate, and in order to better secure our destruction, you have allowed our most cruel enemy to put his inexorable hand on the mouth of the artery through which alone the blood can circulate. Because of you, we must submit ourselves to the colonial and military despotism of Bonaparte. The Americans living near the western waters will necessarily be ruled by those who dispose of their productions . . .

Madison saw no reason to keep reading further. "Proves my point, doesn't it? This good Natchez citizen wouldn't be writing in this vein if he knew the port was about to be reopened. Even assuming that he would, for every one of him, who criticizes the Administration's policy, there is one who supports it."

"Amounting to half a nation of critics. Hardly what I would call a mandate for our side."

Madison smiled. "I see you are determined not to be cheered by the good news."

"This communiqué, what does it mean?" Jefferson shrugged. "The Spanish have decided that, when they get around to it, they will reopen New Orleans to us, which, considering their usual pace, will come in the eleventh hour of their presence in Louisiana. At which point the French will say: Just a moment, citizen-brothers of the American Republic! Don't you realize you are trespassing? This is French property. Your arrangement with the former owners is null and void. And the whole cycle will start anew. I will cheer, Mr. Madison, when the situation calls for cheering; when Monroe secures us a port from Bonaparte for cash. To be perfectly frank, I have no great expectations there either."

"But," Madison started, trying to ward off the waves of pessimism spilling over to him from Jefferson, "not so long ago you claimed your highest hopes were invested in Monroe."

"What would you have me say?"

"I see." Madison sighed. He was beginning to wish the long-awaited letter from New Orleans had never come.

April 14

I t was twelve minutes after nine. Recalling his promise to be prompt, Livingston quickened his step, then thought better of it. Why rush to a meeting sure to test his patience, to say nothing of his liver which, after functioning admirably for weeks, was reverting to its former antics. Mary tended to point to American peach brandy as the culprit, but Livingston knew the guilty party went by another name.

Chewing on his second Balsam of Tulo tablet of the day, Livingston devoutly wished he could share his wife's confidence of success. Still reeling from the impact of *Amélie de Mansfield*, the latest effort of Marie Cottin — in whose novels the virtuous were pursued by a perversely inclined fate through the majority of their pages, to recover birthright, lost offspring and good fortune in the last ten — Mary seemed to think that he, too, had met with a sufficient number of setbacks to warrant imminent victory.

Not bloody likely.

The best one could hope for was that the machinery in Marbois's brain had been turning at about the speed with which Mme Cottin's heroes raced from one funeral to the next. Unless the Minister of the Treasury could present an argument propelling Monroe into action, they might be stalled at the present impasse indefinitely. The object was to convince Monroe of the propriety of overstepping his own authority.

This irked Livingston, because the issue, really, ought to be whether it was desirable for the U.S. to add the vast colony of Louisiana to her already considerable existing territory. The United States was not expansionist. Else there would be something in the Constitution touching upon this point. Assuming he and Monroe took Bonaparte up on his offer, what would Jefferson have to say? To be sure, Jefferson was always sitting knee-deep in maps and fossils, sending his protégés through an uncharted wilderness in search of mountains of salt, antique towers, tribes of giants, and other exotica. Confronted with the purchase of Louisiana, though, would his vision remain so broad as to embrace it. A literal interpreter of the Constitution, could he afford to?

It was all good and well for the opposition to belittle the President as a philosopher and dreamer; that didn't make him any less of a skillful politician. And that he would seek reelection in 1804 was certain, all coy disclaimers to the contrary notwithstanding.

Americans living on the Ohio, along with all Westerners, would, of course, wildly applaud the unexpected acquisition, but what of the rest of the country? More to the point, how would those citizens holding a vote see this unconstitutional extravaganza? To the Federalists, it might be just what the doctor ordered to restore their floundering party back to health.

Considerations of this sort didn't improve the behavior of a man's liver, Livingston decided — though they had carried him before Marbois's handsome house without his realizing it. Trying to think up a plausible excuse for being late, he pulled the brass lever of the doorbell and unbuttoned his topcoat, aware suddenly that the weather had changed overnight and didn't require its wearing.

On hearing footsteps in the hall, Livingston looked up, expecting to see one of the dour-faced servants Marbois imported from Normandy where he had his chateau, but it was the master of the house himself who opened the door.

"My dear . . . " Marbois beamed, causing Livingston to look over his shoulder in the belief that the greeting was addressed to someone else. "Your powers of persuasion are simply miraculous."

Livingston's head tilted elegantly to the left. He knew how to accept a compliment, be it ever so obscure. "Good morning, Mr. Marbois. Sorry I'm late."

"Not at all, my dear sir. Not at all . . . " Leading his caller past the grand staircase with its noble wrought-iron railing, Marbois paced swiftly toward the library that served as his workroom. Monroe was drinking a cup of coffee in a chair near the bureau, apparently in good spirits. "Good morning, Mr. Livingston."

"Indeed, indeed," Marbois smiled. "Now that Mr. Monroe has

agreed to treat on the basis of the entire colony, we can begin the negotiations in earnest. A cup of coffee, Mr. Livingston?"

Relieved of his topcoat by the butler, Livingston found it necessary to open his jacket. Was he hearing correctly? "Yes," he nodded to the silver coffeepot in the butler's hands.

"I'm not sure I can agree to the price of eighty-million francs, though," Monroe said. "Eighty-million francs translates into fifteen-million dollars, Mr. Marbois. Our fellow Americans have an extreme aversion to public debts. How can we, without provoking their displeasure, burden them with the enormous sum of fifteen-million dollars?"

"The price can be argued separately from the treaty," Marbois promised. "Our immediate concern must be with the regularization of the purchase, before Spain or England hears of it. How is the coffee, Mr. Livingston?"

"What of the indemnities due our citizens?" (Livingston had, these past months, literally run out of breath, pressing United States demands for restitution for the seizures, requisitions, and capture of American ships which had been the stock-in-trade of France's First Republic. Bonaparte had steadfastly refused to accept responsibility for the excesses of the Directory. Here was a perfect opportunity to recoup these extensive losses.)

"The First Consul is prepared to remunerate all legitimate claims, I am happy to tell you." The First Consul hadn't mentioned a word to that effect, but Marbois was confident that the thirty million he was asking in excess of Bonaparte's fifty would more than cover all American claims.

Livingston let himself down in a chair facing Monroe, whose granite features mellowed for an affectionate nod. What was this? A happy ending à la Marie Cottin, where even the weather collaborated? All of it without anybody falling prey to some unnamed deadly malady? Did that mean he could expect his liver to reform as well? Entertained by his own thinking, Livingston picked up his cup from the tray on the bureau. "The coffee is excellent, Mr. Marbois."

A rather belated reply, but then, he hadn't noticed until now how remarkably good the coffee tasted.

April 14

W ell, Mary, congratulate me. It's all over. We've done it."

"What, Robert?" Mrs. Livingston hadn't seen her husband this exuberant since the birth of their first child. "What have you done?"

"We've bought Louisiana — the whole colony, kit and caboodle . . . from Bonaparte . . . Monroe and I . . . is now part of the United States."

"Robert, dear, sit down. You're incoherent. You haven't been drinking brandy this early in the day? Where is your topcoat? You and Monroe bought Louisiana, did you say?" Mrs. Livingston looked about for a place to sit herself, surprised to find she was already seated.

Livingston sat down, then jumped up again, too elated to keep still. "Yes, Mary. Imagine it! Imagine Monroe suddenly agreeing to it! Imagine the importance, the momentum, the historic implications — yes, I'll have a glass of brandy, thank you — Can you believe it, Mary? Can you appreciate what your husband has done today?"

"I am trying my best."

"Of course the details still will have to be worked out — the treaty, our claims, the financing, all of that will take some doing and time — but the deed is done, the deal made, the price agreed on. We've got ourselves a huge territory for fifteen million dollars, Mary, a bargain, thanks to Bonaparte's obsession to go fight the English. That's what it boils down to."

"But, Robert, how do you know it's a bargain when the size of the colony is a mystery? You said yourself that nobody knows the boundaries of Louisiana."

"Which may turn it into an even greater bargain than we suspect. What, say, if the Floridas were included in the sale?"

"I don't know . . . " Mrs. Livingston shook her head. "To up and buy a country full of people strikes me as a curious — I don't know — a reckless thing to do. How will the President react to your going over his head like this?"

"Don't worry about the President. This is one instance where he can't say no."

"How many times haven't I heard it said that democracy is possible only in small countries. The last thing the founding fathers wanted was to add more country to a country already considered too big for the experiment to succeed — otherwise they would have provided for the possibility in the Constitution. You said so yourself only the other day."

"What are you trying to say, Mary?"

"Well, Jefferson has the reputation of being a strict interpreter of the Constitution, hasn't he? So aren't you being a little rash in expecting his blessing for what is, after all, an unconstitutional act?"

"Jefferson will be a strict interpreter of the Constitution up until the time he gets word of the sale, when, I guarantee you, he'll turn direction on the spot."

"He's good at *that*, I'll grant you."

"Look, I know Jefferson can be underhanded, vengeful — a manipulator, a hypocrite, what have you — but you shouldn't short-change him by comparing him with Monroe. The President sees further than the length of his own nose. He doesn't have to rely on others for his vision."

"Is that what you think, Robert? That she talked Monroe into changing his mind? Mrs. Monroe, I mean?"

Livingston grinned. "*Somebody* did."

"Oh, Robert . . . " Mrs. Livingston couldn't help smiling.

"Talking about irony . . . You could never guess who is financing the transaction."

"But you only just agreed to the sale. How can you have financing already?"

"When it comes to sniffing out banks, nobody can match Marbois. Why do you think Bonaparte made him his Secretary of the Treasury?"

"All I can say is, the French must have been awfully confident that you were going to buy what they were selling."

"Is there a law against making inquiries? Anyway, no French bank would touch it, Marbois told us. So he ended up with Hope and Baring.

Can you believe it?"

"You mean to tell me that an English bank is prepared to finance a deal the money of which will be used to make war on England?"

"I told you it was ironic."

"Blood and tobacco!" said Mrs. Livingston, an expression that had never crossed her lips before.

"What?"

I couldn't help feeling sorry for Carlos IV, who emerged as the betrayed party in this transaction. Had not Bonaparte solemnly vowed to retrocede the Louisiana colony to Spain rather than ever to let it slip out of French hands? And hadn't he forthwith proceeded to break his vow?

"Poor Spain," I sighed to Alquier, who lost no time to retort (in his best regicidal voice): "When you are stupid, Monsieur, you deserve to be cheated."

Thus, like the betrayed husband, who is always the last to discover the infidelities of his wife, the cheated King, short on insight and lacking that flair for language which might have enabled him to decipher the characters looming on the wall, shuffled about his daily business, blithely ignorant of the injury.

April

Carlos IV was fond of Manuél de Godoy, the only Prime Minister within kingly memory who didn't talk national policy at every turn of the palatial corridors. So whenever possible, His Catholic Majesty left the pleasure of the forge or hunt momentarily for the pleasure of addressing a few amicable words to Manuél; to watch him in the ritual of climbing into his generalissimo uniform; or, as was the case today, to wish him good morning.

"Good morning, Manuél," Carlos wished, and, having done as much, wondered what in the way of amicable words he could say next. The King remembered that there was a specific bit of official information he had come to impart to the Prime Minister, but remembering this was of little help since he couldn't remember at the moment what it was. "But it will come back to me shortly," he promised brightly.

"Has it to do with the Crown Prince's bride, the Princess Maria Antonia, Your Majesty?" Godoy prompted, eager to be of assistance. His past dallyings and present schemings with the Queen notwithstanding, Manuél reciprocated the King's fondness of him.

"No." Carlos shook his ample head. "However, relative to that subject I can tell you that I have recently come upon a letter written by the Queen in which she refers to the Princess Maria Antonia, and to the Princess's mother, Queen Caroline of Naples, in terms which I do not consider fitting. Terms I can scarcely repeat to you, Manuél. ('The slimy offspring of that belching Neapolitan frog', the Queen had described her daughter-in-law. 'That off-scouring of her mother; that poisonous viper; that animal bursting with spleen and venom instead of blood; that half-dead toad; that diabolical serpent . . . ') This is all the more unsettling," he confided, "seeing the King of Naples is my brother and the Princess Maria Antonia my niece."

"It is well known, Sire," Manuél said soothingly, "that mothers, be they queens or not, find it very difficult to praise those their children have married. In a letter shown me by Her Majesty, Queen Caroline of Naples calls his Royal Highness, the Crown Prince of Spain, hideous to look at, with a tubby shape, round knees and legs, a small delicate voice, and utterly dull."

The King sagged onto a nearby bench. "What, I wonder, is the world coming to when princesses of the blood betray their station by committing such uncharitable sentiments to paper? Myself, I could not conceive of permitting considerations of this nature to enter my thinking. It is not Christian. It is not noble. What is the good of educating royal princesses if they abuse their alphabets to leave these questionable legacies? Can we be surprised if the people begin to doubt the judiciousness of the monarchy when the King's Queen behaves no better than they?

"This is where all those republican notions originate, you know, Manuél. France today would not be a republic if the Queen had behaved in a manner befitting her station. Likewise, if the American States today exist in the form they do, we need look no further than His Royal Highness, King George III, who, you can depend upon it, has in some way been remiss in his kingly duties.

"I don't see any danger of that happening in Spain, Sire," Godoy smiled confidently. "A republic, I mean."

"No." Neither did Carlos. "So long as the King remains honorable as king in the eyes of his Creator, the people cannot very well overrule His Divine judgment and pronounce him unfit." Of course, a king shared his throne with a queen . . . "But if it should ever come to that, I must, like my poor unfortunate cousin, Louis XVI, and George III, stand personally to blame."

"How noble you are, Your Majesty," Godoy stammered in admiration.

"That, precisely, is the point, Manuél. It is the duty of kings to be noble. But I must leave you now. My hounds are barking impatiently. I only came by to wish you good morning and, ah yes . . . " Speaking of republics had cleared the King's memory. " . . . to tell you that when you next see the American Ambassador, you may admit to the cession of Louisiana."

"Is this an official communication, Sire?"

"Is this not your king speaking? You can tell Mr. Pinckney he may inform his government that His Catholic Majesty, Carlos IV of Spain, has seen fit to cede the colony of Louisiana to the Republic of France."

News being unable to travel faster than the ships which carry it, summer would arrive in Washington City before word of the purchase reached our President . . .

JULY

July 3, 1803

Tomorrow was the Fourth of July, an event celebrated enthusiastically throughout the country. And what better place to celebrate the Nation's Independence than the Federal City. From the depths and wilds of Washington the people had come — from Hamburg, Carrollsburg, and even further — to flounder happily through the marshy stretches of alder bush on Pennsylvania and New Jersey Avenues and be a part of the festivities. This Fourth of July promised to be particularly memorable. Conrad's boarding house and Stelle's and Lovell's were jammed with citizens, excitedly speculating about an astonishing piece of information that had washed onto native shores the past week.

News of the United States, via her ministers in Paris, having bought Louisiana had spilled into Boston on June 28, courtesy of a ship returning from Le Havre. The incredible tale had swept from Massachusetts through neighboring states with the force and speed of a yellow fever sighting. Before the Administration had been officially informed, Federalist New England was up in arms against it.

"We are to give money of which we have too little for land of which we already have too much," cried Boston's *Columbian Centinel*. All of this for "a great waste, a wilderness unpeopled with any beings except wolves and wandering Indians."

His hat pulled deep over his eyes, Jefferson talked his startled horse past a cluster of reveling pedestrians and toward the heaps of stone and rubble in back of the President's House. Wildair was trotting peacefully alongside the rail fence when the porter came waddling up from inside.

"Mr. Madison's here!"

Jefferson spurred his horse to a wild dash for the yard, where Petit stood waving his arms, shouting: "Mr. Madison is here!" The cook reluctantly accepted charge of the snorting Wildair as the President bounded inside, nearly colliding with Lewis Harvie.

"Mr. Jefferson, sir!" the secretary stammered. "Mr. Madison is waiting for you." Harvie pressed his plump frame against the door, bewildered at the aggressiveness with which Jefferson rushed past him into the study, the smell of horses, and crisp Washington air rushing in with him.

"Is it true, Jemmy?" Jefferson stopped. Madison's glowing face flashed instant confirmation of the question. Jefferson dropped, exhausted suddenly, onto the nearest chair.

"It's true." Madison triumphantly planted the letters from Paris in the President's hands. "Read for yourself."

Unable to either confirm or deny the existence of what was being pronounced a monster, sight unseen, by the opposition, the President and his Cabinet had been relegated to the role of expectant fathers, tensely awaiting official word to discover what they had wrought.

And now here it was. Delivered at last. Every bit the enormity the Federalists claimed. "I can't say it wasn't expected . . . " Jefferson started, unable to concentrate on the dispatches.

"I know. It's quite a shock."

"The question is, what do we do now, Mr. Madison?"

"We wait for the treaty to arrive."

"And then, Jemmy?"

"It will have to be submitted to Congress for ratification.

Jefferson nodded pensively. The Executive, in seizing the opportunity that would so much benefit the country, was committing an act beyond the Constitution. "What must Congress do then, under the circumstances?" His hand tapped absentmindedly against the cage in which the mockingbird sat staring in sleepy fixation. "They must risk themselves and ratify, and do for the people unauthorized what we know the people would have done themselves had they been in a position to do it."

Madison smiled. The President and he had scaled that topic countless times during the past few days. Thomas Jefferson, third President of the United States, considered to be the strictest interpreter of the Constitution, was ready to violate that very Constitution for the future good of the land. "You will be called inconsistent," he teased.

"And what would you call our Federalist friends, formerly so concerned with the plight of their western brothers as to insist on taking New Orleans by force, but who suddenly are screaming hellfire and murder when those same brothers achieve their aim without a shot being fired or a single American life having been lost?"

"The Atlantic States live off the sea. I expect they are fearful of competition."

"Didn't they live off the sea before? When they introduced resolutions in Congress calling for war?"

"Have you considered, Mr. Jefferson, that, in their mad rush to alert the nation to the purchase before the President could, the Federalists have done us a good turn? We now needn't guess at the people's reaction." The country by and large stood behind the President. Natchez and environs were too far away to have been heard from yet, but the West was one area where the response was utterly predictable. "Why," Madison smiled, "even New York approves."

Jefferson returned the smile. "One would have expected New York to respectfully abstain, at the very least. You don't suppose Livingston's being involved has anything to do with that?"

Madison's fine smile remained set. "No more than I suppose Virginia's applause has to do with Monroe's involvement."

"Whom do *you* applaud, Jemmy?"

"I am a Virginian, sir."

"Yes . . . So am I. All the same, it wouldn't be amiss to reserve a round of applause for the American people, who will somehow or other have to come up with fifteen-million dollars." Direct taxes were out of the question. The nation yielded enough indirect revenue to justify taxing the people directly. But that was Gallatin's province. The thrifty Secretary of the Treasury would have his work cut out for him. Jefferson picked up the letters. "May I hold on to these for the night, Mr. Madison?" He had barely skimmed their contents. "I'll see to it that they are returned to you by morning."

"No hurry."

The President sauntered toward the row of potted plants in the recess of a window, meaning to report on a thick-leafed specimen given him by Mrs. Madison. He distractedly picked a dead leaf from a begonia, his intent forgotten. Tomorrow was the Fourth of July. "What better day than the anniversary of our Independence to announce the momentous news?" His sandy complexion flushed at the prospect.

Madison agreed. "The crowd is larger this year than last, have you noticed?" Almost as if it were *expecting* to hear something out of the ordinary. "Dolley tells me the public houses in Alexandria and Georgetown are packed to the brim with celebrants."

"There is good cause for celebration. We have secured our rights by pacific means: Reason has been more powerful than the sword. A little celebrating of our own would be entirely in order." Jefferson stalked toward the corner cabinet. Arriving before the cabinet, he paused, his mind, once again, having wandered from his immediate intent to the historical news. 'What am I looking for?"

"The Madeira, I believe."

"Think again, Jemmy." Bending over to inspect the contents of the pine shelves, Jefferson smiled over his shoulder. "Is this an occasion calling for Madeira?"

"Something with a rather more national flavor perhaps?" Madison smiled.

"You *are* a patriot, Mr. Madison! American peach brandy it is."

* * *

It is the case of the guardian, investing the money of his ward in purchasing an important adjacent territory; and saying to him when he came of age, "I did this for your good; I pretend to no right to bind you; you may disavow me, and I must get out of the scrape as I can; I thought it my duty to risk myself for you."

— **Thomas Jefferson**

BIBLIOGRAPHY

Adams, Henry. *John Randolph.* New York: AMS Press, 1972

Barbé-Marbois, François. *The History of Louisiana, Particularly of the Cession of That Colony to the United States of America,* ed. E. Wilson Lyon. Baton Rouge: Published for the Louisiana American Revolution Bicentennial Commission by the Louisiana State University Press, 1977

Bernardy, Françoise de. *Talleyrand's Last Duchess,* trans. Derek Coltman. New York: Stein and Day, 1966

Bodine, A. Aubrey. *The Face of Virginia.* New York: Bonanza Books, 1980

Bowers, Claude Gernade. *Jefferson in Power, the Death Struggle of the Federalists.* Boston: Houghton Mifflin, 1936

Brant, Irving. *James Madison.* Indianapolis, New York: Bobbs-Merrill, 1941-61

Breton, Guy. *Napoleon and his Ladies,* trans. Frederick Holt, (1st American ed.) New York: Coward-McCann,1966

Bridenbaugh, Carl. *Seat of Empire: The Political Role of Eighteenth-century Williamsburg,*(New ed.) Williamsburg, VA: Colonial Williamsburgh, distrib. Holt, 1958

Brodie, Fawn McKay. *Thomas Jefferson: An Intimate History.* New York: Norton, 1998, 1974

Cable, Mary. *The Avenue of the Presidents,* fwd. Nathaniel Alexander Owings. Boston: Houghton Mifflin, 1969

Carrington, Dorothy. *Napoleon and His Parents: On the Threshold of History.* New York: Dutton, 1990

Castelot, André. *Josephine,* trans. Denise Folliot. New York: Harper & Row, 1967

Chase-Riboud, Barbara. *Sally Hemings.* New York: Viking Press, 1979; also Avon Books, 1980

Chastenet, Jacques. *Godoy: Master of Spain, 1792-1808.* trans. J. F. Huntington. Port Washington, NY: Kennikat Press, 1972

Chidsey, Donald Barr. *Louisiana Purchase.* New York: Crown Publishers:

1972

Chinard, Gilbert. *Thomas Jefferson, The Apostle of Americanism.* 2d ed., rev. Ann Arbor: University of Michigan Press, 1957, 1939

Cooper, Duff. *Talleyrand.* New York: Fromm International, 1986

Criss, Mildred. *Jefferson's Daughter,* illustr. with photos. New York: Dodd, Mead, 1956, 1948

Dangerfield, George. *Chancellor Robert. R. Livingston of New York.* New York: Harcourt, Brace, 1960

Daniels, Jonathan. *The Devil's Backbone: The Story of the Natchez Trace,* map and headpieces by the Dillons. New York: McGraw-Hill, 1962

Dawidoff, Robert. *The Education of John Randolph,* 1st ed. New York: Norton, 1979

Delderfield, R. F. *Napoleon in Love.* New York: Simon and Schuster, 1959

Dillon, Richard H. *Meriwether Lewis: A Biography.* Santa Cruz, CA: Western Tanager Press, 1988

Fleming, Thomas J. *The Man from Monticello: An Intimate Life of Thomas Jefferson.* New York: Morrow, 1969

Gohm, Richard van de. *Antique Maps for the Collector.* New York: Macmillan, 1972

Goodwin, Maud (Wilder). *Dolly Madison.* Spartanburg, SC: Reprint Co., 1967

Graff, Henry F., consulting ed., *The Life History of the United States.* New York: Time-Life Books, 1964

Greenhill, Basil and Ann Giffard. *Travelling by Sea in the Nineteenth Century: Interior Design in Victorian Passenger Ships.* New York: Hastings House, 1974

Guérard, Albert Léon. *Napoleon I: A Great Life in Brief.* New York: Knopf, 1956

Hatcher, William B. *Edward Livingston: Jeffersonian Republican and Jacksonian Democrat.* Gloucester, MA, P. Smith: 1970, 1940

Huber, Leonard V. *New Orleans: A Pictorial History,* fwd. Charles L Dufour.

New York: Bonanza Books, 1980

James, Dorris Clayton. *Antebellum Natchez, (by) D. Clayton James.* Baton Rouge: Louisiana State University Press, 1968

Joelson, Annette. *Courtesan princess: Catherine Grand, Princesse de Talleyrand.* Philadelphia: Chilton Books,1965

Kamen, Henry Arthur Francis. *A Concise History of Spain (by) Henry Kamen.* New York: Scribner, 1973

Katz, William Loren. *Early America 1492-1812,* Minorities in American History, vol. 1. New York: Franklin Watts, 1974

King, Grace Elizabeth. *New Orleans: The Place and the People.* New York: Negro Universities Press, 1968

Klapthor, Margaret Brown. *The First Ladies.* Washington, DC: The White House Historical Association with Nat. Geographic Society, 1975-81

Laussat, Pierre Clément de. *Memoirs of My Life to My Son . . . ,* trans. and introd. Agnes-Josephine Pastwa, ed. and fwd. Robert D. Bush. Baton Rouge: Published for the Historic New Orleans Collection (monograph series) by the Louisiana State University Press, 1978

Lomask, Milton. *Aaron Burr.* New York: Farrar, Straus, Giroux, 1979-82

Malone, Dumas. *Jefferson and His Time.* Boston: Little, Brown, 1948-81

Markham, Felix Maurice Hippisley. *Napoleon.* New York: New American Library, 1963

Mitchell, Broadus. *Alexander Hamilton: A Concise Biography.* New York: Oxford Univ. Press, 1976

Monroe, James. *Autobiography of James Monroe,* ed. and intr. by Stuart Gerry Brown with Donald G. Baker. Syracuse, NY: Syracuse University Press, 1959

Moore, Virginia. *The Madisons: A Biography.* New York: McGraw-Hill, 1979

Morgan, Edmund Sears. *Virginians at Home: Family Life in the Eighteenth Century.* Williamsburg, VA: Colonial Williamsburg, 1952

Morse, John Torrey. *John Quincy Adams.* New York: AMS Press, 1972

Nichols, Frederick D. *Monticello: A Guide Book*. Monticello, VA: Thomas Jefferson Memorial Foundation, 1967

Paris: A Picture Book to Remember Her By, design. David Gibson, produced by Ted Smart. New York: Crescent, 1979

Peterson, Harold L. *American Interiors: From Colonial Times to the Late Victorians*. New York: Charles Scribner's, 1971

Robiquet, Jean. *Daily Life in France Under Napoleon*, trans. Violet M. MacDonald. New York: Macmillan, 1963

Singleton, Esther. *Social New York Under the Georges, 1714-1776*. New York: D. Appleton, 1902

Vidal, Gore. *Burr / Gore Vidal*. New York: Modern Library, 1998

Weider, Ben and David Hapgood. *The Murder of Napoleon*. New York: Congdon & Lattès: distrib. St. Martin's Press, 1982

White House, The. Washington, DC: The White House Historical Association with Nat. Geographic Society, 1962-82

Williams, Henry Lionel and Otttalie K. Williams. *A Guide to Old American Houses 1700-1900*. London: A. S. Barnes, 1962

Wilson, Everett Broomall. *Fifty Early American Towns*. South Brunswick, NJ: A. S. Barnes, 1966